UNDERSTANDING AUSTRALIAN INDUSTRIAL RELATIONS

UNDERSTANDING AUSTRALIAN INDUSTRIAL RELATIONS

SECOND EDITION

ROBYN ALEXANDER
Industrial Relations Division, NSW TAFE

JOHN LEWER
Hunter Institute of Technology, NSW TAFE

Harcourt Brace Jovanovich, Publishers
Sydney   Fort Worth   London   Orlando   Toronto

Harcourt Brace Jovanovich Group (Australia) Pty Limited
30–52 Smidmore Street
Marrickville, NSW 2204

Harcourt Brace Jovanovich Limited
24/28 Oval Road, London NW1 7DX

Harcourt Brace Jovanovich, Inc.
Orlando, Florida 32887

Copyright © 1992, 1990 by
Harcourt Brace Jovanovich Group (Australia) Pty Limited

First edition 1990

This publication is copyright. Except as expressly provided in the Copyright Act 1968, no part of this publication may be reproduced by any means (including electronic, mechanical, microcopying, photocopying, recording or otherwise) without prior written permission from the publisher.

National Library of Australia Cataloguing-in-Publication Data

Alexander, Robyn, date–
  Understanding Australian industrial relations.

  2nd ed.
  Bibliography.
  Includes index.

  ISBN 0 7295 1284 3.

  1. Industrial relations — Australia. I. Lewer, John, date–
  II. Title.

331.0994

Printed in Australia

Foreword

Our industrial relations system is undergoing one of its most significant changes in generations. The foundation for labour market reform for years to come is being completely recast. Our elaborate system of industrial awards is being restructured. Work practices and arrangements which have evolved over years are being reformed. Unions are adapting to new industrial processes and amalgamating at an historically unprecedented rate. Employer and employee organisations, individual management and unions and employees themselves are all actively co-operating in this change. The change is necessary and urgent because of the need to make Australia's economy and industry more efficient and more competitive.

Change of such magnitude requires (among other things) that those involved and affected—whether in industry itself, in administration or in the wider community—understand our industrial relations system. Poor understanding results in poor ideas; poor ideas cause confusion and inefficiency. If the community does not appreciate how the system works, it is ill-placed to agree on effective reform proposals or to ensure that reform is sound and sustainable.

Understanding Australian Industrial Relations introduces the key features of our industrial relations system in a clear and accessible form. It has been valuable in providing students, participants and other readers with important insights into the forces and developments that have produced the system. I am glad—though not surprised—that it is going into a second edition.

Peter Cook
Minister for Industrial Relations

Contents

Foreword	v
Preface	ix
1. The Context of Australian Industrial Relations	1
Objectives	1
Towards a definition	1
Approaches to industrial relations	4
Industrial relations in the broad perspective	8
Industrial relations in the human resource context	10
The industrial relations specialist	12
Summary	15
Questions and activities	16
2. Trade Unions	19
Objectives	19
Introduction	19
Trade union development	19
Organisation and size	25
Type of union	32
Union structure	34
Inter-union organisation	37
Union aims and objectives	37
Methods of achievement	38
Summary	40
Questions and activities	41
3. Employer Organisations	43
Objectives	43
Introduction	43
Types of employer organisations	45
Employer unity	53
Employer 'militancy'	55
Services	59
Other activities	63
Administration	63
Summary	64
Questions and activities	64
4. Government	69
Objectives	69
Introduction	69

Powers and levels of government	69
Functions of government	71
Government as industrial relations legislator	72
Industrial relations and the government's executive responsibilities	75
The judicial system	87
Summary	91
Questions and activities	91

5. Industrial Conflict — 93

Objectives	93
Introduction	93
Approaches to industrial conflict	93
Manifestation of conflict	96
The media and industrial conflict	99
Australia's recent dispute record	101
Summary	104
Questions and activities	104

6. Resolving Conflict — 113

Objectives	113
Introduction	113
A shift to a workplace focus	114
Grievance procedures	115
The tribunal system	119
Tribunal structures	120
Non-compliance	137
Industrial democracy and employee participation	142
Summary	144
Questions and activities	144

7. Conditions of Employment — 149

Objectives	149
Terms and conditions of work	149
The contract of employment	150
Employment legislation	157
Awards	160
Conflict between the sources of law	176
Summary	179
Questions and activities	179

Appendix I — Glossary — 184

Further Reading — 189

Index — 191

Preface

This is the second edition of our book and, as with the first edition published in 1990, we have attempted to provide a plain-English introduction to Australian industrial relations. The dynamic nature of Australian industrial relations means that it is difficult to produce a book which is completely up-to-date. However, we have endeavoured to incorporate reference to significant industrial relations events which have taken place since the publication of the first edition within the context of the book's ultimate goal, which is to provide a straightforward guide to the industrial relations framework.

The use of actual source documentation and contemporary materials as case studies is designed to familiarise readers with these references, the objective being to generate a continued interest in industrial relations developments.

Chapter 1 provides a framework for the study of industrial relations within the context of the overall environment and within the organisation. Chapter 2 outlines the role and functions of trade unions as one of the parties in industrial relations. Chapter 3 discusses employer associations, their role and functions, as another party in industrial relations. Government and its part in the industrial relations process is the topic of Chapter 4. Having identified the principal parties and outlined their objectives, the issue of conflict between them is dealt with in Chapter 5. Chapter 6 looks at the various means of resolving conflict in industrial relations, including grievance procedures, the tribunal systems, the role of industrial democracy and the legal system. Finally, Chapter 7 examines the terms and conditions of employment, particularly the contract of employment, awards and legislation.

The Glossary has been susbstantially enlarged and the Questions and Activities at the end of each chapter have been revised, and in most instances expanded, to give practical insight into recent industrial relations issues and practices.

We would like to acknowledge those persons, both students and teachers, who provided valuable advice and useful suggestions on aspects of the first edition. (We would welcome any further suggestions for improvement in this second edition: a survey is supplied at the end of the book for this purpose.) Further, the continued efforts of Didge Cusick in typing part of the second edition manuscript, Denise O'Hagan as editor and the immeasurable encouragement from families and friends are much appreciated.

With regard to material obtained from the AGPS: all legislation herein is reproduced by permission but does not purport to be the official or authorised version. It is subject to Commonwealth of Australia copyright. The *Copyright Act 1968* permits certain reproduction and publication of Commonwealth legislation. In particular, s.182A of the Act enables a complete copy to be made by or on behalf of a particular person. For reproduction or publication beyond that permitted by the Act, permission should be sought in writing from the Australian Government Publishing Service. Requests in the first instance should be addressed to the Manager, Commonwealth Information Services, Australian Government Publishing Service, GPO Box 84, Canberra ACT 2601.

Robyn Alexander
John Lewer

Chapter 1

The Context of Australian Industrial Relations

Objectives

At the end of this chapter, the reader should be able to:
- define industrial relations;
- identify the parties in industrial relations;
- discuss different approaches to industrial relations;
- identify factors affecting industrial relations;
- discuss industrial relations within the context of human resource management; and
- explain what an industrial practitioner does.

Towards a definition

All Australians are affected either directly or indirectly by industrial relations. Awards of the industrial relations system set the terms and conditions of work for over 80 per cent of wage and salary earners. Governments pass legislation which determines, among other things, how and when people take long service leave and annual holidays. For their part, employers and unions must comply with relevant awards and industrial legislation or face legal action. Finally, the general public becomes vitally interested in industrial relations when affected by industrial disputes.

Despite the importance of industrial relations in our lives as wage and salary earners, employers or consumers, our understanding of the subject is often limited. Moreover, this understanding may be coloured by personal experiences or by the frequent media portrayal of industrial relations as simply concerning conflict between employers and trade unions.

The foundation of industrial relations rests with the employer and the employee in the workplace. The interaction between these two parties and the relationship established between them provides the basis for industrial relations practice.

An employer can be represented at the workplace by a manager or supervisor and at the industrial or national level through an employer association. In either case the employer has certain objectives. These include, as shown in Figure 1.1:

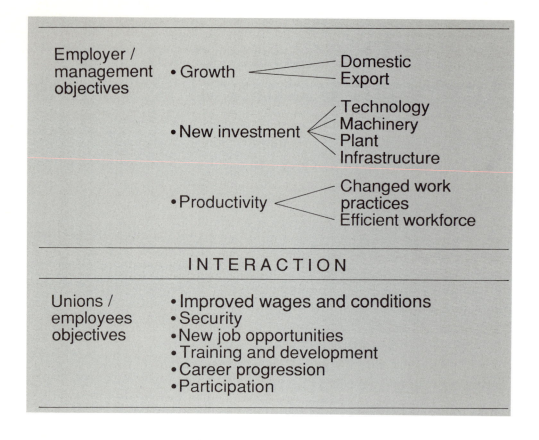

Figure 1.1: The interface of employer/management objectives with union/employer objectives.

- to make an acceptable return on investment;
- to conduct an efficient organisation;
- to have a productive workforce; and/or
- to comply with various government regulations, such as pollution and safety standards.

The employer's objectives are put into practice within the context of an organisation or business. Organisations need employees or 'human resources' to pursue their objectives.

An employee also has objectives concerning work. These may include:

- to earn the best possible wage for the job;
- to have a secure and satisfying job;
- to develop a career; and/or
- to be in a satisfying work group.

Employees can choose to represent themselves as individuals in an attempt to secure their objectives. Alternatively, individuals may undertake collective action through union representation. By way of illustration, an individual can ask the manager for a pay increase on completion of a course relevant to his or her employment. Whether or not it is given depends on the particular circumstances and on the discretion of the manager. Another way to achieve the objective is for the employees as a group, through a union, to put forward a claim to management that a pay increase be given to employees on the completion of a specified course.

It is whether or not employees seek to pursue their objectives with or without the support of a union which distinguishes employee relations from industrial relations. 'Employee relations' is a general term to describe the way in which management deals with employees. 'Industrial relations', however, accepts that the employer is represented through management and their employer associations and employees through trade unions. Therefore, the practice of industrial relations is the interaction of employers and their representatives with employees and their representatives in pursuit of their respective objectives.

The parties, whether it be in an environment which recognises union representation or where employees deal with the employer/management on an individual basis, have varying objectives. This is not to say that there are no common or mutual goals (e.g. industry growth), but there will be occasions when the parties seek differing objectives or when their objectives have different priorities. In any event, disagreement or conflict can be expected.

Interaction between the key industrial parties has repercussions on the general public. Consequently, governments must play a key role in setting the framework for this interaction. In Australia, governments have constructed many of the rules which regulate the way the conflict is handled between the principal parties.

To summarise, the parties in industrial relations are:

- employers, their management and employer associations;
- employees and trade unions; and
- governments and their 'agencies'.

See Figure 1.2.

The term 'industrial relations' encompasses the way in which the above parties interact, particularly within a framework established by governments. There is a diversity of views about the kind of industrial relations framework which is 'best' for Australia. A knowledge of the principal parties and their characteristics, together with an understanding of the functioning of the industrial relations system, will allow these views to be assessed objectively.

Approaches to industrial relations

Hand-in-hand or face-to-face

There are a number of possible approaches to the study of industrial relations: one is that there should be greater emphasis on the common objectives between employers or management and employees and trade unions, and is often described as a 'harmony' between capital and labour. This approach maintains that the industrial objective of both major parties is the creation of wealth through greater efficiency and productivity. Industrial relations should thus

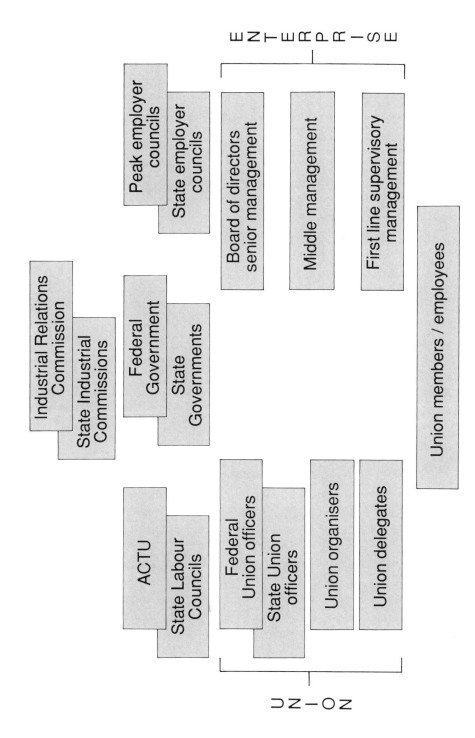

Figure 1.2: The parties in Industrial Relations.

involve the parties operating 'hand-in-hand' as opposed to 'face-to-face'. This is also referred to as the 'unitary' approach to industrial relations.

This view is particularly attractive to employers. Employers often refer to 'employee relations' as discussed—rather than 'industrial relations', which denotes employer–trade union interaction. The 'hand-in-hand' approach assumes industrial relations signifies conflict between the parties and is believed to be outmoded. Industrial relations is regarded as too rigid and should be broadened beyond formal dispute resolution and award-making to include the more informal practices envisaged in employee relations. To foster co-operation, good management practices, communication skills and other means of encouraging the common interests of employees and employers are recommended.

While those persons who adopt the 'hand-in-hand' approach to industrial relations strive to minimise conflict, the 'face-to-face' approach accepts conflict as inevitable—even potentially positive. This view accepts that there is, and probably always will be, a diversity of views held by the parties in industrial relations: on the one hand, management perceives 'profits' as necessary for a number of reasons including new investment, research and dividends. Their employees, on the other hand, see themselves as key to the generation of profits, and therefore deserving of increased wages and improved conditions. Their objectives are different.

The acceptance of differing views is sometimes referred to as a pluralist or multiple perspective to the field of industrial relations. Pluralism is not limited to the field of industrial relations—it is accepted as the basis of democratic society. The presence of a variety of views on issues in the community is not only considered legitimate but to be a right in most democratic countries. For example, there are groups which lobby the government for gun control and those which are against gun control—also, certain groups in favour of the privatisation of government enterprises and others against it.

If a 'face-to-face' approach to industrial relations is adopted, the emphasis shifts from minimising conflict to resolving and regulating it. This approach allows for a diversity of interests but that there must be a way of accommodating this diversity within a framework or system. Figure 1.3 outlines the various methods which can be utilised to resolve conflict in the workplace.

In Australia, the primary method used to resolve conflict has been machinery established by government. Dating back to the turn of the century, federal and state governments have passed legislation to set up tribunal systems for the resolution of differences between employers and unions. The historical presence of a tribunal system to process conflict between parties in the workplace lends credence to the idea of a diversity of interests between the parties. Despite the historical prominence of conciliation and arbitration machinery to resolve industrial conflict, other methods have been used. There is increasing effort to have the industrial parties at the workplace level resolve their differences themselves rather than rely on 'outside' agencies like the

THE CONTEXT OF AUSTRALIAN INDUSTRIAL RELATIONS □ 7

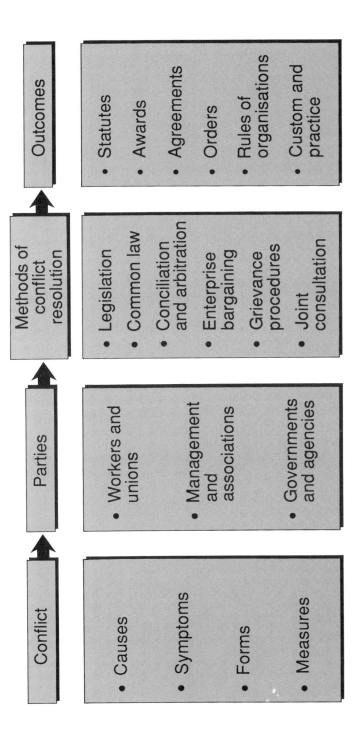

Figure 1.3: Methods and outcomes of conflict resolution.

Source: Adapted from Deery S. and Plowman D., (1991) *Australian Industrial Relations*, McGraw-Hill, Sydney.

tribunal systems. As a consequence, methods like grievance procedures and enterprise bargaining have been attracting greater attention as methods of resolving workplace differences. These are discussed further in Chapter 6. It is government in its role as 'balancer' of the interests of employees vis-à-vis those of employers which sets up the rules or parameters within which the two principal parties resolve their differences. This can be done in a variety of ways but usually involves government legislation.

However, while the accepted industrial relations framework has allowed the expression of views while balancing this diversity, there are those who do not believe that the balancing will be equitable. Some of these people adopt a more radical perspective: in their view, until the means of production is democratically controlled, the framework will always serve the interests of the owners or employers over those of employees.

The particular approach an employer takes to industrial relations will be influenced by his/her values and beliefs. For example, if an employer believes that the majority of workers work primarily for money with little interest in career opportunities, it is likely that he/she will attempt to co-opt the workers' efforts in a 'hand-in-hand' approach. In other words, the employer will see very few issues for potential conflict with employees; the employer makes decisions with or without consultation and communicates them to the employees. This view may also be reflected in the employer's attitude to unions. Trade union influence may be limited and any push by unions for greater involvement in the operation of the organisation may be opposed. If an employer, on the other hand, believes that employees collectively through their trade unions have a substantial contribution to make on issues related to work and the community in general, industrial relations will evolve more in line with the 'face-to-face' approach.

Industrial relations in the broad perspective

There are a variety of factors determining the objectives set by the parties in industrial relations and their ability to achieve these objectives. The events and issues which develop between employers and employees will be determined, in part, by the broader environmental context. As social norms and political, economic, technological and legal factors in a society change, these changes will be reflected in its industrial relations system. For example, the increase in the number of married women in the workforce has led to pressure for equal pay and demands for more flexible working hours.

Further, the technology employed at the workplace has far-reaching consequences for the form of management and employee organisation. One technological characteristic is the type of product or service. This will influence the size of the workforce and duration of employment. (For example, if the product is fresh produce, employment will be plentiful only at the time of harvest.) The type of work undertaken will also influence the composition

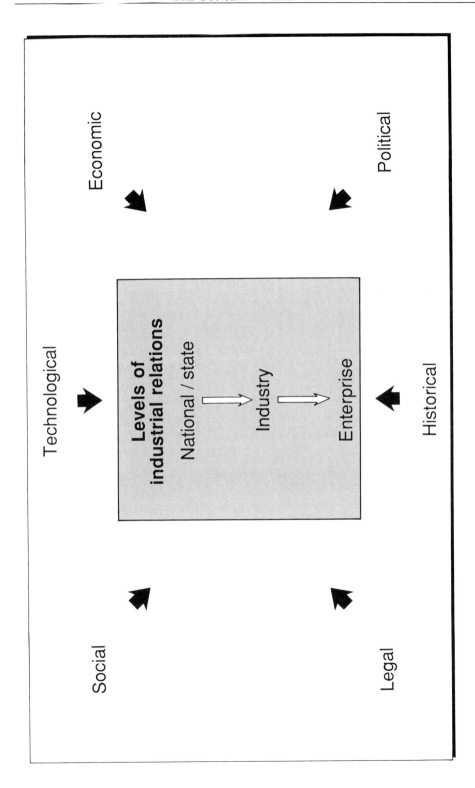

Figure 1.4: Each level of Industrial Relations is affected by environmental factors.

and size of the workforce: if the work is dangerous or necessitates shiftwork, this will be reflected in the number and types of employee applying for the work.

Essentially, the principal industrial relations parties operate within a subsystem of the overall social system. As has been seen, there are a number of factors within the larger system which influence developments in the industrial relations subsystem (see Figure 1.4).

Industrial relations in the human resource context

Similarly, the industrial relations system in an organisation does not operate alone but is influenced by a number of factors.

In its effort to achieve certain results, an organisation sets goals and objectives as part of its planning function. In most instances this is undertaken by senior management. The organisation's goals and objectives are incorporated into its corporate plan. These goals and objectives will have ramifications on the human resources required. It is the duty of those persons responsible for human resource management to develop a human resource plan to meet the organisation's overall goals and objectives. There will probably be industrial relations considerations (e.g. possible redundancies) resulting from the human resource plan (see Figure 1.5).

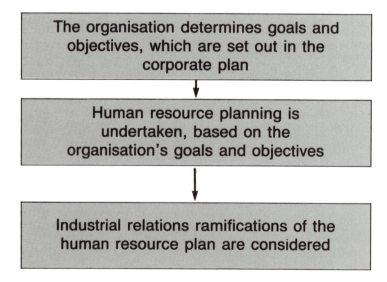

Figure 1.5: Industrial relations in the context of human resource planning.

Industrial relations, while considered an activity in its own right within the human resource function, has considerable impact on other human resource activities (see Figure 1.6). How management addresses these industrial relations

Activity	Industrial relations considerations
Recruitment	• Does seniority or merit apply? • What are the award provisions for the position? • What is the policy on internal versus external advertising?
Selection	• Is there preference to members of the union? • Is there a union/employee representative on the selection committee? • What is the organisation's attitude to union membership—encouraged or discouraged?
Performance appraisal and counselling	• Are there relevant award provisions? • Is there union agreement on disciplinary procedures? • Is there an effective grievance procedure?
Training and development	• Is the union(s) involved in the induction of new employees? • Is the union(s) consulted on training programmes? • Are there union–management agreements on skill development and training programmes? • What are the relevant award provisions for study leave?
Occupational health and safety	• Is the union(s) involved in evaluation of occupational health and safety policy and programmes? • Is the OH & S committee operating effectively from an industrial relations view?
Remuneration management	• Are there over-award payments? • Is the union(s) involved in job evaluation/skills auditing exercises? • Would an enterprise-based agreement be more appropriate to industry award coverage?
Equal employment opportunity and affirmative action	• Is the union(s) consulted on EEO policies and programs? • Is the union involved in the preparation of the affirmative action report?

Figure 1.6: Industrial relations considerations of the human resource management function.

considerations will depend on 'custom and practice' (what has happened in the past) and on the organisation's attitudes or philosophy. Some organisations have an industrial relations policy to assist them in meeting these considerations.

Such a policy not only reflects the organisation's attitude towards industrial relations, but also provides a reference point for decision-making which is consistent with the organisation's objectives. The policy may include statements on issues such as:

- *attitude to unions*. Will they be welcomed, tolerated or resisted? Will multi or single unionism be encouraged?
- *consultation*. Will consultation take place with the unions and/or employees? What issues will be open for consultation?
- *dispute settlement*. How does the organisation expect disputes to be resolved? Are there grievance procedures in place as a result of the policy?

While an industrial relations policy can be a useful tool in industrial relations procedures and practices, it also provides the workforce with a measure of managerial accountability. For example, an industrial relations policy may dictate that management will consult with trade unions; particular circumstances may arise, however, where management does not feel consultation is warranted. This may cause a diminishing of good faith between the parties.

The question of managerial accountability for industrial relations necessitates the establishment of industrial relations indicators, that is, some measurement of whether or not industrial relations is 'good' or 'bad' in a particular organisation. Industrial relations reporting could include information on absenteeism rate, labour turnover rate and monthly calculations of the number of strikes, stop work meetings, grievance meetings and resultant lost time of each.

While industrial relations tends to be incorporated under the umbrella of human resources, the size of the organisation and the degree and level of union activity determine whether or not industrial relations is treated as a separate function or as one of the activities of the human resources or personnel manager. Figure 1.7 details the position of the industrial relations function in a medium-sized manufacturing firm.

The industrial relations specialist

The industrial relations specialist may work in a private organisation or employer association, in the public sector for a government authority or department, or for a trade union. Within a private or public sector organisation the industrial relations activities may or may not be part of the human resource manager's position. Nevertheless, whether it is a private or public sector organisation or a trade union, the duties designated to an industrial relations specialist include:

- acting as an adviser on industrial relations policy;
- maintaining research on the conciliation and arbitration system;
- making representations before tribunals;
- liaising on industrial relations issues (e.g. disciplinary action);

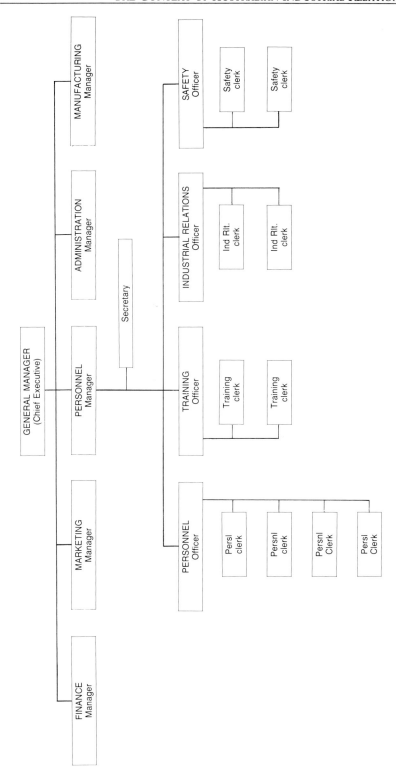

Figure 1.7: The industrial relations function in a medium-sized manufacturing firm.

- negotiating on claims;
- administering industrial legislation;
- interpreting and applying awards and agreements;
- researching industrial relations claims and issues; and
- anticipating changes in industrial relations.

Figure 1.8 shows examples of positions advertised for an industrial relations specialist.

INDUSTRIAL OFFICER
Electrical Contractors Association of N.S.W.

The Association is seeking the services of an Industrial Officer who will be responsible to the Executive Director for:

Research negotation and advocacy concerning Award variations and industrial disputes.

Advice to members concerning all industrial matters including appropriate legislation.

Monitoring current developments in the industrial area with particular emphasis on how such changes could relate to Electrical Contractors.

The Association has a high and respected profile in the industry and accordingly we are looking for a senior person with a wide range of experience in industrial matters.

Salary will be negotiated within the range $30–35,000 dependent upon experience.

Written applications, including details of qualifications and experience should be sent to:-

The Executive Director,
Electrical Contractors Association of N.S.W.
51 William Street,
Sydney, 2011.

RESEARCH OFFICER
AUSTRALIAN TIMBER AND ALLIED INDUSTRIES UNION (N.S.W.) BRANCH

The A.T.A.I.U. is a registered trade union representing in excess of 10 000 members employed within the timber and timber related industries and requires a person to fulfil the role of a Research Officer in its N.S.W. Branch.
DUTIES INCLUDE
Preparing, submitting and negotiating claims.
Appearance and advocacy before Industrial Tribunals.
Conduct of negotiations with employers and employing authorities.
Research, collate, catalogue, file or otherwise deal with records, publications or other research material.
Assist individual members with work related problems.
Some industrial work will be involved, including attending meetings with unions, occasional visits to workplaces.
ESSENTIAL REQUIREMENTS
Commitment to trade union principles and objectives.
Ability to analyse complex problems, prepare a case and support it by argument.
Well developed skills in effective oral and written communication.
A sound experience in research and knowledge of contemporary industrial issues, practises and arbitration system.
Ability to organise and co-ordinate work to meet priorities and deadlines.
SALARY
The commencing salary will be $32,000. Superannuation will be negotiated.
Applications detailing relevant experience and qualifications should be forwarded to:
Acting Secretary
A.T.A.I.U.

Figure 1.8: Examples of positions advertised for an industrial relations specialist.

> **INTERVIEW**
>
> **SUELLEN WHYBRO**
> *Position*:   Human Resources Manager, TNT Express Worldwide
>
> *1. What is the relationship between human resource management and industrial relations in your organisation?*
>
> Responsibility for industrial relations falls under the human resources umbrella. Managers deal with the unions and with some basic industrial relations activities. It is the Human Resources Manager's role to provide advice and assistance to the managers. This means that the Human Resources Manager needs to be familiar with the legislation, such as awards, occupational health and safety, equal employment opportunity and affirmative action. The Human Resources Manager needs to identify the impact of industrial relations on other human resource policies and practices.
>
> *2. How does your organisation link its industrial relations policies to its overall business strategies?*
>
> A yearly strategic plan is developed by the General Manager, with input from senior management, including the Human Resources Manager. This plan incorporates all functions of the business and stems from the mission statement. Human resources is a key strategy in our mission, therefore industrial relations becomes part of the overall human resources strategy, which in turn links into overall business strategies.
>
> *3. What do you see as the future of industrial relations activities within the human resource function in organisations?*
>
> I believe that we will continue to see a more decentralised industrial relations system. The human resources role will be twofold in my opinion. Firstly, the human resources/industrial relations specialist will be required to train line managers in negotiating and consultation techniques. Secondly, the human resources/industrial relations people need to ensure that they are gaining the most effective agreements aimed at meeting the future needs of the company.
>
> *4. In your view, what is the best education and training for someone interested in industrial relations as a career?*
>
> I suppose my view is biased, but I believe that the TAFE industrial relations or a personnel management specialist qualification provides a very solid base. Personally that is where I started and subsequently did a Grad. Dip. in Employee Relations and an MBA which are beneficial for more senior industrial relations people. The really good industrial relations people need to be up-to-date with changes in industry and industrial relations developments which are very dynamic. Hands-on experience is also essential.

Summary

There are three main parties involved in industrial relations in Australia: the employer and employer representatives; the employee and employee representatives or trade union; and government, which includes government agencies. The subject of industrial relations is concerned with the interaction between these parties at either the enterprise/workplace level or the state and national level.

There are a number of approaches to the study of industrial relations. The approach adopted will be determined largely by one's attitudes, values and beliefs. The fact that Australia instituted conciliation and arbitration machinery at the turn of the century to resolve disputes between industrial relations parties suggests that a pluralist or 'face-to-face' approach was recognised and accepted. Whatever system is adopted, it will be influenced by legal, political, social and economic factors. As these factors change, so does the practice of industrial relations.

Within an organisational context, industrial relations is ultimately affected by the organisation's goals, objectives, attitudes and philosophy. While in practice industrial relations has been traditionally restricted to the resolution of disputes and operation of the award structure, there is evidence to suggest that greater interest is evolving in more strategic or long-range industrial relations issues.

Australian industrial relations has been put into the context of the overall social system, and its operation shown with an organisation. In order to understand how the system operates, the respective parties need to be examined and their role, objectives and functions determined.

Questions and Activities

1. Keep a diary of current events in industrial relations. Collect newspaper clippings of an industrial relations nature, summarise and analyse them with respect to various issues (e.g. give an example of the 'hand-in-hand' approach).
2. Obtain the organisation chart for a particular organisation. Determine where the industrial relations function is located. What can be said about the organisation's attitude to industrial relations from the organisation chart?
3. How does a change in government affect industrial relations? What can a government do to affect the industrial relations system?
4. If one accepts that conflict between employers and employees is inevitable, how would this be reflected in the organisation and attitudes of management?
5. Discuss industrial relations considerations of the human resource management function (see Figure 1.7).
6. Read the following 'Monday comment' by Ross Gittins and answer the related questions.

MONDAY COMMENT

ROSS GITTINS
ECONOMICS EDITOR

Productivity and the touchy-feely solution

The more of our top-flight businessmen I hear, the more case studies and research I read, the more I think the push for enterprise bargaining is putting the cart before the horse.

We're agreed we need faster productivity growth and that this requires changes at the enterprise level. The message we're getting from both sides of politics (and most economists) is that the key to gains in productivity is enterprise bargaining: shift wage-fixing to the enterprise level and higher productivity follows. Change the institutions of industrial relations and that causes a change in attitudes and behaviour.

This gets cause-and-effect the wrong way round. It's a top-down solution: change things on the ground in Bankstown by changing laws in Canberra. It's a central solution to a perceived problem of over-centralisation.

What we really need is better industrial *relations* on the ground in Bankstown: more co-operation and trust between managers and workers. When you get better human relations, you start to get the things politicians and economists are seeking: higher productivity, firms better able to compete, and wage rises more in line with productivity growth. When managers and workers co-operate for commercial success, in pursuit of their common goals of higher job satisfaction and monetary reward, wage-fixing falls into place.

Disagreements arise, but are resolved with less emotional and economic cost. The parties probably *will* want to make enterprise-specific arrangements on pay and conditions. But those who want to can do this within the present wage system. They can agree to turn a blind eye toward provisions; they can agree on over-award payments. If they wish to be more formal, they can get the IR Commission to approve a 'certified agreement' under Section 115 of the Act.

Well, better industrial relations would be t'riffic. But if they can't be brought about merely by decisions at the centre to change wage-fixing institutions, how are they brought about? That's the frustration for law-making pollies and lever-pulling econocrats: the initiative for better industrial relations must come from the managers of enterprises. That's not because the behaviour of workers and unions is beyond criticism (hardly), but because enterprises are managed by managers.

Consider the views of the justly feted Dr Michael Deeley, boss of ICI Australia, given to a meeting of EPAC, and issued today as discussion paper 91/02. 'We need to move from seeing employees as an undesirable and variable cost to seeing them as an important investment; as the key to improving performance through fully utilising their talents,'' he says. 'For such a cultural shift to be successful, a company's policies and actions must reflect a change of attitude of management to its employees.

'There is a need to move from a culture where employees are controlled, to one of commitment. This is where employees are trusted and empowered; where management provides support and motivation by focusing on performance and outcome. In a workplace based on commitment, the individual will have a job that is flexibly defined and part of a comprehensive career structure, with opportunities for advancement through skill acquisition.

'The organisational structure is flat, with management systems that emphasise involvement and mutual influence. The consequences for industrial relations is the shift from negotiations to resolve conflicts, to problem-solving involving the company, its employees and their unions.

'Our experience demonstrates that shared goals and values—combined with empowerment and trust—can create more productive workplaces, and benefit both the company and employees. Agreements negotiated at individual sites are the obvious products, but it is the process by which they are reached that is crucial.' Amen to that. Dr Deeley's exposition of what they're doing at ICI, why they're doing it and what the results are is required reading. This touchy-feely, pop sociology approach to productivity and competitiveness is a hard gospel for hard-harded law-makers and economists to accept; that the solutions to economic problems have to do with culture, 'empowerment', job satisfaction and management technique, not just wage fixing systems and government intervention (or the removal of it).

We need to be clear on the link between productivity and enterprise bargaining. Sure there are, in some areas, once-only gains in labour productivity to be had by bribing workers to give up restrictive work practices. But the *fundamental* sources of productivity growth remain increased capital investment and technological advance.

Dr Deeley's touchy-feely approach facilitates these fundamentals. Well-motivated, trusting workers agree more readily to the introduction of new technology and to the full exploitation of its potential. And every time a manager accepts a worker's idea on how the job may be done better, a tiny but cumulative advance in technology occurs.

Source: *Sydney Morning Herald*, 13 May, 1991.

a. Is the ICI experience an example of a 'hand-in-hand' or 'face-to-face' approach?
b. Define 'enterprise bargaining'.
c. What action(s) are recommended for successful enterprise bargaining?

Chapter 2

Trade Unions

Objectives

At the end of this chapter, the reader should be able to:
- discuss the major events in trade union development;
- identify ways in which employees are represented in Australia;
- explain the objectives and role of trade unions; and
- distinguish between responsibilities and functions of the various levels in trade unions.

Introduction

Trade unions are associations of workers that have joined together to protect and better their wages, hours of work, and conditions of employment. Trade unions are accepted by most Australians as having a legitimate role in any democracy. Legislation supports the formation of unions, the recruitment of members to unions and the recognition of the conditions gained through union efforts. Although unions can be seen as only one type of vested interest group (others are environmental, ethnic, women's, or disabled groups), their efforts often receive greater scrutiny and elicit more emotional responses. Unlike those of other groups, their actions are often seen as challenging conventional managerial rights or the community interests.

While unions may be accepted as legitimate representatives of the collective interests of their membership, the public's perceived parameters for their actions are unclear. Unions, the economy and politics seem to be connected in the minds of a majority of the public. Consequently, if the public believes there is a problem, unions are often implicated (Table 2.1). In this context, it is valuable to examine how unions developed, their role, and their objectives.

Trade union development

Trade unions came into being because employees are able to exercise less power in relations with their employers as individuals than as a group. As far back as the 1830s, workers were combining into unions to provide mutual aid in cases of injury, sickness or death and to seek better wages from employers.

Table 2.1: Trade unions are seen as having a significant effect on the economy.

Bodies most responsible for Australia's economic problems	Total (%)	18–24 years	25–34 years	35–44 years	45–59 years	60+ years
Federal Government	33	37	37	32	31	27
State Government	5	6	6	4	4	3
Trade unions	42	36	38	46	45	45
Management	10	10	9	9	10	11
Arbitration Commission	1	—	1	1	1	2
Don't know	10	10	8	8	9	13

Source: *Sydney Morning Herald* Survey, 16 October, 1986.

During the 1850s, the foundations of the present-day labour movement were laid. A number of events took place which consolidated the unions:

- substantial economic growth, including the goldrushes;
- the influx of immigrants, many of whom with trade union experience, radicalised the workforce;
- economic growth led to labour shortages; consequently, employers granted better conditions to some workers. This stimulated demand for similar conditions by other workers; and
- unions began to organise on a broader level, forming trades hall councils to assist individual unions.

Economic prosperity for most of the latter half of the nineteenth century contributed to union growth and strength. This all changed during the 1890s. The country experienced severe economic depression, export prices slumped, overseas loan money became scarce, credit was restricted, and unemployment spread. Working conditions began to deteriorate. Several of the larger unions, notably the maritime, pastoral and mining unions, took part in large-scale strikes. For the most part, the unions were defeated because of their weak bargaining position and because the colonial governments of the time sided with the employers.

Reduced power in the workplace led unions to take political action. They lobbied for legislation beneficial to workers and against government funds being given to aid employers affected by the recession. Ultimately the trade unions formed the Labor Party in 1900.

With Federation in 1901, the concept of conciliation and arbitration was written into the Constitution and subsequently embodied in federal legislation in 1904. The legislation also encouraged the organisation of representative bodies of employers and employees. This official recognition of trade unions strengthened their position. By 1926, 55 per cent of the workforce was unionised.

Over the years, unions have made considerable gains in working conditions and wages for Australian workers (see Figure 2.1). The 1970s brought a number of changes both economically and socially which have had an impact on

1860s
- Melbourne Trades Hall formed.
- 'Free selection before survey' to open up land to settlers without capital.
- Manufacturing industry growth begins as does the economic 'boom'.

1870s
- Sydney Trades and Labor Council formed.
- The 'new unionism' unskilled workers are organised.
- Victorian Supervision of Workrooms and Factories Act (first major occupational health legislation).

1880s
- NSW Trades Union Act (1881)—union rights and registration.
- Trades and Labor Councils formed in Hobart, Brisbane and South Australia.
- Five Intercolonial Trade Union Congresses were held in the 1880s.

1890s
- Sudden economic slump.
- 'Great Strikes' maritime, Broken Hill and shearing.
- Foundation of Labor parties in the colonies.
- Victorian Factory Act establishes wages boards.

1900s
- NSW Industrial Arbitration Act 1901 (compulsory arbitration).
- Victorian Rail Strike—first strike by government employees.
- Federal Conciliation and Arbitration Act 1904 (Commonwealth Arbitration Court).
- 'Harvester judgment' (1907) Justice Higgins establishes 'basic wage', a 'fair and reasonable' minimum weekly wage.

1910s
- 'Whybrow's case'—High Court restricts federal awards to named respondents (preventing 'common rule').
- General strikes in Sydney and Brisbane.
- 'Mildura Fruit Pickers Case' Justice Higgins awards women 54% of basic wage.

1920s
- 44 hour week for timber workers and engineers 1920. Arbitration court restores 48 hour week in 1922.
- ACTU established 1927.
- Bruce-Page government defeated over attempts to abolish the federal arbitration system.

1930s
- Basic wage cut by 10% during depression.
- Aborigines specifically excluded from the Federal Pastoral Industry award and were not included until 1966.
- Female wage 54% of male wage.

1940s
- 1 week's leave and 2½ days sick leave standard (1941).
- 2 weeks' paid annual leave introduced (1945).

cont.

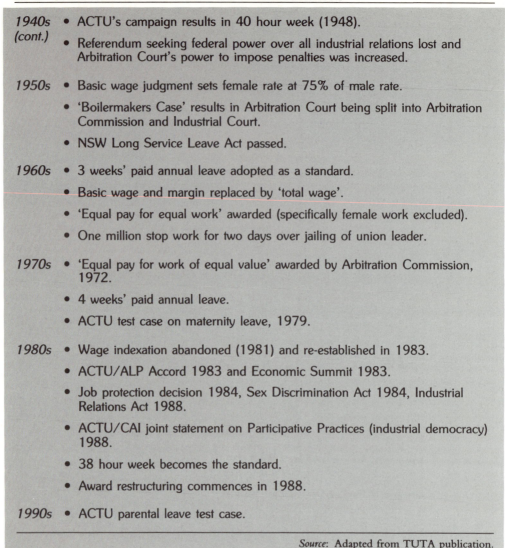

Figure 2.1: A summary of key events in trade union history.

the role and operations of unions. The mid-1970s were characterised by 'stagflation' (i.e. high inflation, little economic growth and high unemployment). In an effort to control inflation, wages were increased in line with changes in the consumer price index. This is known as wage indexation, and was used in a number of forms for most of the 1970s and part of the 1980s. Furthermore, since the early 1970s, the composition of the workforce has undergone significant changes. New social issues emerged and unions—as worker representatives—had to respond to these changes. Unions, through the Australian Council of Trade Unions (ACTU) took up a number of important issues:

- *Equal pay*: the 1969 and 1972 Equal Pay Cases before the Federal Commission opened the way for equal pay for women employees.
- *Maternity leave*: the 1979 Maternity Leave Case before the Commission entitled women employees covered by federal awards for up to 12 months' maternity leave.
- *Redundancy protection*: the 1984 Job Protection Test Case set requirements for employers to notify, consult and award severance pay in the event of loss of employment through new technology or organisational restructuring.
- *Paternity leave*: the 1990 decision of the Federal Commission opens the way for male employees covered by federal awards after 12 months' service to share the caregiving following the birth of their child. Specifically the decision allows:
   a. up to one week's paternity leave at the time of confinement of their spouse,
   b. an additional unbroken period of up to 51 weeks' unpaid leave in order to become the primary caregiver of the newborn child,
   c. ability to work part-time for up to two years under certain conditions following the birth of the child.

Figure 2.2 is an extract from the Full Bench decision on paternity leave of the Australian Industrial Relations Commission.

The adoption of the Prices and Incomes Accord (the Accord) between the Australian Council of Trade Unions (ACTU) and the ALP in 1983 marked a new approach by trade unions. The overall thrust of the labour movement shifted its emphasis from the 'distribution' of benefits, to include trade union involvement in the means of creating wealth and expanding production.

The basic premise behind the Accord was that, in return for union co-operation in setting wages policy, a Labor government would pursue policies encouraging full employment and a rise in living standards. Between 1983 and 1991 there were six versions of the Accord.

While union involvement in economic decision-making at a governmental level was accepted as part of the Accord, business support for the concept was not wholehearted. Some industries, notably the metal industry, have increasingly involved unions in business decision- and policy-making, but others have been more cautious.

> **How much power do trade unions have?**
>
> The power we [the unions] have is the power of an organisation in a pluralist democracy. We represent people. We bargain. We don't pretend to have any power beyond that.
>
> *Source*: Bill Kelty, Secretary of the ACTU, *The Bulletin*, 2 April, 1991.

EXTRACT ONLY

AUSTRALIAN INDUSTRIAL RELATIONS COMMISSION
Conciliation and Arbitration Act 1904
s.25 notification of industrial dispute

Federated Miscellaneous Workers Union of Australia

and

Angus Nugent and Son Pty Ltd and other
(C No. 23285 of 1988)

s.59 application for variation

Shop, Distributive and Allied Employees Association
(C No. 23321 of 1988)

Various employees   Saddlery, leather and canvas industry
                                     and wholesale and retail trade

JUSTICE COHEN
DEPUTY PRESIDENT MOORE
DEPUTY PRESIDENT POLITES
COMMISSIONER GRIFFIN
COMMISSIONER TURBET   MELBOURNE 26 JULY 1990

Parental leave

DECISION

The matters before us constitute a test case for parental leave in federal private sector awards. The claims are brought by the Australian Council of Trade Unions (ACTU) on behalf of its affiliates against a background of existing provisions for maternity leave and adoption leave introduced as standards in private sector awards by decisions of full Benches of the Australian Conciliation and Arbitration Commission on 9 March 1979 and 16 August 1985 respectively.

In relation to eligibility for paternity leave the ACTU proposed similar certification to that required in respect of maternity leave. We have adopted the basic format of the ACTU proposal, but we have taken account of the concerns expressed by CAI as to the possibility of abuse of paternity leave. For the extended period of paternity leave a statutory declaration will therefore be required confirming that the purpose of the leave is for the employee to become the primary care-giver of the child. The declaration will also set out any period of maternity leave to be taken by the employee's spouse and the employee will declare that he will not engage in any conduct inconsistent with his contract of employment whilst on leave.

CAI submitted that if the Commission were to grant any paternity leave entitlements, we should exclude employers with 100 employees or less. No such restriction exists in relation to maternity leave and we are not satisfied that such a restriction should be placed on the availability of paternity leave.

Figure 2.2: An extract of the Australian Industrial Relations Commission decision on parental leave.

The election of the Labor Government in March 1983 increased substantially the profile of the labour movement. During the early 1980s the Labor Government-ACTU wages strategy, as evidenced by the earlier versions of the Accord, was on the overall economic framework within which wages and conditions were determined. From 1986 onwards the focus shifted to specific industries and local or enterprise level industrial relations practices. This shift of focus from macro-economic (national) to micro-economic (local) conditions is expected to have a continuing effect on the practice of industrial relations in the 1990s. All parties agree that industrial relations reform is needed at the enterprise level but there have been differing strategies. For their part, the unions and the government, through later versions of the Accord, saw industrial reform and increased productivity best achieved through initiatives encouraging skill formation, multi-skilling and career development for workers in return for pay rises. This strategy was endorsed by the 1988 and 1989 National Wage Decisions of the Federal Commission which set down a number of measures (Structural Efficiency Principle) linking wage rises with award changes (award restructuring) that lead to increased productivity and greater efficiencies (see Figure 2.3).

Under the umbrella of 'award restructuring', employers and unions have turned some of their attention to enterprise level industrial relations practices and conditions in an effort to make enterprises more efficient, and consequently to secure wage increases for workers. While the concept of enterprise level bargaining is supported by the industrial parties, there is considerable discord over the form it should take. Some employer groups, notably the Metal Trades Industry Association, favour a form of 'managed decentralism', where the Commission would have considerable power to oversee the industrial relations developments resulting from enterprise bargaining. The MTIA concern is that enterprise bargaining will lead to excessive overaward payments and restrictive work practices for those groups which enjoy industrial strength. Other employer groups want to see the entire industrial system deregulated so that employers can negotiate directly with employees, with little or no role for unions or the conciliation and arbitration machinery. For their part, the unions, like the employers, do not have a unified position on how to proceed with enterprise bargaining. Some unions are prepared to negotiate employer-by-employer, overhauling awards and accepted practices, whereas other unions will not accept that traditional 'industry standards' are negotiable. Whatever approach is adopted by a union will be determined largely by its size and even more so by its organisation.

Organisation and size

By international standards, unionisation in Australia has been considered widespread (Table 2.2). The Australian Bureau of Statistics survey of trade union membership sets the level of unionism as at August 1990 at 41 per cent.

> *The National Wage Case Decision*
> *12 August, 1988*
> *Extract from the Principle*
>
> **STRUCTURAL EFFICIENCY**
>
> Increases in wages and salaries or improvements in conditions allowable under the National Wage Case decision of 12 August 1988 shall be justified if the union(s) party to an award formally agree(s) to co-operate positively in a fundamental review of that award with a view to implementing measures to improve the efficiency of industry and provide workers with access to more varied, fulfilling and better paid jobs. The measures to be considered should include but not be limited to:
>
> - establishing skill-related career paths which provide an incentive for workers to continue to participate in skill formation;
> - eliminating impediments to multi-skilling and broadening the range of tasks which a worker may be required to perform;
> - creating appropriate relativities between different categories of workers within the award and at enterprise level;
> - ensuring that working patterns and arrangements enhance flexibility and the efficiency of the industry;
> - including properly fixed minimum rates for classifications in awards, related appropriately to one another, with any amounts in excess of these properly fixed minimum rates being expressed as supplementary payments;
> - updating and/or rationalising the list of respondents to awards;
> - addressing any cases where award provisions discriminate against sections of the work-force.
>
> Source: TUTA 1989 Year Book

Figure 2.3: An extract from the 1988 National Wage Decision.

There are two obvious facts about the state of Australian trade unions—the percentage of trade union members in the workforce has dropped (Figure 2.4) and there are substantial variations in union membership between the public and private sector and men and women (Table 2.3).

The declining rate of unionisation has been attributed to a number of factors:

- growth in the number of women in the workforce who have historically not been as attracted as men to unions (45% of males and 35% of females are union members);
- the growth in jobs has been primarily in part-time work rather than full-time work. Part-time workers are less likely to join unions (25%) than full-time workers (45%);

Source: *Australian Financial Review*, 23 April, 1991.

Table 2.2: A comparison of union membership by country, 1961–1985.

Countries	1961	1968	1974	1981	1983	1984	1985
	As a percentage of wage and salary earners						
Australia	59	51	55	57	58	57	NA
Canada	30	30	32	36	38	38	37
Japan	34	34	34	31	30	29	29
Sweden	68	71	80	91	94	95	NA
United Kingdom	43	45	51	56	54	53	51
USA	30	31	29	23	21	19	18
West Germany	31	37	40	42	43	42	NA

NA = not applicable.

Source: Kumar, P. et al., *The Current Industrial Relations Scene in Canada*. Industrial Relations Centre, Queens University, 1987.

Table 2.3: Proportion of all employees who were members of a trade union and sector, March to May 1982 to August 1990

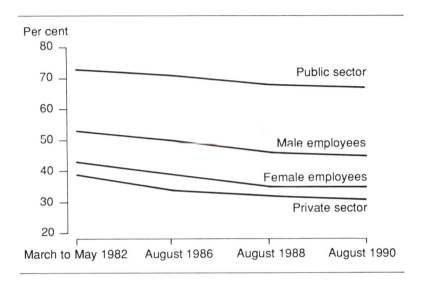

Source: ABS, Trade Union Members Australia, August, 1990. Catalogue no. 63250.

- industry growth is occurring primarily in those areas where unionisation is weak and difficult to achieve (e.g. in white-collar, high technology and personal services areas). See Table 2.4;
- unions have relied too much on the tribunal system; consequently, there is little 'shop-floor' representation to encourage new memberships;
- lack of resources because of low membership fees and small average membership;
- poor perception by the public of trade unionism because of adverse media coverage and mediocre union public relations.

The organisation of union members in Australia is not uniform. For years it has been said that there are too many unions in Australia. By 1906 there were over 300 unions and it was never below this number until June 1990, when 295 unions were identified. This does not mean that all trade union members belong to small organisations: over 55 per cent of unionists belong to only 14 unions. The number of large unions is expected to increase at the expense of smaller unions as a result of the *Industrial Relations Act 1988*, which not only makes union amalgamations easier, but also permits only unions of more than 10 000 members to be registered under the Act. Many unions will be forced to amalgamate.

The growth in white-collar areas of work, the increase in the number of women workers, and the trend towards part-time and contract work all pose significant challenges to trade unions.

Table 2.4: Proportion of all employees who were members of a trade union and industry, August, 1990.

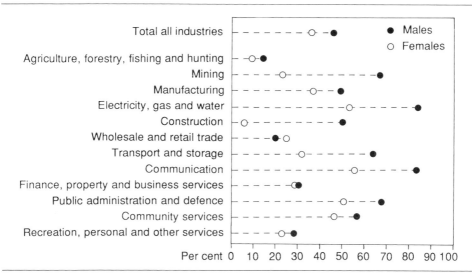

Source: ABS, Trade Union Members Australia, August, 1990. Catalogue no. 6325.0

Union ranks fall 9pc in 10 years

By BRAD NORINGTON Industrial Editor

MELBOURNE: The trade union movement is facing a bleak future after figures released yesterday showed memberships have declined by 9 per cent over the past decade, despite strong employment growth.

The result is disturbing for the ACTU because it shows that efforts to combat the trend with union mergers and improved services are not working.

The figures released by the Australian Bureau of Statistics, reveal that 42 per cent of the 6.1 million workforce were union members in August last year.

As part of a continuing slide, this follows 46 per cent union membership in 1986 and 51 per cent in 1976.

The most serious declines were in the private sector and among employed youth, where memberships have fallen to far below the overall average.

The private sector workforce grew by 25 per cent over the past four years, but union memberships increased by only 2 per cent to 32 per cent.

Union memberships in the public sector have remained high but also reflected the trend as the workforce increased 2 per cent but union numbers fell by 5 per cent to 68 per cent.

The figures show that 46 per cent of the men belonged to unions at the time of the 1988 survey. Only 35 per cent of women were members.

The level of memberships increased with age, from 27 per cent for the 15–19-year age group to a peak of 51 per cent for the 55–59-year age group.

Trade union statistics reveal that the size and composition of the workforce has dramatically shifted as service industries have grown compared with manufacturing, and that the private sector has increased at the expense of public enterprise.

Unions have failed to keep up with change and lacked the resources to organise in new areas of economy growth, particularly in finance, communications, tourism and other service-based areas.

Source: abridged article from *Sydney Morning Herald*, 7 June, 1989.

Figure 2.4: Rate of unionisation in Australia decreases.

Union amalgamation efforts are seen as a measure to bolster union influence in these areas through better financed and more vigorous organisations (Figure 2.5). Unions, through the ACTU, are also trying to improve community perception of them through various marketing strategies, particularly targeting youth, women and white collar workers. Figure 2.6 outlines a number of initiatives which the ACTU has taken in this area.

Union amalgamation scheme gathers pace
By MARK DAVIS

The ACTU's strategy to reshape the Australian labour movement through a round of union amalgamations is gathering pace, with more than 60 union mergers now on the drawing board.

An internal ACTU document on the state of play of amalagamations shows 61 separate amalgamations are being planned by almost 100 of Australia's 320-odd unions.

The document identifies how far each of the planned amalgamations has proceeded, showing that in 23 cases, unions have opened formal discussions, while in a further 24 cases, unions' decision-making bodies have taken the next step of formally deciding to amalgamate.

A further 12 of the 61 planned amalgamations have progressed through the various legal and administrative hurdles to the relatively advanced stage where the Industrial Relations Commission has referred the merger proposal to a ballot of union members.

Under the legislative framework for union amalgamations, which was streamlined by amendments to the Industrial Relations Act passed by Parliament late last year, mergers take at least six months and in most cases, from nine to 12 months.

If most of the amalgamations now on the drawing board proceed according to schedule, the ACTU will be able to point to significant changes in the structure of the union movement by early next year.

The peak union council has been pursuing a strategy of strengthening Australia's thinly stretched network of craft-based unions through a round of mergers along broad industry lines.

The ACTU document shows that the following 12 proposed union mergers have reached the stage where the commission has referred the proposal to a ballot of union members for ratification:

- A five-way merger designed to create a new finance industry union through amalgamation of the Australian Bank Employees' Union, the Australian Insurance Employees Union, the AMP Staff Association, The Trustee Company Officers' Association and the Woolbrokers Staffs' Association.
- Australian Teachers' Union-ACT Teachers' Federation-NT Teachers' Federation.
- Waterside Workers' Federation-Australian Foremen Stevedores' Association.
- Shop, Distributive and Allied Employees' Association-Mannequins and Models' Guild-Hairdressers and Wigmakers' Federation.
- Australian Professional Engineers' Association-Australian Professional Scientists' Association (merger endorsed by membership ballot).
- Municipal Officers' Association-Australian Transport Officers' Federation-Technical Services Guild (ballot closes next month).
- National Union of Workers-Commercial Travellers' Guild-Commonwealth Foremen's Association (merger endorsed by membership ballot).
- External Plant Officers' Association-Telecommunications Technical Officers' Association.
- Independent Teachers' Federation-NT Independent Schools Staff Association.
- Public Sector Union-Meat Inspectors' Association.
- Seamen's Union of Australia-Professional Divers' Association.
- Victorian State Building Trades Union-Slaters, Tilers and Roofing Industry Union.

Source: Australian Financial Review, 11 April, 1991.

Figure 2.5: Some of the union amalgamations being undertaken.

ACTU stepping up drive for union membership

By SIMON LLOYD

The Australian Council of Trade Unions has embarked on a major upgrading of its marketing efforts in response to the union movement's falling membership numbers and tarnished image.

The ACTU has openly acknowledged that trade unionism carries stereotyped perceptions in the general community. It is beginning to address these negative attitudes through active and, more importantly, professional, marketing.

Membership of trade unions has dropped to about 41 per cent of the workforce, with under 35 per cent of workers in the 20-24 age group now belonging to a union.

In 1989 the ACTU spent about $500,000 on an advertising campaign focusing on lower paid workers.

Now, in a hitherto uncharacteristic move, the ACTU has begun calling for expressions of interest from public DBXations and media consultancies to make its communications more effective.

The ACTU has also started a drive for high-profile corporate sponsors of its work education package, now in its third year.

In addition, the ACTU will soon publish a new quality magazine, entitled *Workplace*, which will be mailed direct to union and business leaders, senior public servants, federal and State MPs, financial institutions, lawyers academics and journalists.

Last month, the ACTU also published a 16-page supplement in the women's magazine *Cleo*, aimed specifically at young female workers, and launched by the Prime Minister's wife, Mrs Hazel Hawke.

Consideration is now being given to a repeat of the exercise because of the importance the ACTU attaches to women in the workforce.

The ACTU's communications campaign officer, Mr Andrew Casey, said the invitation for expressions of interest from public relations companies stemmed from a growing number of inquiries from individual unions to the ACTU requesting advice on media and marketing consultancies.

'Unions want public relations input and want the ACTU to help in the process,' Mr Casey said.

Mr Casey said that PR consultancies which were, or were willing to become, respondents to the new industrial award for PR workers would be treated favourably.

Unions were now recognising the need to communicate more effectively, and some were already making 'quite brilliant' inroads into the task, Mr Casey said.

He cited among others the Metal Workers, the Australian Bank Employees Union and the Flight Attendants Association for their internal and external marketing programmes.

'We [the union movement] have to change to survive and expand,' Mr Casey said.

'One of the challenges is being able to communicate to the membership and potential membership.'

Belying the widespread view that corporate sector management is vehemently anti-union, top Australian companies have in previous years committed substantial funding to the education package. Sponsors have included Ansett, Coles Myer, ICI, Ampol and CRA.

Source: Australian Financial Review, 9 April, 1991.

Figure 2.6: The ACTU is trying to overcome poor public perception of trade unions through various public relations activities.

Type of union

There have conventionally been attempts to classify unions in various ways. There are, however, a number of pitfalls in trying to classify unions precisely—particularly in light of expected amalgamations and realignments. Nevertheless, a distinction between craft, industrial and general unions is a useful aid to understanding.

Craft unions

These unions recruit members mainly on the basis of their craft or trade, irrespective of the industry involved. An example of such a union is the Electrical Trades Union (ETU). While a union may be termed 'craft', very few Australian unions qualify as genuine craft unions. Although some unions are dominated by members who have completed a trade and who work across industries, these unions also enrol trades assistants and related workers. They are therefore not purely restricted to 'craft' employees.

Industrial unions

These unions restrict membership to all employees in a particular industry. The industrial union is often regarded as the ideal form of unionism, cutting as it does across craft and occupational divisions. The ACTU 1987 'Future Strategies for Trade Unions' envisaged that ultimately there would be 20 industry-based unions in Australia. The recent formation of the Finance Sector Union made up of the amalgamation of five unions is an example of an industrial union (Figure 2.7).

Industrial unionism can be of benefit in limiting demarcation disputes—that is, disputes between members of different unions over the exclusive right to perform particular work. It is also of benefit in reducing competing union representation in negotiations with the employer over conditions of employment. Disadvantages include the creation of a powerful pressure group, which could disrupt the entire organisation unless management accedes to its demands. Also, a large, powerful organisation may not be as receptive as a small organisation to input from individual union members on matters of policy-making. As with any large organisation it must ensure that there are good channels of communication so that the concerns or problems of members receive prompt attention.

General unions

Membership in general unions is open to a variety of occupations and skills in any number of industries. The level and extent of membership depends on the diligence of the union in recruiting and servicing members. The National Union of Workers and the Federated Miscellaneous Workers are examples of general unions.

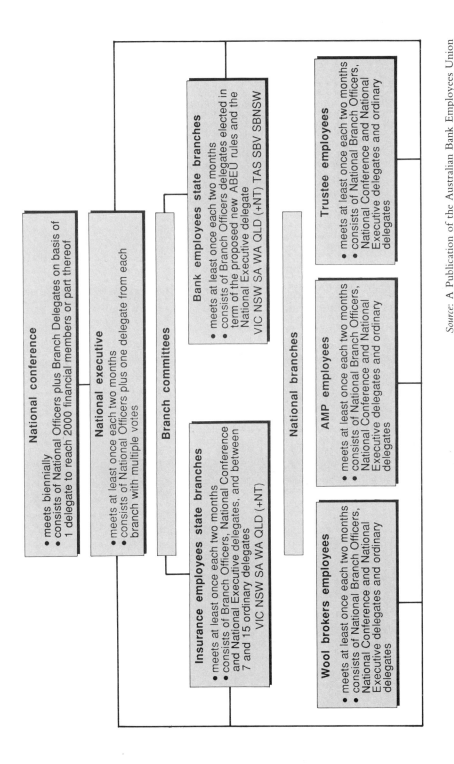

Figure 2.7: The structure of the new Finance Sector Union of Australia which amalgamated the Australian Insurance Employees Union, the Australian Bank Employees Union, the AMP Staff Association, the Trustee Companies Officers' Association and the Wool Brokers' Staff Association.

Source: A Publication of the Australian Bank Employees Union

Finally, there is the classification of staff association or house union. These organisations are usually formed to represent white-collar employees who do not want to be seen as unionists in the traditional sense.

Union structure

There are state and federal trade unions (depending on whether the union conforms to state or federal legal requirements). In order to have legal status, a union must be registered under the relevant state industrial legislation and/or the federal *Industrial Relations Act*. Only a registered union can participate within the system of conciliation and arbitration. If a union is deregistered it is unable to participate. Its members no longer have the benefits of an award, and are open to 'poaching' from a registered union.

While the internal structure of Australian unions can vary considerably in detail, there are certain features that can be regarded as typical. A simple model of a federal union structure comprises four levels:

1. *Workplace, plant or shop*. The workplace is theoretically where union members get to know the union. A member's first contact with the union is usually through the job representative (also referred to as 'shop steward' or 'job delegate'). As a consequence, in order to establish a union 'presence' the role of the job representative becomes crucial. Further, the role of the union representative takes on greater significance if there is a trend towards greater negotiation and consultation at the enterprise level of organisations. Figure 2.8 outlines the role of the job representative and Table 2.5 calculates the time spent on the various tasks undertaken by a job representative/delegate.

Table 2.5: Tasks undertaken by delegates.

	Task undertaken (% of delegates)	A lot of time spent on task (% of delegates)
Handle individual grievances	88	39
Negotiate physical working conditions	63	19
Negotiate about work practices	61	21
Recruit members	65	12
Participate on joint consultative committees	48	22
Negotiate other employment conditions	48	16
Prepare newsletters	37	12
Negotiate wage rises	27	10
Negotiate about allocation of overtime	23	5
None of the above	2	21

Population: Delegates at Australian workplaces with more than twenty employees.
Figures are weighted and are based on responses from 1138 delegates.

Source: Callus, R. et al., 'Industrial Relations at Work', The Australian Workplace Industrial Relations Survey (AWIRS), AGPS 1991.

THE JOB REPRESENTATIVE

When you start work, your first contact with the union will usually be through the job representative, also referred to as a shop steward or a job delegate.

The job representative is elected by union members at the work place as their representative. She/he is a vital link between those members and the union.

THE ROLE OF THE JOB REPRESENTATIVE

Recruitment
The job representative recruits new members to the union and provides workers with forms which may need to be filled out for union membership.

Health and safety
Job representatives often also act as health and safety delegates in the workplace.

Grievances
The job representative investigates grievances at the workplace and keeps union members informed of problems and outcomes.

Awards
The job representative makes sure that all the work carried out at the workplace is in accord with the award or local agreements.

New technology
The job representative informs the union of the introduction of any new work practices or technology in their workplace.

Information
The job representative keeps you informed about all union matters and makes sure that union circulars, notices of meetings, and union journals are brought to your notice.

Representation
The job representative represents you on local matters which affect your interests and helps to solve problems in the workplace.

The job representative can also:

- explain to you what your entitlements are under the award, including correct wages and working conditions;
- advise you where to go for help in a range of welfare issues, including the types of service provided by your union; and
- explain the decisions and policies of the union to the members in the workplace.

Source: (Adapted from) *ACTU Youth Book,* 1988/89

Figure 2.8: Role of the job representative.

At larger workplaces there may also be shop committees or combined union committees to coordinate union issues and activities. For example, a particular health and safety problem may come before the committee to get broader support before it is taken up with management.

2. *District or Regional.* Sub-branches based on localities comprise the district or regional level of the union. These convene general meetings of members, usually at monthly intervals.
3. *State.* At the state level there are branch offices in the relevant state capital which are directed by an annual conference. There is a state council or

committee of management which meets monthly. These bodies are made up of part-time officials.

There is also a state secretary and state organisers, who may be either elected or appointed by the committee of management—depending on the union rules—and who are responsible for the day-to-day operation of the union. They attend district meetings of members, take up issues of concern with management, and provide advice and assistance to individual members and job representatives. A diary of the typical workday of an organiser is shown in Figure 2.9.

DIARY EXTRACT

6:45 a.m.	Left home for Trades hall to pick up messages and leaflets.
7:15 a.m.	Arrived at the Showground to talk to members about the possible amalgamation between the union and either the Building Workers' Industrial Union (BWIU) or the Plumbers and Gasfitters' union. Passed out leaflets on the pros and cons of amalgamation. Answered queries on the amalgamation. Some members uneasy about joining BWIU because it now contains non-craft workers from the former Builder's Labourers Federation. Others voiced anxiety over the Union being swallowed up by the larger BWIU.
7:45 a.m.	Visited a site in Bondi, four members working. Checked if members were financial. Spoke briefly about the amalgamations and later interviewed site manager about 'top-up insurance'. Since the changes to Workers Compensation, employers are being asked to increase their insurance cover of employees to make up the difference. Employer would not make any commitment at this time. Grumbled: 'When will all these add-ons end?'.
8:30 a.m.	Came across an appalling site in Dover Heights. The scaffold had no ladder or rails. Electric cables were running through pools of water and in some places the cables were frayed. At 'smoko' the men were sitting on the concrete floor having their break. No messroom with table or chairs. The foreman became very aggressive. I pointed out to him various breaches of safety standards and regulations. In his view, provided the men are willing to work, it doesn't matter. Told him he had 24 hours to fix the site up and that I would be contacting the Safety Inspector.
10:00 a.m.	Interviewed a foreman at a factory in French's Forest over the sacking of an apprentice. Foreman said the apprentice was 'cheeky'. He was attempting to paint the ceiling of an office without covering up the floor. When asked to put down a drop-sheet, he allegedly swore at the tradesman. Interviewed site members about the incident.
1:00 p.m.	Rang union office for messages and picked up a sandwich.
2:00 p.m.	At a site in North Sydney saw a painter using banned 18" rollers. With protracted use these rollers have been shown to affect arm muscles and back of the neck. After checking that the painter is a financial member, rang the contractor who claimed not to know anything about the situation. Contractor is notorious for using these rollers. Took the rollers with me.
4:00 p.m.	Back to office to catch up on administrative work. Will go out and have a meal before union executive meeting at 6:30 p.m.

Figure 2.9: Daily Diary of Activities—State Organiser, Operative Painters and Decorators Union.

4. *Federal*. The federal level consists of a council or national conference—the union's highest policy-making body, which is made up of elected members and meets on an annual or biennial basis.

There is also an elected federal executive, which meets frequently to administer the day-to-day aspects of policy. In addition, the federal executive oversees the activities of the full-time federal officials—that is, the federal secretary and other staff of the federal office. The federal level of the union handles federal award negotiations and Commission appearances.

Inter-union organisation
National representation
The Australian Council of Trade Unions is the central trade union organisation in the country. Over 150 unions are affiliated to the ACTU, representing 2.6 million workers. The ACTU's primary task is to represent the union movement at the national level. Specific duties include:
- helping affiliated unions settle disputes;
- presenting submissions to the National Wage Case and other major hearings before the Federal Commission on behalf of affiliated unions;
- presenting submissions and lobbying the Federal Government on economic, legal and industrial issues which affect its members;
- maintaining international links with overseas trade union bodies; and
- providing advice to affiliates and researching issues affecting working people, such as occupational health and safety, migrant and women workers.

The ACTU is governed by decisions of the biennial congress. The congress consists of delegates from affiliated unions, delegates from the trades and labor/trades hall councils, and the Federal Executive. Implementation of policies passed by congress is the responsibility of the Federal Executive.

The elected Federal Executive includes a president, secretary, assistant secretaries and delegates representing industry groupings. It must also include at least three women. The day-to-day activities of the ACTU are managed by the elected full-time officials and specialist staff.

State representation
The ACTU is represented in each state by a Trades and Labor or Trades Hall Council. There are also some provincial councils (e.g. Newcastle and Geelong) that are directly affiliated to the ACTU. The state councils have the same concerns as the ACTU but operate on a state basis. They are also responsible for implementing ACTU policies within that particular state.

Union aims and objectives
The aims and objectives of individual unions are usually set out in their constitution and rules. The overall aim of a union is to protect and advance

the interests of its members. Specific objectives include improved economic and working conditions, security of employment, the provision of services to members, the setting up of affiliations, and political influence in policy-making.

Improved economic conditions

Better financial reward for work is the primary objective of unions. This can be achieved through shorter working hours, increases in paid annual leave, or improved wages and salaries.

Improved working conditions

Unions seek to improve members' physical working conditions by ensuring workers have regular work breaks, adequate amenities and safe physical surroundings. Unions take up claims on behalf of individual union members relating to workers' compensation and related matters.

Security of employment

Unions attempt to protect members against arbitrary or discriminatory dismissals. Also, unions act on behalf of members should redundancies or transfers eventuate from industry restructuring or technological developments.

Services to members

Most unions provide welfare and legal assistance for members. Some have credit union facilities, recreational outlets (e.g. holiday flats, clubs) and educational assistance (e.g. scholarships).

Affiliations

Unions usually have a number of affiliations, either to assist them in pursuing their own objectives or—as part of their commitment to the labour movement—to assist other organisations or workers generally. Examples of affiliations are international trade union secretariats such as FIET (International Federation of Commercial Clerical, Professional and Technical Employees) or the International Metalworkers Federation and the ACTU overseas aid agency, APHEDA.

Political aims

The Australian Labor Party has been seen historically as the political arm of trade unions. This has changed in recent times as the party has endeavoured to become more broadly based. Nevertheless, the union movement maintains a significant influence in policy-making through their assured representation at ALP conferences.

Methods of achievement

It is the method by which trade unions attempt to improve members' economic

INTERVIEW

MARK RYAN
Position: Federal Industrial Officer, The Australian Journalists' Association.

1. Mark, could you briefly outline the role and aims of the AJA?

To represent AJA members in all their industrial and professional concerns. Apart from the normal industrial activities of award matters, negotiation, disputes etc, it involves the following 'professional' activities: investigation of complaints concerning breach of the AJA Code of Ethics; submissions to various inquiries; including regular submissions to the Australian Broadcasting Tribunal on the renewal of TV and radio station licences, Parliamentary inquiries and so on regarding defamation law, seeking to obtain payment of copyright royalties. Many of these 'professional' concerns also indirectly offset the working conditions of members.

2. Briefly, what does your position with the union entail?

The AJA has some 12 500 members employed in the private and public sector. The overwhelming majority of members have their rates of pay and conditions of employment governed by awards of the Australian Industrial Relations Commission. There are 2 industrial officers based in the Federal Office and a third part-time Federal Industrial Officer based in our Victorian Branch Office who mainly looks after superannuation matters. My main responsibility is in relation to private sector awards. This entails meetings with members, negotiations with employers, advocacy before the Commission and advice to Branch officials.

3. You often refer to the employers as the 'bosses' and you feel uncomfortable with the term 'the troops' which employers sometimes use to refer to your members. Do you see industrial relations in terms of capital versus labour?

Yes. It being expressed usually as an attempt to alter the power relationship between employers and employees. This goes beyond the mere attempt to gain wage increases. For example, ACTU Test Cases over recent years (maternity leave etc.) are good examples of a change in the exercise of power at a macro level.

4. What would you see as the most important steps and considerations that need to be taken to settle industrial disputes?

Regardless of the type of dispute involved for example, workplace disputes versus industry-wide disputes, it is essential to assess the strengths and weaknesses of both sides. Secondly, to assess what is the appropriate tactic to be employed, remembering that industrial action, of whatever sort, is a means to an end rather than an end in itself.

5. Finally, you work in the print and electronic media. How do you feel the media generally reports the field of industrial relations?

Reporting industrial relations falls into two categories—as a specialist area and as part of general news. In the first category there will be analysis of what is going on, why the dispute has occurred or what submissions were put to a National Wage Case hearing. In the second category will be a straight news story, for example closure of the Government Printing Office. Both these types of coverage are usually well done. Where the story covers a dispute the major failing for someone involved in industrial relations is that both the causes of the dispute and terms of settlement of disputes are little publicised, particularly where the story or stories have concentrated on the effects of the dispute on the public.

standards which receives most public attention. The extent of trade union power tends to dominate the public's attitude to unions. The unions are often thought to be the cause of any economic ills the community may be experiencing. Unions do not operate alone, however, and what they can achieve is largely determined by the prevailing environment.

In recent years, under the Federal Labor Movement, unions have liaised more closely through the ACTU with government in economic decision-making. They have sought to achieve their objectives by co-operating with government through the Accord. Ultimately, the effectiveness of this, or any method, is determined by union members. While the union movement as a whole may see the co-operative approach as the best avenue for improved living standards and secure employment, individual unions must still answer to the internal industrial pressures from members.

Another method a union uses to achieve its objectives is direct negotiation or collective bargaining with an employer at the enterprise level. This has normally been done to achieve over-award benefits which do not form part of the award. Unions can make gains through direct negotiation also during periods of labour shortages. In recent years, there has been greater reliance on direct negotiation between employers and unions under the auspices of the industrial commissions. The 1988/1989 measures in the structural efficiency principle set down by the Federal Commission, whereby workplace efficiency is sought through award restructuring, has contributed to an increase in the use of consultation and negotiations between the parties at the workplace or enterprise level.

Unions can additionally use political pressure to achieve their objectives. Individual unions, state trades/labor councils and the ACTU all lobby government for initiatives favourable to workers. Conversely, if a government intends to pass laws considered adverse to workers' interests, industrial campaigns will ensue.

The conciliation and arbitration machinery has had a considerable role in protecting and advancing the interests of unionists. This is discussed at greater length in subsequent chapters.

Finally, unions use industrial pressure to assist in achieving their aims, including work-to-rule, overtime bans, and strikes. These may be used in direct negotiations or when the dispute is before an industrial tribunal, although the member of the tribunal will usually attempt to stop any industrial action during the conciliation and arbitration phase. Employers may also use some direct action to assist in countering union pressure.

Summary

People combine into collective organisations known as trade unions in the realisation that they will have more influence as a group than as an individual.

There is a wide range of views about the usefulness of unions. Some regard them as an essential element in a democratic state, as vehicles of expression for working people. Others take a more political stance, and see unions as the means of overtaking the means of production and ensuring that workers have control. Still others feel that unions have outlived their usefulness, because 'management is more progressive nowadays'. In reality, it is difficult to generalise about unions. They are all different, and their actions and development depend on leadership, membership attitudes, economic and political factors.

While the major aims and objectives of trade unions have not changed significantly since their inception, changes in the composition of the workforce and in the nature of work have had an effect on trade union operations. How the union movement addresses these and other contemporary challenges will determine its effectiveness in achieving its objectives and future influence in the community.

Questions and Activities

1. Why would the ACTU rules insist on at least three female representatives on the executive?
2. Why is the workplace often considered the most important level of a union?
3. After reading Figure 2.5 what, in your view, are the advantages of unions amalgamating? Are there potentially any disadvantages?
4. Profile a particular union by getting relevant information (rules, new member information and the journal). What are its objectives? What services does it offer? Is the membership of the executive reflective of the general membership? What are the major issues of concern?
5. After reading Figure 2.6 list some of the initiatives which unions are taking to improve the community's perception of them. What other measures could unions be taking?
6. Read the following article and answer these questions.
    a. In Kelty's view, who does the ACTU represent?
    b. What is meant by 'power of an organisation in a pluralist democracy'?
    c. In your view, is the 'power' of the ACTU at the top or spread through all society?

Are the unions too powerful?

Kelty says the role of the union is as a social bargainer, balancing a democracy's liberal democratic ideal and social concern. He says the criticism of alleged excessive ACTU power is the criticism of 'extremists'.

The Bulletin asked him what right did the union movement have to exercise such influence.

'Because the power we have is the power of an organisation in a pluralist democracy. That's the power we have. It's a pluralist democracy. We represent people. We bargain. We don't pretend to have any power beyond that.

But, by definition, Kelty represents a diminishing band.

'By *fact*, we represent a reducing proportion of the workforce directly—not by definition. A lot of our strategies and objectives are not designed simply to raise wage rates. Look at the question of low paid workers. Union membership is actually a much smaller proportion of low-paid workers. Most of what we will do in terms of minimum rates will not be about unionised members, it will be about women and non-unionists working in difficult industries for us to organise. Why? Because in the final analysis, it is about social concern. Superannuation is for everybody, not just unions. It's a social concern. Child care isn't limited to union members. If you are social bargainers, clearly you've got to represent directly and indirectly a lot of people.'

But Kelty really has tremendous power. Isn't it nonsense to say he doesn't?

'I don't think so. I think power is often exaggerated. Power is the processes of government, the power of individuals is inflated. Keating as Treasurer doesn't wave a magic wand and fix up the economy. I don't have a view of society that all power resides at the top. Power and the ability to influence ideas goes through all society.

'Like China and the Soviet Union are now realising, you can't just have so-called power just at the top. Power has got to be something spread through the whole society.'

Source: *The Bulletin*, 20 June, 1989.

Chapter 3

Employer Organisations

Objectives

At the end of this chapter, the reader should be able to:
- consider the variety of ways employers have combined to pursue their interests, especially within the industrial relations system;
- discuss the issues of employer unity and the growth of employer 'militancy'; and
- list the services provided by employer associations.

Introduction

In Chapter 2, the activities and functions of trade unions are discussed. It is now appropriate to consider the role of employer associations.

The Australian industrial relations system has fostered the collective representation of employer interests in the same way as it has with trade unions. Indeed, the systems of conflict resolution and the administration of awards and other rules could not be conducted efficiently without substantial membership of employer associations among the society's retailers, manufacturers, distributors and the like.

While there is no one agreed definition of employer associations, all are essentially characterised by groups of business enterprises which have combined to pursue common goals. Their affairs are in accordance with a registered constitution and rules, and they often have elected and employed officers. The aims and objectives of the Confederation of Australian Industry (CAI) provide a useful and general guide to the goals pursued by employer associations:

- to promote industry, trade and commerce;
- to promote unity of purpose and action by employers in all matters affecting their welfare and interest;
- to improve relations between employers and employees;
- to represent employers, industry, trade and commerce before any courts, tribunals, commissions or committees; and
- to represent the interests and views of employers, industry, trade and commerce at government level.

Source: CAI Information Brochure

These objectives indicate the desire of employer organisations to improve the business environments of their members, to limit labour costs, and to provide accurate and concise information and advice. This is further illustrated in the condensed objects of the Retail Traders' Association set out in Figure 3.1.

Name of Association

1. The Association shall be known as 'The Retail Traders' Association of New South Wales'.

Office

2. The principal office of the Association shall be at RTA House, 120 Clarence Street, Sydney, or at such other place as the Council may from time to time determine.

Objects

3. The objects for which the Association is established are:
   a) To protect promote and advance the interests of Retail Traders in the State of New South Wales and in all other States or Territories from time to time constituting the Commonwealth of Australia.
   b) To promote and maintain good relations between the members and their employees and between the members and manufacturers, producers, distributors and consumers of goods sold by the members.
   c) To protect and promote the interests of the members generally by all lawful means.
   d) To secure to the members the advantage of unity of action in all matters affecting their interests.
   e) To organise the employers in the retail trade with a view to improving conditions in the trade.
   f) To act as an organisation or industrial union of employers under the laws of the Commonwealth of Australia or of any State within the Commonwealth.
   g) To bring any industrial dispute or claim relating to industrial matters before any Commonwealth Court, Commission or other Commonwealth Industrial Tribunal or before any State Court, Commission, Board, Committee or other Industrial Tribunal, or before any other body or Tribunal constituted for the purpose of dealing with industrial matters.

Figure 3.1: The Retail Traders' Association of New South Wales—constitution and rules.

Underlying any employer organisation's objectives is the desire to ensure its continued operation. Significant efforts are made to encourage membership and to discourage the emergence of other organisations which might compete for members. Registered employer associations will often argue against the formal recognition by industrial tribunals of any new employer associations which may seek to enrol members of the current associations. Trade unions are equally concerned about their own organisational security.

It is customary to refer to employer associations as being on the 'opposite side of the coin to trade unions'. This description is acceptable to some degree but is limited by a colloquial view of the nature of industrial relations (trade unions versus employers and management), and it overlooks the occasions on which unions and employers have acted in unison—demonstrated, for example, by trade union support of employer association submissions to government when considering issues such as tariff protection from imported goods.

Employer associations perform a critical role in Australia's industrial relations system. Some trade unions have even supported the development of combinations of employers within their industry to assist the union to achieve its objectives. Although this may appear illogical (why should unions support the formation of employer groups?), employer associations do make much of the union's task easier. For example, associations inform their members of changes to awards. Union organisers can rely on member companies being told of the changes and are therefore able to concentrate on other activities. At a practical level, if a union organiser encounters an employer association member who is not abiding by an award condition, then the association can usually be relied upon to ensure that the member's error is corrected. The alternative method of formal award enforcement involves legal processes which can be lengthy and costly. Finally, conventional wisdom suggests, it is simpler for unions to negotiate with one employer group than with hundreds or perhaps thousands of individual firms.

There is pressure to encourage workplace negotiations (enterprise bargaining) which some view as a device to reduce trade unions' capacity to achieve changes with large numbers of employers via a small number of employer associations.

Types of employer organisations

Not all organisations which outwardly appear to be employer associations actually have an industrial relations purpose. Often a group of employers in an industry will combine with formal rules of associations and hold meetings to achieve common objectives. A group of Health Professionals, for example, could act collectively to lobby government to enact legislation restricting those without certain qualifications from working in the industry. While this organisation can be viewed as an employer association (common objective, they employ people, and they have a constitution and rules), it differs significantly from 'conventional' employer associations.

As the concern here is industrial relations, the employer organisations of interest are not those which exist mainly as trade or professional associations but those which are primarily concerned with assisting their members resolve industrial conflict and administer employment law. Obviously, many employer organisations do provide commercial and related services (as discussed in detail below); however, their primary function is to represent their members' interests in the industrial relations system. Of these organisations, two main categories can be identified:

- *Industry associations.* These represent the interests of employers in a particular industry. The Printing and Allied Trades Employers' Federation of Australia (PATEFA), for example, has as its members employers who are engaged in commercial printing and packaging. The Registered Clubs Association of NSW, as its name implies, is an organisation with a membership of some 1500 licensed clubs in New South Wales. Industry associations develop very specialised knowledge.

INTERVIEW

KEN STENNER

Position: Industrial Officer, Printing and Allied Trades Employers' Federation of Australia.

1. Ken, what are your responsibilities as an industrial relations specialist?

To assist member companies achieve and maintain industrial harmony and compliance with legislative award provisions.

More specifically, I provide advice to members on award provisions, interpretations and precedents; dispute resolution and legislative and regulatory requirements (e.g. Occupational Health and Safety Act, anti-discrimination legislative provisions and training guarantee requirements).

Dispute resolution either through negotiation between employers, employees/unions or as an advocate on behalf of a member organisation is another important aspect of my job.

Other responsibilities include presentation of training sessions, research of issues and precedents, telephone inquiries and preparation of circulars for members.

2. What training and education do you have for a career in industrial relations?

I received informal training in the workplace in payroll, personnel management and industrial relations at various management levels in administrative, construction, primary manufacturing and service areas.

A short stint as a union delegate rounded off my informal training prior to commencing tertiary studies.

My formal education in industrial relations commenced with the Advanced Certificate in Industrial Relations at Sydney Technical College. Following this I completed the Graduate Diploma in Labour Relations and the Law, a two year part-time course conducted by the University of Sydney.

3. What role do you see industrial relations having in organisations in the future?

A vital one which works with employers to gain optimum organisational performance through harmony in the workplace while ensuring management's ability to manage is not impaired. I see industrial relations responsibilities infiltrating all areas of organisations and rather than being seen only in a troubleshooting role, will become complementary to all other management functions from supervision through to strategic planning.

Greater emphasis will be placed upon formulating industrial agreements which are specifically appropriate to the requirements of individual enterprises.

Responsibilities for many day-to-day industrial issues will be devolved to line managers and supervisors to become part of their normal duties.

4. What role do you see industrial relations specialists having in the future?

The specialist, while maintaining the legalistic role of adviser and advocate in tribunals, will diversify into other human resource management areas including training and career development.

As well, the specialist will become more closely involved in operations management through strategic planning and implementation of industrial relations practices designed to anticipate potential problems. It will be more of a proactive role instead of being an industrial firefighter.

- *Umbrella organisations.* These groupings, represented by organisations like the Australian Chamber of Manufactures and the state-level employers' federations, have members from a diversity of industries. Individual companies without the services of an industry association often join an umbrella group. A significant function of these associations also involves representing the industrial relations interests of smaller associations which have affiliate membership. These join umbrella organisations like the Employer's Federation of NSW because they often do not have the resources necessary to provide full industrial relations services to their membership.

Figure 3.2 is a sample of the over 250 associations separately registered under the NSW *Industrial Arbitration Act*, and illustrates the diversity of employer organisations.

Accommodation Owners' Association of Australia—P. James, Aston House, 297 Elizabeth Street, Sydney
Aerated Water and Cordial Manufactures' Association, The—Henry M. Deakin, Schweppes (Aust.) Pty. Ltd. 43 O'Riordan Street, Alexandria.
Apparel Manufacturers' Association of NSW. (Division of the Chamber of Manufacturers of NSW)—L. J. Alexander, 60 York Street, Sydney.
Architects' Association, Practising—M. A. Maine, 196 Miller Street, North Sydney.
Asbestos Cement Manufacturers' Association of New South Wales, The—L. W. Farrar, 3rd Floor, Scripture Union House, 129 York Street, Sydney.
Auctioneers and Agents' Guild — C. L. Allen, Anderson Real Estate, 71 George Street, Parramatta.
Australian Agricultural Co., The—J. Henry, General Superintendent, off Hunter Street, Newcastle.
Australian Gas Light Co., The—J. E. Hooper, P.O. Box 944 North Sydney.
Australian Iron and Steel Proprietary Limited— T. M. L. Snelson, 20 O'Connell Street, Sydney.
Australian Medical Association, The New South Wales Branch of the—Dr R. Cable, 2nd Fl., 33-35 Atchison Street, St Leonards.
Automotive Industries of New South Wales, Chamber of—W. R. Lowrie, 33 Riley Street, Potts Point.
Bakers' Association Broken Hill, Master—R. F. L. Carpenter, Argent Street, Broken Hill.
Bakers & Pastrycooks' Association of NSW, Family— H. J. Hol, 81 Meadow Street, Tarrawanna.
Beauty Therapists, The Advance Association of—Mary Kay, 271 Pitt Street, Sydney.
Blood-Horse Breeders' Association of Australia (New South Wales Division)—J. Brady, 154 Elizabeth Street, Sydney.
Boarding-house Proprietors' Association of New South Wales, The—F. J. Howland, 33 Macquarie Place, Sydney.
Bonded and Free Stores Employers' Federation, The Sydney—H. R. Beardsmore, c.o. Perry Johnson, Beardsmore & Wilton, 39-41 York Street, Sydney.
Bread Manufacturers' Association of New South Wales, The Country—C. Cracknell, 1 Stafford Road, Artarmon.
Bread Manufacturers' of New South Wales—B. Hume–Phillips, 167 Kent Street, Sydney.
Bread Manufacturers of New South Wales, The Independent—L. Gullick, 49 Blue Gum Crescent, Frenchs Forest.
Brewers' Association of New South Wales—J. McBlane, 95 York Street, Sydney.
Brick Manufacturers' Association of New South Wales, The—T. Edwards, 115 Wellbank St., N. Strathfield (P.O. Box 192, Concord).
Bricklayers' Association, The Central Coast Master—Mrs. J. M. Smith, 21 Bellevue Crescent, Terrigal.
Bricklaying Contractors' Association of New South Wales, Master—W. G. Byerley, c.o. Aubrey F. Crawlye, 56 Hunter Street, Sydney.
Broken Hill Proprietary Newcastle Iron and Steel Industry—C. R. Hall, General Manager, Newcastle Works.
Builders' Association of New South Wales, Central Cumberland Branch, The Master—E. Webb, 48 Macquarie Street, Parramatta.
Builders' Association of New South Wales, The Master—R. L. Rocher, 52 Parramatta Road, Forest Lodge.

> Builders' Association of New South Wales, St. George Branch, The Master—C. H. Schofield, Builders' Exchange, Hill Street, Hurstville.
> Building Lining Contractors, New South Wales, The Association of— G. A. Cooke, 308 Great North Road, Abbotsford.
> Burns, Philp and Company Limited—E. T. lee, 7 Bridge Street, Sydney.
> Bus and Coach Association (NSW)—G. E. Gourlay, 27 Villiers Street, North Parramatta.
> Butchers' Association, Sydney Master—A. C. Bender, Daking House, Rawson Place, Sydney.

Source: *1988 Official Directory*, Labor Council of NSW

Figure 3.2: A sample of employer organisations registered under the NSW Industrial Arbitration Act.

Peak employer bodies

Employer groups have developed national associations to pursue their interests. The major 'umbrella' peak employer bodies are the Confederation of Australian Industry (CAI), formed in 1978, and the Business Council of Australia (BCA). The CAI is controlled by a board of directors who are nominated by a number of regional employer groups. As its objectives (discussed earlier) demonstrate, the CAI broadly exists to counter the ACTU as the peak trade union organisation but also to pursue employer concerns (its pro-active role), especially in the determination of government policy. An extract of the Presidential address to the CAI's Ninth Annual General Meeting (1986) illustrates the wide role occupied by the CAI.

> In the area of business regulation, CAI has since 1980 consistently led the argument for less interference by governments and their regulatory agencies, estimated by the business regulation review unit to involve some 16,400 commonwealth public servants at an aggregate cost of $700 million per annum.
>
> CAI has commended the government for the serious attempts it has made to limit and reduce regulation. In particular, CAI has welcomed the establishment of the business regulation review unit, streamlining of customs clearance procedures, reductions in export controls and the commitment of the states to uniform food standards. Each of these initiatives has resulted in substantial savings for industry. However, much more must be done.
>
> No single business regulatory action has attracted more attention this year than takeovers. CAI has strongly argued that government intervention powers to restrict and regulate takeovers should not be increased and was pleased with the Government's decision not to strengthen the merger provisions of the Trade Practices Act by lowering the threshold test. Restructuring of Australian industry in the current period, on efficiency grounds, is essential if we are to compete successfully overseas [. . .].
>
> To defeat the superannuation claim, CAI devoted an unprecedented level of resources to the fight.
>
> We conducted a major media campaign with advertisements in both the print media and on television.
>
> We published a widely discussed booklet which looked at productivity growth, its derivation and the relationship between productivity growth and the economy's ability to support increased labour costs such as the projected superannuation payments.

> We ran an eighteen day submission in the Arbitration Commission which left no doubt that the union productivity claim had no basis in valid economic reasoning.
>
> *Source*: CAI Annual Report 1985/1986

Although a number of the specific issues discussed in the address are from the mid-1980s, they demonstrate the CAI's continuing desire to: influence general government policy direction (e.g. by pursuing an acceptance of less business regulation); argue the case for and against specific legislative changes (e.g. by not altering the merger provisions of the Trade Practices Act); and to represent their members' views in major industrial relations issues and cases (e.g. the ACTU superannuation claim in the Arbitration Commission).

Another significant peak employer body is the Business Council of Australia (BCA) formed in 1983. It consists of the Chief Executives of some of Australia's largest companies. The BCA guiding 'philosophy' and objectives are:

> Democratic governments best pursue the national interest and encourage growth by setting a competitively neutral environment for productive financial and commercial activities and the creative use of human and capital resources. The generation of profits, the life-blood of every private sector economy and the underpinning of private fixed capital investment, is essential to Australia's global competitiveness and economic wellbeing.
>
> Accordingly, the Council and its members in the workings of Council, will promote the following:
>
> - the business community is the basic wealth-creating and job-creating element of society and is dependent on community acceptance and support to continue that wealth and job creation.
> - the corporate responsibility and long term interest of business enterprises produce standards of high integrity and effective self-regulation.
> - a system of competition, entrepreneurship, risk-taking and rewards in an open and free international and domestic market environment is vital to economic and social progress and is the only way of providing best value to customers.
> - building and reinforcing at the enterprise level, the genuine sense of co-operation, responsibility and mutual respect between management and individual employees which maximises employee satisfaction and improves economic performance.
> - business must work with every elected government in and under the law, while strongly advocating smaller less costly government and opposing corporatist approaches which erode market-based resource allocation and freedom of choice.
> - the role of business leadership in creating a society which is self-reliant, competitive and innovative and which distributes wealth with equity, consistent with risk, incentive and the contribution of the individual.
>
> *Source*: BCA Annual Report, 1985–86

The BCA's objectives reflect the general thrust of peak employer body concerns. This is noticeable in a number of commonly occurring key phrases, such as 'smaller less costly government', 'market-based resource allocation', 'system of competition', 'incentive', and 'mutual respect between management and individual employees'.

Consistent with these objectives, in 1987 the BCA issued an important policy statement, 'Towards an enterprise based industrial system'. The introduction to the statement is set out as follows:

1.1. The Business Council, after a great deal of internal consultation, intensive work by a committee of Chief Executives, and discussion and decision-making in meetings of the full Council, has committed itself to pursue a major new direction for Australia's idnustrial relations system.

1.2. The Council's overriding objective is to create an industrial relations environment where:
- people can work more effectively and with greater satisfaction;
- the highest possible productivity becomes the common goal for all; and
- healthy enterprise performance provides the best outcomes for employers and employees alike.

1.3. The Council seeks a fundamental reorientation of the system:
- away from one largely focused outside the enterprise, adversarial in nature, and conducted by intermediates positioned between management and other employees;
- towards one which is centred on the enterprise, develops a high degree of mutual trust and interest, and strengthens the direct relationships between employers and employees.

The Business Council believes that, because of the economic challenges facing Australia and an increasing community awareness of the shortcomings of the present system, there is now a significant opportunity to move away from our traditional industrial relations problems to a more positive system for the future.

The Business Council recognises that much of the responsibility for implementing this reform rests with company management.

Source: BCA policy statement, 24 March, 1987

The BCA policy encourages plant or enterprise level negotiation to resolve conflict, while fostering an industrial relations 'culture' within companies which relies upon direct employer/employee communication with, some have argued, less trade union involvement. To some extent, the BCA's policy and its accompanying sentiments, well exampled by *The Australian's* editorial (Figure 3.3), have gained support. In the submissions at the April 1991 National Wage Case hearing, the ACTU, the Federal Government and most national employer groups (except the Metal Trades Industry Association—a major, national association) wanted the Commission to depart, either somewhat or totally, from centralised wage-fixation to a wages system based on 'enterprise bargaining'. This, they argued, would create a more efficient and productive workforce utilising the gains achieved under award restructuring. Essentially it was contended that entepise bargaining better takes into account the circumstances of each organisation whereas 'across-the-board' increases are paid regardless of the productivity, efficiency or capacity-to-pay of each company.

In a controversial decision, the Full Bench of the Industrial Relations Commission rejected the drive to set up a framework of enterprise bargaining,

THE AUSTRALIAN

WEDNESDAY MARCH 25, 1987

A breath of fresh air for industry

IF Australia is to increase its standard of living, it has to be more competitive. To be successful, our industrial enterprises have to break away from the stultifying industrial relations club atmosphere and have a refreshingly productive new relationship with their workforces.

The policy statement published yesterday by the Business Council of Australia (BCA), advocating a complete revision of our industrial thinking to end the assumption that conflict is inevitable, is a document that could lead to that new relationship.

Business management, unionists—whether shop-floor members or organisers—and politicians right across the political spectrum cannot afford to ignore the document's suggestions.

If the BCA document were implemented we would see annual or biennial negotiations between management and workers leading to binding and enforceable fixed-term agreements; agreements including performance-based rewards and profit sharing; negotiations taking place between management and employees without outside interference; unions organised on an industry basis, with one union for each factory or enterprise; non-compulsory union membership; and both workers and management having equality under the law.

What a breath of fresh air this would be amid the mouldering piles of confrontation-style agreements fought out between management and unions in industrial courts and tribunals over the years!

Managements would again have to shoulder the responsibility of management of labour, something they have left to union delegates, industrial relations officers, industrial commissions and national wage negotiations for too long. No longer would someone divorced from a factory or office decide what each worker was worth, but the people running the enterprise and providing the manpower would do so together.

Similarly, workers would not have their futures decided by unseen union leaders or the votes of union members in other enterprises or even other States.

But unionists would have to agree to the simple rule that if an agreement is good enough to sign, it must be good enough to stick to for a fixed term.

The BCA document is not a union-bashing diatribe. It offers a bright future for all Australian workers away from the awful mess that we have allowed the arbitration and conciliation system to become. It also offers the possibility of taking Australia away from the disruptive demarcation disputes and industry-wide conflicts that have cost this country so much in lost production and exports.

The BCA consists of the chief executives of 80 of Australia's largest companies. Those most concerned with drawing up this document have reputations for success and enlightenment. They deserve a hearing.

If we are to continue to have a caring Australia, with the revenue to allow us to be suitably compassionate, we must have a vigorous, successful private enterprise system. This document makes a valid contribution to this end.

Source: The Australian, 25 March, 1987

Figure 3.3: Report on BCA policy.

arguing that the concept is not new and, in the past, has led to 'excessive wage levels, excessive improvements in conditions of employment and restrictive work practices of which employers and others have subsequently complained'.

The MTIA's arguments against organisation or enterprise based bargaining included:

- enterprise bargaining cannot work without enterprised-based unions. In the metal industry, well-organised craft unions have exploited their ability to establish over award payments in certain companies and then achieved a 'flow-on' to other employers in the industry; and
- based upon the award restructuring experience, enteprise bargaining needs a whole new management and workplace culture which does not exist.

Source: Newcastle Herald, 17 April, 1991

In October 1991 the National Wage bench decided to agree to enterprise bargaining but with reservations. The decision allowed unions and employers to negotiate wage rises in return for improved productivity at the enterprise level. Agreements are then certified using Sections 112 and 115 of the Industrial Relations Act. The Commission was still concerned that enterprise bargaining seriously increased the risk of excessive wage increases 'flowing on' in a deregulated environment.

Employer unity

Unlike the experience of the labour movement, where the ACTU has demonstrated considerable skill in limiting the disaffection of its membership, the peak employer bodies have had to contend with problems which, as industrial relations experts would describe, relate to their level of 'internal authority'. In other words, very significant employer groups (such as the National Farmers Federation and the Master Builders' Federation) have, for example, sometimes dissolved their affiliation with the CAI or have openly disagreed with the policies the CAI has pursued. It is common, therefore, to find a number of employer associations putting their own submissions in national wage cases while the ACTU dominates the union submissions.

In an illustration of the difficulties associated with establishing a 'single employer voice', in December 1987 the Metal Trades Industry Association resigned from the CAI. In the MTIA Annual Report 1987, it was stated:

> The National Executive of MTIA formally advised the Confederation of Australian Industry of its resignation from that organisation in May 1987 to take effect from December 1987. The National Executive's unanimous vote on the decision to resign reflects the long-standing dissatisfaction with the present structure and role of the CAI. The decision was taken after many months of constructive effort by MTIA to bring about changes which would make the CAI more effective as an industrial relations peak body. It was felt that the CAI's resources were channelled too much into commerce and industry policy areas to the detriment of the industrial relations function. However, MTIA remains committed to the establishment of an effective peak employer organisation which could represent all areas of the private sector in industrial relations matters.

The fallacy of a unified business voice

IS THERE really a need for a unified business voice in Australia? It has become an article of faith in a number of business quarters that there needs to be a stronger, and clearer, business position on a wide range of issues supposed to affect business.

The core of these issues is usually deemed to be wages, with taxation, industry protection and governmental red tape running a close second.

The past week must therefore have provided advocates of a more coherent national business lobby with despair. There has been the spectacle of disarray among competing employer groups over the coming national wage outcome and the revelation of a further diminution of the already castrated, and ill-named, Confederation of Australian Industry.

The only glimmer of light for advocates of a higher profile might have been today's talkfest on competitiveness by the business community's would-be Republican Guard, the Business Council of Australia.

The traditional view has been that there is a genuine community of interest for business—or more accurately in this context, employers—in at least one crucial area, that of wages. And the traditional view has been that employers should always say 'no'.

Yet even that has been shattered in recent weeks with the CAI arguing before the national wage full bench that any decision on a wage increase should be deferred, the sectoral group the Metal Trades Industry Association saying it agrees with proposals on wages put by the unions and other motley business groups arguing variations on the theme.

The lack of unity reflects a fact that will always dog arguments for a monolithic counterweight to the ACTU—employers, in truth, have very little in common.

Employer groups are built out of corporations, not individuals. Corporate bodies are legally separate, can be bound by various laws, are of widely varying mass and service different markets.

The industrial relations agenda of a capital-intensive company is, for example, different and inherently less pressing than that of a labour-intensive employer who is relatively more sensitive to labour cost increases. Decisions that affect capital costs are, on the other hand, more likely to affect the capital-intensive corporations.

The CAI itself consists of employer groups rather than individual companies and is the result of the 1977 merger of the national body of the State-based employer federations and the national umbrella group for the State chambers of manufacturers. While the employer federations had focused mainly on industrial relations issues, the manufacturers were more concerned with trade issues.

In its heyday, which really only lasted from its formation in 1977 until about 1983–84, the CAI's membership included a diverse range of employer associations ranging from all-purpose groups clustered in one geographic area to the more specific industry-based employer associations such as those covering the metal and building industries.

But from the outset the interests of the two main factions were difficult to reconcile, reflecting a strand in employer politics that dates back at least to the turn of the century and the debate over the so-called New Protection, in which the tariff was linked to the introduction of compulsory arbitration.

Then, manufacturers were protected from 'unfair competition' from imports in return for accepting that labour had to be protected from 'unfair competition' in the labour market by an arbitrated minimum wage.

The CAI's backbone is intact with the membership of the State-based employer federations and chambers of commerce that coalesce a wide range of small to medium-sized companies across the industry and commerce spectrum.

But the confederation has been weakened by departures, beginning with the resignation of the National Farmers Federation in 1983 in response to the CAI's perceived closeness to the arbitration system and followed by the builders, the bankers, the MTIA and the Australian Chamber of Manufactures.

There is no persuasive evidence that this attrition has adversely affected national wage outcomes. Indeed the evidence is that wage-cost pressure was relatively benign during the Accord years, which straddle the economic boom of the 1980s.

And while the weakening of the CAI could be seen as limiting the private sector's ability to influence the broader agenda, the lobbying vacuums created by the defections have inevitably been filled, often by those groups that departed.

Groups such as the NFF and the ACM have played major independent roles in shaping the debate on micro-reform, trade policy and debt in recent years and the decline of the CAI as a general spokesman for major industry sectors has also been offset by the BCA's emergence.

The BCA, which emerged from the Australian Industries Development Association, is undeniably elitist. Its membership is limited to the top executives of about 80 Australian companies that are, with a few exceptions, the nation's largest corporations.

Like all aggregations of businesses, the BCA is constrained by the tendency for competing interests to be resolved by the adoption of a 'lowest-common-denominator' position.

But it has been able to effectively use research to bolster its own views and to function similarly to US style think-tanks by adding fuel to the micro and macro-economic debate.

The BCA was, for example, able to spur the industrial relations debate by producing substantial arguments in favour of deregulation of the labour market at a time when there was an emerging consensus within the orthodox IR school that highly centralised wage-fixing was an impediment to economic reform.

An underlying theme of today's BCA conference—that the business sector is capable of winning half of the potential productivity gains to the year 2000 regardless of what the Government does—will, if grasped by delegates, represent another BCA contribution.

There is now a consensus for economic reform. The emergence of several significant corporate lobby groups should not hinder the process. It is a natural reflection of the diverse interests of the corporate sector and is infinitely preferable to any attempts to shore up cross-factional lobbies like the CAI which will never adequately service their constituents.

Source: *Australian Financial Review*, 1 March, 1991

Figure 3.4: Lack of unity amongst employers.

The article 'The Fallacy of a Unified Business Voice' (Figure 3.4) notes the continuing disaffection of the 'sectional' MTIA voice from the CAI and adds:

> The lack of unity reflects a fact that will always dog arguments for a monolithic counterweight to the ACTU—employers, in truth, have very little in common. Employer groups are built out of corporations not individuals. Corporate bodies are legally separate, can be bound by various laws, are of widely mass and service different markets!

Apart from inter-organisation rivalries and differences, employer associations have also had to develop strategies to accommodate the competitive relationships within their own membership. The Retail Traders' Association, for example, consists of companies which openly compete in the marketplace. Trade unions have often exploited the fact that most employer associations are groups of competing companies. Although an employer association may have a common line against, for example, a wage increase, this can waiver if one member is suffering losses in an industrial campaign whose fellow members have not been involved in the industrial action. Unions may use a technique known as pattern bargaining, when they isolate an individual company (or a small group), employ direct bargaining with possibly industrial action, and thereby gain a concession. This concession (say, a wage increase or shorter working hours), once granted, can then be pursued through the relevant employer association to the rest of the businesses in the industry.

In such circumstances it is difficult for the employer association to 'punish' the member who gave the wage increase. If the association's rules did allow for expulsion of the member, the member's business activities would still continue and it could possibly join another association to regain access to the services lost. Unlike the effect that expulsion would have on a union member, especially in an industry with compulsory unionism, the effect on the employer in this case would be negligible.

Employer 'militancy'

The 1980s have witnessed the emergence of a number of employers who have been prepared to suffer considerable economic losses in protracted industrial disputes eventually to 'win' against their employees' trade union. Often, the employers have been supported and encouraged by their employer organisation. In the Mudginberri case of 1985, for example, a small export-oriented abattoir in the Northern Territory claimed that the Australian Meat Industry Employees Union (AMIEU) had breached Sections 45D and 45E of the *Trade Practices Act* in a dispute over a new award. The Federal Court found in favour of the employer, and damages were ultimately awarded against the union. Part of the AMIEU's assets were subsequently seized under a court order to pay the damages.

This willingness of employers to use legal action to secure punitive damages against a trade union has loosely been termed 'employer militancy'. It stems from a view that trade union action should be strictly within the limits of all law: for example, that a return-to-work order of an industrial tribunal must be obeyed in all circumstances. It also stems from the demise of various penal sanctions (bans clauses, deregistration of trade unions etc.) of the arbitration system since the 1970s as effective deterrents to the use of trade union power.

The growth of employer militancy has been associated with the emergence of a political 'philosophy' known coloquially as the 'New Right'. In industrial relations circles this is characterised by a group known as the H.R. Nicolls Society (see Figure 3.5). Essentially, this political movement seeks:

- the greater use of market forces, especially in the determination of wages;
- to lessen government intervention; and
- to reduce trade union power by diminishing the significance of the conciliation and arbitration system.

H.R. Nicholls Society attacked by trades hall

MEMBERS of the H.R. Nicholls Society were well-known but not well-respected, according to a recent resolution of Newcastle Trades Hall Council (NTHC).

In an oblique reference to remarks by Newcastle's Lord Mayor, Ald McNaughton, who will open THE New Right society's conference in Newcastle next weekend, NTHC slammed the group's members.

Ald McNaughton said he saw nothing wrong in opening the conference and described the society's members as 'well-respected'.

The NTHC resolution called the members 'ridiculous and dangerous New Right bigots'.

But the unions stopped short of protest action, contending that Newcastle people knew that 'the answers to our regional problems do not lie in a return to industrial anarchy.'

The resolution said the choice of the 'industrial and predominantly working class' city of Newcastle as a venue for the conference was 'provocative in the extreme and consistent with the confrontationist approach of the ... society'.

'Its stated policies are absolute freedom of the market, almost total abolition of the public service, total abolition of the Arbitration and Conciliation Commission, abolition of the trade union movement, putting Aborigines on reserves, abolishing Parliament and cutting all welfare benefits.

It would appear that the intent of the Society in holding their conference in Newcastle is to make inroads into the strong tradition of regional co-operation that has been developed by unions, employers, government and the community.

The aim of the H.R. Nicholls Society is to eliminate such tripartite co-operation in favour of the absolute freedom of market forces,' the resolution said.

Source: The Newcastle Herald, 13 February, 1988

Figure 3.5: Trades Hall takes a jaundiced view of 'New Right' society.

The Dollar Sweets case (1988) is regarded as another major instance of employer militancy. Essentially, the company involved (Dollar Sweets) used the common law of torts (civil wrongs) to sue the Confectionery Workers' Union (CWU). Its members had been on strike in support of a pay claim. The employer asked the court to issue an injunction (a legal device used to restrain a person or organisation from certain action) to stop the employees from striking. Damages of $175 000 were awarded against the CWU. This case re-emphasised to employers that, along with the sanctions used in the Mudginberri case, significant common-law remedies were still available. These exist outside of the arbitration system. As Pamela Williams noted in the *Australian Financial Review* (Figure 3.6) when commenting on the Dollars Sweets case:

> The main point is that injunction proceedings have rarely been used by employers simply to bludgeon unions [...] With both Dollars Sweets and Mudginberri, the difference is that the companies were small employers, backed by a large, highly politicised employer organisation determined to press the case to its conclusion.

The 1989 Pilots' dispute highlighted how much of the tactics of the New Right have been accepted. Peter Costello, a prominent New Right protagonist and a barrister involved in the Dollar Sweets case commented on the Pilots dispute in an article for the *IPA Review* (October–December) 1989:

> Some employers may take the lesson when confronted with the next ban: cancel the award, sue the workers, bring in the military...

Along with an array of tactics used by and against the domestic pilots who were seeking a 29.47 per cent pay increase, in October 1989 an application was lodged in the Victorian Supreme Court by the airlines seeking damages against the pilots' union (the Australian Federation of Air Pilots). In summary, the court held that damages were payable because the union had conspired to unlawfully interfere with the airlines business by, *inter alia* intimidating pilots to stop them from working. The case shows the power of industrial torts. Also a number of observations have been made of the judgment (*Ansett Transport Industries (Operations) Pty Ltd v. Australian Federation of Air Pilots*):

- much of the common law used in the case was created by a 'demonstrably anti-union British judiciary'; and
- the effect of the decision is that all industrial action initiated by Australian trade unions is unlawful.

Plainly, the issue of employer militancy is one which is clothed very much in approaches to industrial relations and views about politics. On the one hand there are those employers and their associations which see industrial relations as being the means of resolving industrial disputes in a manner endorsed by the system of conciliation and arbitration. They are not necessarily dismissive of the full range of legal avenues available, but their emphasis is on a non-confrontationist approach. Alternatively, there are those employers and their organisations which actively pursue all legal processes to curtail union action. Typically, they see the arbitration tribunals as impediments to their 'rights'

Dollar Sweets case wasn't a precedent

There has been much strong talk in recent years about landmark legal actions on unions and employers setting tough industrial precedents as protection against industrial disputes.

But while this week's surprise $175,000 damages settlement by the Confectionery Workers Union to the little Melbourne company, Dollar Sweets, is undoubtedly a first, the legal action preceding it was nothing more than weekly fare for any good industrial lawyer.

Indeed, contrary to the impression created by the publicity machine trumpeting the Dollar Sweets case, there has been a steady stream of common law actions since the early 1970s when penal powers in the Conciliation and Arbitration Act lapsed into disuse.

The rhetoric espoused by factions of small business this week has also claimed that Dollar Sweets has proved common law protects individual rights and a small business need never be trampled by militant unions again.

But without in any way diminishing vindication of Dollar Sweets against the appalling behaviour of a pig-headed union, it must be said that Dollar Sweets is probably one of the worst recent examples of interlocutory injunctions under common law.

The employer waited five months in 1985 for legal relief which was probably accessible within a week. The option to sue the Confectionery Workers Union was there from the start.

Instead the company waited while its new backers, the then Melbourne Chamber of Commerce, spent tens of thousands of dollars on legal research to press a fairly common industrial case.

Dollar Sweets and the Mudginberri dispute, which relied on sections 45D and 45E of the Trade Practices Act, have been used as political footballs over the past three years.

The two disputes have been presented on countless occasions as the first real legal breakthroughs in winding back union power.

But in reality, both the secondary boycott provisions of the Trade Practices Act and the common law torts are widely used by employers and well respected by unions.

The Confederation of Australian Industry lists no less than 24 examples of the recent use of various tort actions in its Resource Book on Industrial Action.

But what divides these innumerable cases and the Dollar Sweets and Mudginberri cases, is that most employers are simply seeking to resolve a dispute and wield the interlocutory injunction as a bargaining tool, much as unions use pickets.

In fact, employers rarely turn to the courts for a perpetual injunction. It is a little like defamation, in that the number of actions which actually get to court is miniscule.

Some lawyers in the industrial community have questioned the Chamber of Commerce and Industry's political motivation in spending $120,000 on legal and research costs to launch a case which should have cost only $20,000.

The case could also have been instigated months earlier, before the company approached the brink of collapse.

In fact, out of his $175,000 settlement, the managing director of Dollar Sweets, Mr Fred Stauder, is expected to pay back about $80,000 to the Chamber of Commerce's fighting fund.

The main point is that injunction proceedings have rarely been used by employers simply to bludgeon unions.

The threat of injunctions and damages action is often made but in the bluff and bluster of industrial disputes, unions generally cave in quickly. in other cases, the injunction is obtained and becomes a critical factor in routing the dispute.

With both Dollar Sweets and Mudginberri, the difference is that the companies were small employers, backed by a large, highly politicised employer organisation determined to press its case to its conclusion.

The National Farmers Federation made it a condition of support for Mudginberri that the abattoir would proceed with legal action against the Australasian Meat Industry Employees Union through to an action for damages, rather than dropping the law when the dispute was resolved.

There is no doubt the examples of Mudginberri and Dollar Sweets have been a daunting spectacle for a few small and bloody-minded unions.

But for most unions and employers, the so-called big wins are not the way to resolve disputes.

And there is unlikely to be a rash of new actions fired by this week's settlement.

Source: Australian Financial Review, 14 April, 1988

Figure 3.6: The Dollar Sweets case: A major instance of employer militancy.

to manage, and as a system which distorts the true operation of market forces. Evaluation of the appropriateness of tactics used by the employers of the 'New Right' rests largely upon which stance is adopted.

Services

Most companies have neither sufficient resources nor the specialist personnel needed to keep up-to-date in the array of laws, award and regulations which affect their businesses. Nor do they usually have sufficient bargaining power individually to influence the decision-making processes of other parties in the industrial relations system, such as governments and trade unions. Employer associations provide these benefits and services.

Industrial relations

Employer associations typically provide advice on awards and other related legislation (e.g. long-service leave, workers' compensation), telephone enquiry services, help in negotiations with trade unions, and expert representation before industrial tribunals. A letter seeking to recruit members to the Employers' Federation of NSW stresses the importance of this service:

> Employers today face multiple obligations in relation to their staff. These include strict adherence to Award rates and conditions, and regulations covering Annual Holidays, Long Service Leave, Workers Compensation, Employment Protection and Redundancy, Health and Safety, to name some areas which are covered by Legislation.
> Failure to be aware of and comply with these obligations may result in prosecution and fines and will undermine the relationship between you and your staff, so important to the achievement of harmony and business growth.
> We seek to keep our members fully informed in straightforward terms of all such obligations under these increasingly complex changes, providing you with the best possible professional advice at the lowest possible cost.
>
> *Source*: Letter of the Membership Officer, Employers Federation of NSW

Figure 3.7, a copy of page 1 of *Employers' Review*, illustrates how members are informed of important industrial relations cases.

Safety and occupational health

Employer associations also offer assistance in implementing safety laws. The Australian Chamber of Manufactures (NSW Division), for example, has a Health, Safety and Environment Unit charged with the task of monitoring changes in safety laws and procedures, and representing the Chamber's view on many safety and occupational health committees and boards.

Personnel management

This service includes salary information, especially in determining over-award payments, superannuation schemes, employee benefits (e.g. child-care crêches, medical services), recruitment, selection, and advice on anti-discrimination laws.

EMPLOYERS' FEDERATION OF NEW SOUTH WALES

EMPLOYERS' REVIEW

15 November 1990   Vol. 62 No. 21

Transport Appeal Successful

The appeal by the Employers' Federation of New South Wales and Chamber of Manufactures of New South Wales against the decision applying the second structural efficiency adjustment to the Transport Industry (State) Award was successful.

BACKGROUND

On 29th June, 1990, his Honour Mr Justice Sweeney of the Industrial Commission of New South Wales varied the Transport Industry (State) Award to apply the second adjustment available under the Structural Efficiency Principle of the State Wage Case decision of 4th October, 1990. In awarding the increase, his Honour gave effect to an agreement reached between the Road Transport Association (R.T.A.), the Long Distance Road Transport Association and the Workers; Union, N.S.W. Branch (T.W.U.).

The Employers' Federation was concerned that the decision did not properly implement the Structural Efficiency Principle and offered minimal benefits to our members.

Accordingly, a joint appeal was lodged by the Federation and the Chamber of Manufactures of New South Wales against his Honour's decision to be heard as a matter of urgency by the Industrial Commission of New South Wales in Court Session.

The Appeal proceedings commenced on 3rd September, 1990, before their honours the Vice President Mr Justice Cahill, Mr Justice Bauer and Mr Justice Maidment. The decision of the Commission In-Court-Session was announced at the conclusion of the appeal proceedings on Friday, 16th November, 1990.

APPEAL UPHELD

In a unanimous decision, the Federation and the Chamber were granted leave to appeal, the appeal was upheld and the decision of his Honour Mr Justice Sweeney of 29th June, 1990 was set aside.

The award was varied in accordance with an exhibit tendered by the Federation and the Chamber during the proceedings, with the exception of two issues which the Federation and the Chamber have been reserved leave to apply for: a minimum payment for a casual employee of four hours for each start, and the payment of wages by electronic funds transfer at the discretion of the employer.

BENEFITS FOR MEMBERS

The particularly beneficial aspects of the appeal decision are:-
- The operative date of the award variations, with the exception of the long distance work provisions, is the first complete pay period to commence on or after 10 September 1990 rather than 29 June, 1990.
- A new Clause 3D, Long Distance Work, will apply from the first complete pay period to commence on or after 29 June, 1990. This clause will particularly benefit members involved in long distance work by providing a new rate system for paying long distance drivers.

Continued Page 3

EMPLOYERS' MANUAL
The Employers' Manual, a valuable reference with a wide variety of essential information, is now available.
   Order your copy now.
   Use the coupon on P2
   Or call (02) 264 2000.

INSIDE...

Award Classification—4
Worker or Non-worker—5

Registered by Australia Post Publication No. NBQ0859 ISSN 0728-635

Source: The Employers' Federation of NSW.

Figure 3.7: How employer association members are informed of important decisions.

Training and development

Supervisory skills courses, management training, production engineering and training program designs associated with award restructuring are services provided by most employer associations. The Chamber of Manufacturers present involvement, for example, in education and training includes:

EDUCATION & TRAINING

Member companies are assisted with the development and management of industry training programs by provision of:
- Introductions to specialist consultants to help plan and assess training needs
- Information on business responsibilities under new legislation and award restructuring
- Specific classroom and in-house programs in quality management, quality assurance and quality control through the Australian Organisation for Quality
- Seminars and briefings on current topics to help members keep up to date with relevant trends and policies on education and training
- Materials to support education and training programs and advice on issues related to education and training
- Representation on committees responsible for efforts to improve the skills of the manufacturing workforce.

Source: The Australian Chamber of Manufacturers, NSW, booklet.

Commercial services

These include advice on the *Trade Practices Act* and associated consumer laws, contractual and standards information, and insurance brokerage. A 'Checklist of benefits available only to MTIA members' set out in Figure 3.8 details these services.

Apprenticeship

Employer associations provide indentures, training and apprenticeship cancellation. All the services are readily accessible, with much information routinely being sent to the members in circulars and newsletters.

Table 3.1 illustrates how, in a day-to-day sense, a commercial printing firm would access the services of their employer association, PATEFA.

Table 3.1: A diary account of the use of the PATEFA—first quarter, 199X

1. *Visited at plant by safety inspector.* Rang PATEFA: got advice on the rights of the inspector to examine equipment.
2. *PATEFA monthly newsletter arrived.* Update on changes to tax law. Also, information provided on newly elected printing trades union officials and forthcoming industry exhibition.
3. *Contacted by PATEFA—conducting wage survey.* Will be provided with up-to-date 'going' rates at next industrial meeting.
4. *Circular setting out new award wage rates from National Wage Case.*
5. *Rang PATEFA to discuss liability of supplier for defective products under Trade Practices Act.*
6. *Attended regional PATEFA annual dinner.* Discussed new equipment on the market. Very enjoyable social occasion.

✓ CHECK LIST of benefits
AVAILABLE ONLY TO MTIA MEMBERS

Industrial Relations and Human Resource Management

- ☐ Wage rates and conditions of employment
- ☐ Supply and interpretation of Federal and State awards – by phone or in person
- ☐ Recruitment, selection, induction, disciplinary procedures, termination, redundancy
- ☐ Classifications of labour at the plant
- ☐ Settlement of industrial disputes, negotiations with unions, plant conferences, hearing before tribunals
- ☐ Training courses for supervisors
- ☐ Employee participation and communication
- ☐ Equal opportunity legislation
- ☐ Discrimination legislation
- ☐ Technological change
- ☐ Manpower planning
- ☐ Apprenticeship
- ☐ Occupational health and safety
- ☐ Workcare
- ☐ Management improvement techniques (JIT etc)
- ☐ Superannuation advice
- ☐ Briefings for members on current issues
- ☐ I.R. Management at construction sites
- ☐ Representation on Conciliation and Arbitration and other statutory bodies

Trade and Commercial

- ☐ "Developing Enterprises Club" for operators of small businesses – accent on education, training and exchange of views
- ☐ Trade Practices legislation
- ☐ Contractual matters
- ☐ Government purchasing
- ☐ Tariffs/Customs
- ☐ Export
- ☐ Research and development
- ☐ Statistical and survey information
- ☐ Standards
- ☐ Government assistance measures
- ☐ Industries Assistance Commission
- ☐ Defence manufacturing and offsets
- ☐ Industrial Supplies Office
- ☐ Technology liaison officer with CSIRO
- ☐ Trade and commercial groupings
- ☐ Taxation advice
- ☐ Legal and regulation issues
- ☐ Specific industry sector matters

Information Services

- ☐ Comprehensive regular production of a wide range of publications

Source: MTIA Annual Report, 1987.

Figure 3.8: Checklist of benefits available only to MTIA members.

The persons providing the advice to the company include industrial officers (many with formal qualifications in industrial relations such as TAFE's Advanced Certificates) and legally trained specialists. They are supported by clerical and administrative staff, who would (in the examples illustrated in Table 3.1), edit and publish the PATEFA newsletter, distribute the National Wage Case circular and organise the regional annual dinner, among many other tasks and responsibilities.

Other activities

Although most of the services provided are designed to meet the day-to-day needs of their members (the micro level), employer associations also represent their members' collective interests at the 'macro' level. For example, the Metal Trades Industry Association:

- appears at and makes submissions in major cases (such as National Wage hearings) before industrial tribunals.
- makes submissions to government on the level of protection it claims that its members need from overseas competitors.
- represents its members' concerns to government (federal and state) on issues as diverse as immigration policy, taxation, and industry restructuring.
- is a member of government committees and other agencies that have a role in the metal and related industries.

Administration

Many employer associations only operate in one state, although some have combined with equivalent organisations in other states and formed federations. Typically, the state branches are independent in most respects (including finance), leaving the federal organisation with limited powers that are largely used to determine national policy.

All employer organisations have elected from and by their membership office-bearers who normally make up a governing body. For the day-to-day management tasks most associations use an executive committee structure, with subcommittees to deal with such specific areas as industrial relations. The elected officials act in an honorary capacity. Those organisations that are large enough employ full-time or part-time staff to carry out the services provided to their members, while smaller associations may have only a secretary as chief executive officer. These are associations which very often affiliate with the 'umbrella' organisations discussed earlier.

Membership fees can be determined in a number of ways: as a percentage of the number of personnel employed, or on the basis of a measure of the size of the business by using turnover figures and other accounting data. The costs of membership can be deducted against the company's income and are therefore tax-deductible. Trade union fees are allowable as a deduction for personal income tax purposes.

Summary

Employer associations are a critical party in Australia's industrial relations system. While much of their task is involved in settling disputes and in making and varying awards, they also represent their members' interests and advise them in fields such as training, commercial matters and trade.

In the 1980s, national 'peak' employer bodies have had to contend with major difficulties in controlling an often disaffected membership.

Questions and Activities
1. Contact an employer organisation and find out:
    a. its objectives;
    b. the services it offers its members; and
    c. its resources for training and research.
2. Why have national peak employers been 'plagued' by such a high level of membership dissatisfaction?
3. After reading the editorial from *The Australian* (Figure 3.3) do you feel that the BCA's policy is 'a breath of fresh air'?
4. Summarise the information provided in the Pamela Williams article from the *Australian Financial Review* (Figure 3.6). Do you feel that 'militant' employee action is warranted?
5. Write a letter to the potential member of an employer association outlining the benefits of membership. See Figure 3.8 for further background.
6. Employers complain that trade unions and their members often do not accept the 'umpire's decision' when industrial tribunals make judgments which are unfavourable to the union's case. For example, unionists may take industrial action when a tribunal fails to reinstate a dismissed colleague.
    a. Check newspapers and other sources for evidence of the decisions of industrial tribunals being ignored or openly challenged.
    b. If you were a member of a tribunal and faced with arbitrating an emotive dispute, such as a reinstatement case, what steps could you take to ensure that, if you found against the union, the decision would be accepted?
    c. Read the abridged article: 'The paralysis of corporate regulation'. If Westfield's arguments are accepted, discuss the view that employers expect a higher level of responsibility of trade unions than they do of themselves.

INSIDER

MARK WESTFIELD

The paralysis of corporate regulation

The legal and judicial system in Australia has reached the stage where it is paralysed in the face of major corporate transgressions. Yet, it falls with its full weight on perpetrators of petty crimes.

A desperate single mother who finds a credit card and attempts to buy a $400 television set is hounded through the courts, yet when businessmen and their legal advisers orchestrate a breach of the corporations law involving $400 million or so, the authorities freeze.

Sure, there is a lengthy and expensive investigation, but when it comes to the nitty gritty, the laying of charges and prosecution through the courts, the record of the authorities is abysmal.

This is the inescapable and irrefutable fact of corporate regulation in this country in the wash-up to the disastrous 1987 stockmarket crash and some of the extravagant behaviour which preceded it.

Insider trading on a massive scale and manipulation of huge sums of shareholders' money to benefit a few at the cost of many go unpunished in this society. By contrast, misdemeanors like shoplifting and petty theft and assault attract penalties vastly disproportionate in terms of the amounts and suffering involved.

Why should people in the street toe the line when businessmen and their facilitators flout the law and take part in corporate raids involving money beyond the imaginations of average Australians, to be rewarded by lack of punishment for their actions?

> '*Why should people in the street toe the line when businessmen flout the law?*'

Does this paralysis stem from pressure from the legal fraternity on the judiciary and prosecuting bodies, who both spring from the law after all, and who may be persuaded to look after their own kind?

Until this year, the corporate authorities used the excuse of lack of funds for their failure to prosecute some of the individuals involved in bringing about the collapse of some of the country's best known corporations and attracting such opprobrium for this country in overseas markets.

This excuse is no longer valid. The new, Federally-funded Australian Securities Commission (ASC) has been guaranteed at least $20 million over the next four months alone to launch prosecutions against some of the nation's more extravagant operators. This is three times the total annual budget of its predecessor, the NCSC.

How can this country ever hope to regain any semblance of a reputation in global markets while the corporate landscape is exploited by an opportunistic minority?

The only 'punishment' for the lack of response is that investors, both overseas and local, will decline to invest as freely as they otherwise would in Australia's markets. The withdrawal of investment funds will affect every level of business in this country, although its effects will not be immediately obvious.

Sure, there has been some support for shares on the stock exchange in recent weeks, but compared with the main trading centres Australia has fallen well behind. Wall Street and London are both trading at levels above their 1987 pre-crash highs. It may be coincidental, but as a result of a flexing of the authorities' muscle in those countries a number of people have been jailed.

In the end, it is very much in the market's interests for at least some of those responsible to be brought to justice. There is little indication to date that this will happen.

Source: Sydney Morning Herald, March 8, 1991.

Questions and Activities (continued)

7. The National Farmers' Federation and its State Associations have strongly pursued a range of policies aligned with 'employer militancy'. After reading the following article, 'The right to hire and fire should rest with the boss', consider the following:
   a. The article refers to the Australian Farmers' Fighting Fund which assisted in mounting the appeal on behalf of Troubleshooters Available. Discuss the view that it is inappropriate for a party not directly concerned with an industrial dispute to be materially involved.
   b. List the policies/views outlined in the article. Analyse how they are consistent with employer militancy and discuss the language used in the article.

The right to hire and fire should rest with the boss

COUNTRY VIEW
NSW Farmers

From the NSW Farmers' Association

THE Australian Farmers' Fighting Fund has enjoyed a major victory, in the Federal Court to uphold the right of subcontractors to work outside the industrial award system.

In 1989 the Melbourne-based building/sub-contracting firm, Troubleshooters Available, proved before the Industrial Commission that building unions had deliberately tried to force labour hired out by Troubleshooters from building sites in Sydney and Melbourne.

Just over a week ago an appeal against this decision by the building unions was rejected by a full bench of the Federal Court.

Industrial Relations Minister, Peter Cook, attacked the decision saying it appeared to mean that an employer could take a worker's job and give it to someone else who agreed to call himself a contractor.

'If that is what the law means, then the law is an ass' Senator Cook said.

It is sad that the union movement has distorted industrial reality so much that a court case was needed to uphold the right of any person to employ whomsoever they wish.

Opposition Industrial Relations spokesman, John Howard, described Senator Cook's outburst as 'hysterical and unjustified' and said it showed 'the depth of the Federal Government's commitment to the centralised industrial relations system'.

Senator Cook's reaction is easily explained. He has served as Secretary of the Trades and Labour Council in Perth and as a junior vice-president of the ACTU.

The industrial history of Australia has shown that trade union movement has rarely accepted 'umpires' decisions' when they go against them.

By coincidence, only days after the Troubleshooters decision, Senator Cook has released a paper which includes, among its proposals, changing the legislation to bring in the mythical 'right to strike'.

If you lose in the courts, then change the law that the courts are interpreting to suit you.

The paper offers options which fall into three categories.

First, leave the system as it is. Such an option always has to be left in but if you did not want to change the system, you would not have the paper prepared in the first place.

Option two looks at bringing in the industrial relations package, successfully fought against by farmer groups and others in 1987, that was a thinly disguised attempt to make unions immune from most legal actions outside the conciliation and arbitration system.

On the other hand, it strengthened the Industrial Relations Commission's power to impose penalties for unauthorised industrial action.

In reality, the 'Industrial Relations Club' fortified its own walls, but the common man was left further exposed to the jungle of trade union warfare against the community and its productive sectors.

> Option three also gives unions immunity from virtually all existing legal sanctions against industrial action, both within and without the arbitration system, but only where industrial action meets certain criteria such as having been endorsed by a secret ballot of members.
>
> An affirmative vote for union action by a secret ballot would then reinforce the 'right to strike' provision.
>
> However, secret ballots take much time and an affirmative vote may need a second ballot to be overturned once leaders of both sides agree on terms for a settlement.
>
> In reality, the secret ballot provision exists in law now under the Industrial Relations Act which allows the Industrial Commission the right to order secret ballots.
>
> The Industrial Relations Club seems reluctant to exercise its own right.

Source: The Sun-Herald, 31 March, 1991.

Questions and Activities (continued)

8. Adopting the role of the State President of an industry association, write a letter to a member of some 22 years' standing who recently granted an over-award concession of a 20 per cent annual leave loading contrary to the association's policy on over-award bargaining. You know that threats of industrial action had been made in support of the claim.

9. *An illustration of how employer associations seek to restrict the registration of association with similar coverage.*

   In 1989 the Australian Federation of Construction Contractors (AFCC) with 21 members (mainly large construction firms) sought registration in the Western Australian State industrial relations system. The Master Builders Association (with 392 members but of small to medium sized builders) objected to the registration.

   The Western Australian Industrial Relations Act, 1979 includes in its objects:

   - Section 6: (e) to encourage the formation of representative organisations of employers and employees and their registration under this Act and to discourage, so far as practicable, overlapping of eligibility for membership of such organisations;
   - and in Section 55(5) the Full Bench can refuse an application for registration if: 'a registered organisation whose rules relating to membership enable it to enrol as a member some of or all of the persons eligible' the members of the organistion seeking registration 'unless the Full Bench is satisfied that there is good reason, consistent with the objects prescribed in sec. 6, to permit registration'.

   It was conceded in evidence that there was very considerable overlap between the eligibility rules of the AFC and the MBA.

   Questions
   a. Why does the legislation seek to minimise overlapping coverage of employer associations (and trade unions)?
   b. Do you feel that the AFCC should have been granted registration? What additional information would you need to help make a decision?

Answer

In a majority decision (with one member dissenting) the Full Bench granted registration, because, in their judgment, 'good reasons' did exist. These included:

- that the AFCC was already playing an important role in industrial relations, especially as it had federal registration.
- registration would not lead to industrial disharmony as there appeared to be a good working relationship in WA between the AFCC and the MBA; and
- the problems associated with overlapping membership were more relevant to trade unions than employer organisations.

Application by the Australian Federation of Construction Contracts (WA). Full Bench of the IRC. (Sharkey P., Fielding and Beech C.C.) (No. 2185 of 1985) 14/3/90.)

Chapter 4

Government

> **Objectives**
> At the end of this chapter, the reader should be able to:
> - explain the functions of government;
> - discuss the role of government in industrial relations; and
> - outline the judicial system and its role in industrial relations.

Introduction

While the foundation of industrial relations rests with the employer and the employee at the workplace, this relationship is affected by another party—the government. Governments, as society's elected representative bodies and their employees, are charged with certain responsibilities or 'powers' which affect the industrial relations process.

Powers and levels of government

Australia has a written constitution which not only sets out the system of government but also details how the responsibilities of government are to be divided between the state and federal levels of government.

Those persons who drafted the Constitution at the turn of the century established a system of government which divided the power of government into three separate fields:

- legislative
- executive   } powers of government
- judicial

Legislative power is used to make, or to enact, laws or statutes. This power is vested in the elected representatives of parliament.

Executive power is allocated to the Prime Minister and to ministers who, through the Governor-General, are ultimately responsible for the execution or implementation of the laws.

Finally, judicial power is given to the High Court and the system of courts in order to interpret and enforce the laws. Each power, or 'arm', is generally regarded as being separate according to the Constitution. In other words, those persons responsible for making laws do not have the authority to enforce them. For example, a taxation official may claim that a person has breached a tax law, but only a magistrate or court has the power to enforce the law by fining or otherwise punishing the person if they are found guilty (Figure 4.1).

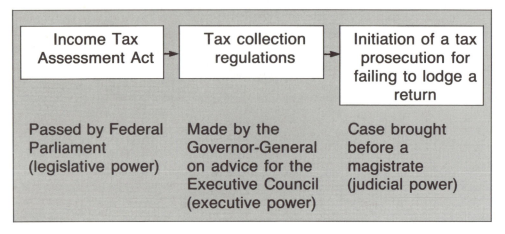

Figure 4.1: An illustration of the legislative, executive and judicial powers of government.

In Australia there are six state and one federal governments, and two self-governing territories (the Australian Capital Territory and the Northern Territory). The Constitution details the responsibilities of Federal (Commonwealth) Government, with all remaining powers not specifically assigned being the responsibility of the states.

Section 51 of the Constitution details most of the Federal Government's powers, including defence, foreign affairs, interstate trade, and commerce. Figure 4.2 summarises the powers relevant to industrial relations. As well, there are concurrent or shared powers between the state and federal governments, one of which being industrial relations.

Section 51(xxxv) of the Constitution gives the Federal Government the power to legislate for the settlement of interstate industrial disputes.

At the time of Federation there was substantial opposition to the inclusion of any Federal industrial relations power in the Constitution. It took the Great Maritime Strike (1890), the Miners Strike (1892) and the Shearers Strike (1894) to convince those persons at the Constitutional Conventions leading up to Federation to include among the powers of the Australian Parliament, the power 'to make laws with respect to conciliation and arbitration for the prevention and settlement of industrial disputes extending beyond the limits of any one State.' The process of conciliation and arbitration was seen by its strongest advocate, Henry Bourne Higgins, second President of the commonwealth industrial tribunal, as a 'substitute' for 'the rude and barbarous process of strike and lock-out'.

In addition to the Federal Government's circumscribed industrial power contained in Section 51(xxxv) of the Constitution, it can pass laws relating

> **A. Federal**
> *Section 51.* The Parliament shall, subject to this constitution, have power to make laws for the peace, order, and good government of the Commonwealth, with respect to:
>
> - (i) Trade and commerce with other countries and among the states;
> - (ii) Taxation;
> - (v) Postal, telegraphic, telephonic, and other like services;
> - (vi) The naval and military defence of the Commonwealth and of the several states and the control of the forces to execute and maintain the laws of the Commonwealth;
> - (xx) Foreign corporations, and trading or financial corporations formed within the limits of the Commonwealth.
> - (xxiii.a) The provision of maternity allowances, widows' pensions, child endowment, unemployment, pharmaceutical, sickness and hospital benefits, medical and dental services, benefits to students and family allowances;
> - (xxix) External affairs;
> - (xxxv) Conciliation and arbitration for the prevention and settlement of industrial disputes extending beyond the limits of any one state;
> - (xxxix) Matters incidental to the execution of any power vested by this Constitution in the Parliament or in either House thereof, or in the Government of the Commonwealth, or in the Federal Judicature, or in any Department or officer of the Commonwealth.
>
> *Section 109.* When a law of the state is inconsistent with a law of the Commonwealth, the latter shall prevail, and the former shall, to the extent of the inconsistency, be invalid.
>
> **B. State**
> Have the right to pass any law relating to industrial relations which is not inconsistent with a federal law.

Figure 4.2: Summary of constitutional powers dealing with industrial relations.

to the terms and conditions of employment of Commonwealth Government employees. Otherwise the states have legislative responsibility for industrial matters like annual holidays and long service leave.

In the case of conflict between state and federal laws (provided both governments are able to pass laws in that particular area), federal law shall prevail over state law, as provided in Section 109 of the Constitution. This is referred to as the paramountcy of federal legislation. This also applies to conflict between federal and state awards (which is discussed further in Chapter 7).

Functions of government

Legislation is passed by the elected representatives in state and federal parliaments. It is introduced as a bill and if, after consideration and any amendments, it is passed by parliament it becomes an act or statute.

Once proposed legislation becomes an Act of Parliament, it is then the responsibility of the executive arm of government to administer it. As an example, government may introduce legislation setting up a scheme to give employers financial incentives to employ long-term unemployed persons. Once the proposed legislation is passed by parliament and becomes an act, it is the responsibility of a particular government department or authority to administer the act. The department's public servants will provide advice to employers and unemployed persons, assess applications for consideration under the act, and undertake any other action necessary to give effect to the legislation.

Governments are elected largely on the policies they offer the electorate. There are many other factors which affect voters, such as the current government's past performance, the personality of candidates, and the media coverage and advertisement given to each party's campaign. When a government comes to power it will seek to implement its 'platform' of policies. This can often be achieved by amending current statutes and by using its executive power to change regulations.

Government as industrial relations legislator

Governments pass legislation using their majority in parliament—legislation which will depend on the constitutional powers given to government and on the issues it considers important. Governments can pass laws only within their constitutional powers. A law outside of its power is said to be *ulta vires*, and is invalid.

The federal industrial relations power is restricted to passing legislation to establish tribunals for the settlement of interstate industrial disputes using conciliation and arbitration. Most other industrial relations legislation is the responsibility of the states. This concurrent responsibility for industrial relations is one of the reasons for the complexity of Australian industrial relations. Any question of jurisdiction—that is, whether a matter is a federal or state responsibility—is ultimately decided by the High Court. This has added to the view that Australian industrial relations is not only complex, but also legalistic. The High Court has heard many cases, involving appearances by a large number of lawyers arguing complicated submissions, to decide on the meaning of industrial powers in the Constitution. The exact wording of the Constitution is subject to varying constructions or interpretations, which is left to the High Court to resolve.

The legislative restrictions on the Federal Government have meant that it cannot pass laws concerning specific employment conditions, unless these are related to Federal Government employees or are concerned with the Territories. As a consequence, legislation on annual holidays, long-service leave and occupational health has come from the states.

A number of developments have recently suggested that some of these limitations are being eroded. The federal *Affirmative Action (Equal Employment*

Opportunity for Women) Act 1986 was passed to improve the employment status of women through affirmative action by employers. However, what constitutional power does the Commonwealth Government have to legislate in this area when its legislative industrial power is limited to conciliating and arbitrating interstate disputes? In this case, the Government used its right to pass laws dealing with foreign affairs rather than the industrial power (see Figure 4.2). Australia, like many other countries, has signed a treaty with the International Labour Organization (ILO) calling for government action to give women equal opportunities with men to compete for all jobs. As a signatory to this international agreement, the Federal Government—using its constitutional foreign affairs power—had the authority to introduce legislation related to affirmative action for women.

Figure 4.3 details significant federal and state industrial legislation. The key laws are those which regulate our system of industrial relations, and consequently the way unions and employers interact. These acts establish:
- procedures for gaining access to the tribunal system;
- the objectives and composition of the various industrial tribunals which resolve disputes between employers and trade unions; and
- the responsibilities of the respective government departments through the appointed ministers to carry out activities related to industrial relations.

AUSTRALIAN CONSTITUTION
FEDERAL OR COMMONWEALTH LEGISLATION
Industrial Relations Act 1988
Trade Practices Act 1974
Trade Union Training Authority Act 1975
Maternity Leave (Commonwealth Employees) Act 1973
Human Rights and Equal Opportunity Commission Act 1986
Racial Discrimination Act 1975
Affirmative Action (Equal Employment Opportunity for Women) Act 1986
Sex Discrimination Act 1984

NEW SOUTH WALES
Industrial Arbitration Act 1940 and Industrial Arbitration Regulations
Trade Union Act 1881
Annual Holidays Act 1944
Long Service Leave Act 1955
Essential Services Act 1988
Occupational Health and Safety Act 1983
Factories, Shops and Industries Act 1962
Anti-Discrimination Act 1977
Employment Protection Act 1982
Industrial Arbitration (Enterprise Agreements) Amendment Act 1990

VICTORIA
Industrial Relations Act 1979 and Industrial Relations Regulations
Equal Opportunity Act 1984
Occupational Health and Safety Act 1985
Labour and Industry (Annual Holidays) Order 1967

cont.

SOUTH AUSTRALIA
Industrial Conciliation and Arbitration Act 1972
Long Service Leave Act 1987
Equal Opportunity Act 1984
Occupational Health, Safety and Welfare Act 1986
QUEENSLAND
Industrial Relations Act 1990
Holidays Act 1983
WESTERN AUSTRALIA
Industrial Relations Act 1979
Industrial Relations Commission Regulations 1985
Equal Opportunity Act 1984
Factories and Shops Act 1963
Long Service Leave Act 1958
Trade Unions Act 1902
Occupational Health, Safety and Welfare Act 1984
TASMANIA
Industrial Relations Act 1984
Long Service Leave Act 1976
Industrial Safety, Health and Welfare Act 1977
Industrial and Commercial Training Act 1985
NORTHERN TERRITORY
Annual Leave Act 1981
Industry and Employment Training Act 1985

Figure 4.3: Industrial Relations Legislation.

The significance of the *Industrial Relations Act, 1988* as an act of parliament and its objects are discussed in Figure 4.4.

Industrial Relations Act 1988

No. 86 of 1988

An Act relating to the prevention and settlement of certain industrial disputes, and for other purposes

[*Assented to 8 November 1988*]

BE IT ENACTED by the Queen, and the Senate and the House of Representatives of the Commonwealth of Australia, as follows:

PART I—PRELIMINARY

Short Title
  1. This Act may be cited as the *Industrial Relations Act 1988*.

Commencement
  2. This Act commences on a day or days to be fixed by Proclamation.

Objects of Act
  3. The objects of this Act are:

(a) to promote industrial harmony and co-operation among the parties involved in industrial relations in Australia;
(b) to provide a framework for the prevention and settlement of industrial disputes by conciliation and arbitration in a manner that minimises the disruptive effects of industrial disputes on the community;
(c) to ensure that, in the prevention and settlement of industrial disputes, proper regard is had to the interests of the parties immediately concerned and to the interests (including the economic interests) of the Australian community as a whole;
(d) to facilitate the prevention and prompt settlement of industrial disputes in a fair manner, and with the minimum of legal form and technicality;
(e) to provide for the observance and enforcement of agreements and awards made for the prevention or settlement of industrial disputes;
(f) to encourage the organisation of representative bodies of employers and employees and their registration under this Act;
(g) to encourage the democratic control of organisations, and the participation by their members in the affairs of organisations; and
(h) to encourage the efficient management of organisations.

...

Regulations

359. (1) The Governor-General may make regulations, not inconsistent with this Act, prescribing all matters:
(a) required or permitted by this Act to be prescribed; or
(b) necessary or convenient to be prescribed for carrying out or giving effect to this Act.

---

1. The Federal government used its industrial power and a number of other powers from the Constitution.
2. Assented to by the Governor General. An Act does not take effect until this assent is given.
3. This law was passed by the Senate and House of Representatives using their legislative powers.
4. These are objectives the Act seeks to achieve.
5. Under this Section, regulations which are necessary for aspects of the Act to take effect can be made.

Figure 4.4: Objects and Regulations of the *Industrial Relations Act 1988*.

Industrial relations and government's executive responsibilities

As discussed earlier, in addition to legislative functions, governments must ensure that the laws passed by parliament are executed or implemented. It is this executive arm which particularly demonstrates the importance of government in influencing the industrial relations system.

Government as economic and social manager

While the Federal Government's direct role in industrial relations is limited to the establishment of machinery for the settlement of interstate industrial disputes, it has a substantial indirect role in setting the social and economic environment within which the industrial relations system operates. It can be said that what goes on in the overall economy will, in large measure, determine what happens within the industrial relations framework.

For example, if the price of goods and services is escalating, what will trade unions and their members be seeking from employers? Obviously, increasing inflation will influence employees to seek wage increases. Another example of the way in which economic factors affect industrial relations is the case of unemployment: when unemployment is high, trade unions are unable to make as many gains for their members as when it is low. High unemployment allows employers to withstand union demands, on the basis that there is a good supply of labour if employees leave because of wages and conditions. Conversely, if the economy is buoyant and unemployment is low, it is the unions which are in a good position for gaining concessions from employers.

Government is seen as being responsible for the management of the economy. In its pursuit of economic stability government has a number of tools available, including fiscal (e.g. federal spending) and monetary (e.g. interest rates) policies. Action taken by government in these areas will affect the relationship between employers and trade unions in the industrial arena.

Probably the best example is with personal income taxes. In the usual case, wage and salary earners will seek wage increases by making a demand on employers through thir trade unions. However, income increases can also be delivered to wage and salary earners by lowering the amount of income

Source: *The Bulletin*, 20 June, 1989

tax they pay to the government, thus increasing the amount of take-home pay for the worker. This is referred to as a 'wage/tax trade-off'. Unions and their members in effect trade off expected wage increases from employers by paying less tax to the government. The result not only goes to satisfy the workers but is advantageous to the employer, who otherwise would have had to finance the full wage increase. The government must obviously face a loss of revenue (see Figure 4.5).

Possibility of using tax cuts to appease unhappy workers

By ROWLEY SPIERS

The Federal Government has raised the possibility of using tax cuts to appease disenchantment with the wage rises flowing from the National Wage Case.

The Government has already paid a round of tax cuts on January 1 as part of the Government's Accord Mark VI package.

However, the Minister for Industrial Relations, Senator Cook, acknowledged yesterday that the Industrial Relations Commission's decision to reject the Accord package and instead award only a phased wage rise of 2.5 per cent had raised the prospect of using even further tax cuts as a wage trade-off.

He told Parliament: 'There will be greater pressure on the Government to do more on the tax-cut front in exchange for wages.' But he appeared to tie the prospect of tax cuts to an Accord Mark VII.

Senator Cook also repeated his criticism of the IRC decision to opt for the percentage wage increase rather than the flat $12 rise sought.

'In our view, that is not a fair outcome and is certainly not the outcome we sought.

Earlier in the day, he also described the IRC's deflection of the Accord's 3 per cent superannuation claim to a requested national retirement income conference as jeopardising the Government's retirement income strategy.

The Minister for Finance, Mr Willis, told Parliament the IRC had 'legitimate concerns' about a wage break-out occurring if the country shifted towards wage bargaining at the enterprise level because of the wage outcomes flowing from previous union campaigns outside centralised wage-fixing.

However, he argued the situation was different this time because it would have occurred during recession when bargaining power was weak.

The transitional bugs could have been sorted out and a culture for enterprise bargaining developed while the danger of a break-out was low.

The Opposition argued yesterday that the IRC had found enterprise bargaining incompatible with a centralised wage-fixing system.

'If we are ever to have a productivity break-out in this country,' the Opposition spokesman, Mr Howard, told Parliament, it would be 'necessary to dismantle Australia's rigid, outmoded centralised wage fixation system.

'What an infernal nerve the Industrial Relations Commission has to say to the ordinary workers and businessmen of this country that they are not mature enough to decide how best to run the enterprises they own and work for,' he said.

To maximise productivity and wage standards, company employers and employees should be free to negotiate their own deals outside the regulations of the current award system.

The only Government intervention would be the setting of a minimum wage and the usual safety and health regulations.

The finance minister, Mr Willis, responded by claiming the Opposition policy was 'fatally flawed' because it would not have the power to enforce a minimum wage on all voluntary agreements.

Source: *Australian Financial Review*, 18 April, 1991.

Figure 4.5: An example of how Government as 'economic manager' can affect industrial relations.

Industrial relations is also affected by government's social welfare policies. For example, an increase in family allowance benefits gives families increased disposable income and eases the pressure on the wages system at least from those groups affected.

Increasingly, the concept of the 'social wage' (all government non-wage allowances and benefits) is being considered part of the negotiating agenda in industrial relations. Discussions between the principal parties in industrial relations are going beyond the industrial wage received by workers. A great deal of the outcome of discussions on wages and salaries rests with the social and economic policies pursued by government.

The spending priorities of governments in education, housing, pensions and benefits are now accepted issues for consideration by industrial relations parties. While the effect of government social policies at the local level may not seem significant, at the national level unions and employer associations are making their views known. This action by the principal parties recognises the role of government in managing the economy and determining the standard of living of Australians. Developments in this broader arena for a large part affect developments in industrial relations. Therefore, the industrial parties are seeking greater input in these broader (macro) level policies which subsequently determine their actions at a local (micro) level.

In carrying out their executive responsibilities as determined by legislation, governments establish departments and authorities under appointed ministers. These departments and authorities are also vested with the responsibility of carrying out the various policies for which the governments have been elected.

Government as administrator of industrial relations policy

The Federal Minister for Industrial Relations is responsible for the Department of Industrial Relations (DIR) and for a number of other tribunals and authorities, including the Affirmative Action Agency, the Australian Trade Union Training Authority, and the National Occupational Health and Safety Commission (Worksafe Australia).

The role of the Commonwealth Department of Industrial Relations, as outlined in its 'mission statement' objectives, is 'to assist the Government', in achieving its 'wider economic and social objectives' (see Figure 4.6). The later part of the 1980s saw the priority in this area being microeconomic and labour market reform. In other words, as part of the government's economic agenda was the desire to create a more efficient workforce through increased labour flexibility and skill development at the workplace or enterprise level. There are a number of industrial relations ramifications of this economic priority.

The major DIR program designed to assist in achieving this goal has been the 'Workplace Reform Program' which ties in with the DIR mission objective of 'promoting and assisting the achievement of a competitive, efficient and

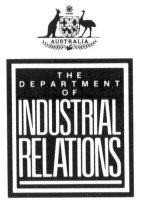

Mission statement

The mission of the Department of Industrial Relations is to assist the Government in achieving its industrial relations and wider economic and social objectives through policies and programs aimed at:

- promoting and assisting the achievement of a competitive, efficient and flexible labour market;
- providing and maintaining an effective industrial relations system which is fair to all parties;
- promoting fair wages and conditions for all workers while assisting Australia's economic and industrial performance;
- fulfilling the responsibilities of the Government as an employer to ensure fair and responsible treatment of its workforce; and
- maintaining a working environment which enables the Department's staff to develop their skills and abilities and contribute to their full potential.

Source: *DIR Annual Report, 1989–1990.*

Figure 4.6: Mission Statement of the Commonwealth Department of Industrial Relations.

flexible labour market'. The DIR has taken a number of initiatives in this area including:

- funding assistance for innovative projects designed to assist employers and unions improve working arrangements at the workplace;
- assistance with the training of managers and union officials on the 'management of change';
- the establishment of a network of Workplace Resource Centres to provide expert technical services to firms;
- publication of a range of booklets, videos, and guidelines on the implementation of Workplace Reform. The Department also sponsored the first comprehensive survey of workplace industrial relations practices (see Figure 4.7).

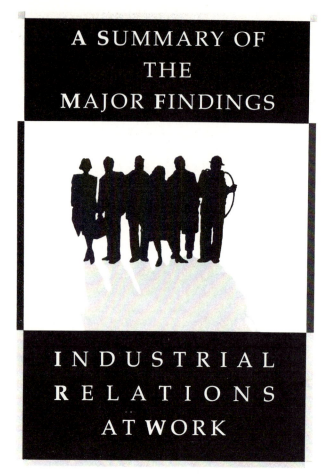

Source: Commonwealth Department of Industrial Relations, AGPS, 1991.
Figure 4.7: An example of a Commonwealth Department of Industrial Relations funded project.

With respect to its 'social' objectives and responsibilities, since 1988 the Government has required all Departments to assess the 'social impact' of their programs and policies. This initiative requires government managers to take account of the four elements of social justice—equity, equality, access and participation—in the programs and services offered by the government. For its part, the Department of Industrial Relations established the Social Justice Section which promotes the recognition of social justice objectives in initiatives taken by the DIR. As part of the award restructuring process, the section, in recognition of women's over-representation in low-pay occupations, has been responsible for the publication of advice and guidelines on ensuring a 'fair deal' for women in the development of new award classifications and training programs as part of the restructuring process.

The Commonwealth DIR and most State equivalents have departmental responsibilities to investigate complaints and give advice about award entitlements. The Awards Management Branch of the Commonwealth Department of Industrial Relations operates in every state and Territory:

- to investigate complaints;
- to educate employers, employees and the community about rights and duties under federal awards; and
- to instigate proceedings where there has been a breach of a particular award.

Table 4.1 shows a summary of data on the activities of the Award Management Branch.

Table 4.1: Awards management branch summary of activities 1989–1990.

Award inquiries	184 680
No. establishments visited	8 067
No. employers in breach	4 253
Total payments to rectify breaches	$ 4 092 153
No. employees receiving payment	15 486

Source: Adapted from *DIR Annual Report, 1989–90*.

Of recent concern to the government has been evidence that employers have not been meeting their obligations to contribute to award-based superannuation resulting from the 1986 National Wage Decision (see Figure 4.8).

A further responsibility of the Department of Industrial Relations derives from Australia's membership of the International Labour Organisation (ILO) and the Organisation for Economic co-operation and Development (OECD). The ILO is the United Nation's agency primarily responsible for labour issues. It establishes international labour standards and gives technical assistance on labour-related matters. The DIR acts as the secretariat responsible for Australian Government's ILO membership and overseas the implementation of ILO conventions in Australia.

> # Pay super or else, bosses told
> ### By BRAD NORINGTON Industrial Editor
>
> The Federal Government has warned it will prosecute employers who avoid paying superannuation after revealing that more than a million workers have not been paid entitlements worth $700 million.
>
> The Minister for Industrial Relations, Senator Cook, said yesterday that many employers had failed to pay the contributions of at least 3 per cent required under occupational award-based schemes.
>
> The evidence, he said, suggested that employers were not as careful about their employees' superannuation rights as they were about their own.
>
> 'I appreciate that some of this non-compliance to pay may be caused by employer ignorance. But I suspect part of the problem comes from groups which have fought against award-based superannuation and are now reacting to it with hostility.'
>
> He said $6.3 million had been allocated to the Awards Management Branch of his department so that 110 inspectors could investigate complaints of employers breaching awards. The ACTU has also mounted a campaign to ensure that superannuation entitlements are being paid and to retrieve contributions still owing.
>
> The ACTU president, Mr Martin Ferguson, said a new ACTU strategy to ensure compliance involved:
>
> - Requiring employers to take part in registered award-based superannuation schemes.
> - Creating a database to identify Federal and State awards which had no provision for superannuation.
> - Putting superannuation on workers' pay slips with dates of payments.
> - Extending award superannuation to part-time and casual employees.
>
> The ACTU believes unions should retrieve unpaid superannuation by taking employers to court if necessary.
>
> The latest concerns arise from the national wage case decision of 1986 which approved an Accord claim for unions to negotiate a 3 per cent wage claim, paid instead as occupational superannuation contributions by employers.
>
> Since then, more than two-thirds of the workforce—4.5 million employees—have gained superannuation as an award entitlement. It was made legally enforceable last year by the Government in amendments to the Industrial Relations Act.
>
> Senator Cook said that in the past only the higher paid who worked in one job all their lives had access to superannuation.
>
> Now that superannuation had been granted under award-based schemes, workers were being denied their rights.

Source: *Sydney Morning Herald*, 28 March, 1991.

Figure 4.8: An example of the role of the DIR's Award Management Branch.

In 1990, Australia ratified the ILO's Convention 156, Workers with Family Responsibilities, 1981. The Convention aims to prevent discrimination against all workers with responsibilities for dependent family members and ensure equality of opportunity in employment. The Convention requires the Government to promote a broad public understanding of the principles of equal opportunity for men and women workers, particularly those with family responsibilities. The DIR in implementing the measures contained in the Convention has set up a Work and Family Unit to advise the Government as well as provide information to employers, employees and unions on relevant strategies for implementation of the ILO Convention.

INTERVIEW

JOE TAURO
Position: Senior Awards Officer, Awards Management Branch, Department of Industrial Relations, Sydney.

1. What is the primary responsibility of the Awards Management branch?

The objective of the awards management function is to assist in the comprehensive management of federal awards by working with award parties to improve the structure and simplicity of awards, maximise awareness of award obligations and entitlements, and maximise compliance with award provisions.

In achieving this objective the Department's role includes:

- co-operative arrangements with award parties through the Federal Awards Management Advisory Committee (FAMAC);
- provision of education, information and advisory services;
- enforcement activities including the investigation of complaints into award breaches and initiating legal proceedings where necessary; and
- undertaking targeted inspection programs on an industry/project basis.

2. Can you give an example of the typical award inquiry you would receive?

Award enquiries cover the whole spectrum of employment conditions; however, one which best typifies an employee enquiry would be:

I have just been terminated by my employer. What are my entitlements—do I receive;

- wages in lieu of notice to terminate;
- redundancy pay
- what happens to my 3 per cent award-based superannuation?

3. What has the Branch done to improve public understanding of awards?

In 1990-1991 the Branch has focused its educative activities on increasing the awareness of employers of their obligations for award-based superannuation. This was seen as a priority project by the industry partners. Priorities over coming years will revolve around improving the structure and simplicity of federal awards. This is intended to make awards more meaningful and understandable documents for both employers and employees.

The Branch also provides a national award information and enquiry service which is being expanded to include both federal and state awards.

4. What skills are needed to be an Awards Officer? What training does the Department offer?

The services of the Awards Management Branch and hence, Awards Officers, are complementary to those provided by the parties to an award, i.e. employer organisations and unions. For those people who are not members of either organisation, the awards management function provides a 'safety net' to maximise compliance with the provisions of the relevant award. Therefore, Awards Officers need to be familiar with the Industrial Relations Act (1988) and other legislation governing industrial relations in Australia. They must be able to read, comprehend and interpret awards so that they know what provisions apply to the respondent parties. They need to be able to set priorities and work independently

> (continued)
>
> to plan and carry out work-site inspections. As greater importance is now placed on providing information to the relevant parties about their rights and obligations under federal legislation and awards, Awards Officers require good interpersonal and presentation skills. A high level of written and oral communication skills are essential for liaising with employers, employees, unions and employer organisations.
>
> The Department provides an eight-week induction course to new Awards Officers. The following list is only a sample of topics covered in the training.
>
> - understanding the Industrial Relations Act and other relevant legislation;
> - the process of making a federal award, its contents, obligations and rights of respondents to that award;
> - how to plan, implement and report findings of work-site inspections;
> - communication skills for dealing with employees, employers, unions and employer organisations.
>
> On-going training is provided, usually in-house, to meet the technical, managerial, and personal development needs of Awards Officers.

Finally, to ensure that government has access to accurate advice, the DIR oversees a number of consultative arrangements. An example of these is the National Labour Consultative Council (NLCC), which is a tripartite consultative body made up of representatives from the ACTU, CAI and government (Figure 4.9). The NLCC meets quarterly as a regular and organised forum at which the key parties in industrial relations can discuss industrial relations, employment and training matters of national concern.

Commonwealth Government representatives
- Senator the Hon. P. Cook, Minister for Industrial Relations (Chairperson)
- Mr G. Glenn, Secretary, Department of Industrial Relations

Representing public authorities as employers
- Dr D. Williams, CEO, Australian Submarine Corporation

Confederation of Australian Industry (CAI) representatives
- Mr J. Clark, Executive General Manager, BHP
- Mr B. Powell, MP, Printing and Allied Trades Employers Federation
- Mr B.M. Noakes, Director General, CAI National Employers' Industrial Council
- Mr C. Anderson, Managing Director, Renison Goldfields Consolidated Ltd

Australian Council of Trade Union representatives
- President
- Mr W.J. Kelty, Secretary
- Mr R. Scott, Junior Vice-President
- Mr W. Mansfield, Assistant Secretary

Figure 4.9: National Labour Consultative Council (NLCC) membership as at 30 June, 1990.

Government as a major employer

To carry out its executive responsibilities, government needs to employ personnel; it is, consequently an employer in its own right. There are government employees at the local, state and federal levels responsible for implementing government legislation and providing services. Teachers, police officers, nurses and telecommunication workers are all considered to be government employees in one form or another. Indeed, government employs almost one-third of wage and salary earners in Australia (Table 4.2).

Table 4.2: Employed wage and salary earners (in thousands): public and private sectors, June 1977 and 1987.

Year	Public sector				Private sector	Total
	Commonwealth	State	Local	Total		
1977	388.8	952.8	124.0	1465.2	3471.6	4936.9
1987	442.5	1161.2	156.6	1760.3	3989.6	5749.9

Source: Adapted from ABS Labour Statistics, 1987.

In its role as employer, the government has a significant impact on the industrial relations system:

- The Department of Industrial Relations represents the Federal Government before the Federal Commission in national wage cases. It develops and presents submissions based on the governmental economic and labour market priorities at the time. As well, it represents government before the Federal Commission in matters affecting employees in the Australian Public Service and in certain Commonwealth authorities.
- The Commonwealth Government Public Service employs some 165 000 staff under 200 federal awards, represented by over 60 unions. The Commonwealth government is, as a consequence, a major employer in its own right and the terms and conditions provided to its own employees affects developments in the private sector. Figure 4.10 illustrates a government initiative for its own employees which could influence private sector developments.

  Another example was the Whitlam Government of 1972–1975 which first introduced four weeks' annual leave for the Australian Public Service, which was subsequently passed on to the private sector.
- Government provides a proving ground for many of its own policy initiatives. Governments cannot expect the private sector to implement labour market initiatives such as affirmative action for women or industrial democracy unless it undertakes reforms in these areas as well. The public sector is therefore often under a great deal of public scrutiny, particularly in areas related to industrial relations.

THE SENATE

MEDIA RELEASE

BOB McMULLAN
SENATOR FOR THE ACT.

TAX OFFICE LEADING THE FIELD IN WORK BASED CHILD CARE

SENATOR BOB MCMULLAN, PARLIAMENTARY SECRETARY TO THE TREASURER, TODAY ANNOUNCED THAT THE AUSTRALIAN TAXATION OFFICE HAS TAKEN THE LEAD IN IMPLEMENTING GOVERNMENT POLICY ON THE PROVISION OF WORKBASED CHILD CARE IN THE COMMONWEALTH PUBLIC SECTOR.

"THE TAX OFFICE, WITH THE ASSISTANCE OF THE PUBLIC SECTOR UNION HAS BEEN EXAMINING A NUMBER OF PROPOSALS OVER RECENT MONTHS," SAID SENATOR MCMULLAN.

"I AM PLEASED TO BE ABLE TO ANNOUNCE THAT DISCUSSIONS HAVE COMMENCED WITH THE ESSENDON CITY COUNCIL ON A PROPOSAL FOR A JOINT VENTURE IN THE MELBOURNE SUBURB OF MOONEE PONDS."

"THE PROPOSAL INVOLVES THE ESTABLISHMENT, ON A PARTNERSHIP BASIS, OF A NEW COMMUNITY BASED CHILD CARE CENTRE. A NUMBER OF PLACES WOULD BE AVAILABLE FOR THE CHILDREN OF STAFF WORKING IN THE TAX OFFICE'S NEW MOONEE PONDS OFFICE."

ALTHOUGH DETAILS HAD YET TO BE FINALISED, SENATOR MCMULLAN SAID THAT: "AS A KEEN ADVOCATE OF PUBLIC SECTOR WORK BASED CHILD CARE, I AM VERY PLEASED WITH THE LEADING ROLE BEING TAKEN BY THE TAX OFFICE. I LOOK FORWARD TO OTHER COMMONWEALTH AGENCIES FOLLOWING THIS LEAD."

"THE PROPOSAL REPRESENTS:
- A FIRST STEP TOWARDS IMPLEMENTATION OF THE GOVERNMENT'S ELECTION COMMITMENTS ON WORK BASED CHILDCARE FOR ITS EMPLOYEES:
- GOOD HUMAN RESOURCE MANAGEMENT, ENABLING OPTIMAL RETURNS FOR THE TAX OFFICE'S INVESTMENT IN RECRUITING, TRAINING AND RETRAINING ITS STAFF:
- THE FRUITION OF THE COMBINED EFFORTS OF THE PUBLIC SECTOR UNION AND ATO MANAGEMENT:
- GOOD CORPORATE CITIZENSHIP, WHEREBY THE TAX OFFICE IS ASSISTING TO MAINTAIN, UPGRADE AND EXPAND CHILDREN'S SERVICES IN THE LOCAL GOVERNMENT AREA; AND
- CO-OPERATION BETWEEN LOCAL, STATE AND FEDERAL GOVERNMENTS."

9 January 1991

Figure 4.10: An example of a government initiative which can be seen as providing an industrial relations model.

To summarise, government has considerable impact on the industrial relations system and is considered a party in its own right. Government's roles include:

- *Legislator*. Federal and state governments pass laws regulating the implementation of industrial relations in Australia. Governments can be said to shape the industrial relations framework.
- *Economic manager through its economic and social policies*. It sets the environment within which employers and unions operate. Government, as a consequence,

influences activities within the industrial relations framework.
- *Employer in its own right.* Governments are employers in Australia. Approximately one in three workers is employed in the public sector. The pay rates, conditions of work and industrial relations initiatives in the public sector therefore influence industrial relations activities in the private sector.
- *Industrial relations model.* Government is expected by the community to set an example concerning industrial relations policies. Policies and programs related to industrial relations, such as migrant education, employment of the disabled and affirmative action for woman, are often implemented in the public sector as a model for the private sector.

The judicial system

There are federal courts and state courts in Australia. The federal courts consist of the High Court of Australia and the Federal Court. The state courts comprise the state supreme courts, the district or county courts and the local or magistrate's courts. See Figure 4.11 for an illustration of the court system.

Each of these courts can be involved in the industrial relations process. To illustrate the role and impact of the judicial system on industrial relations, the responsibilities of the High Court, the Federal Court, a Supreme Court and a Magistrate's Court are outlined below.

High Court

The Australian Constitution, which established the parameters for Australian federation, is interpreted and enforced by the High Court of Australia, the supreme judicial body in the country. The High Court, in its interpretation of the Constitution, has had a profound impact on the system and practice of Australian industrial relations. Section 51(xxxv) of the Constitution has been the subject of more legal battles than virtually all other sections combined. With each decision a new or different light is thrown on the meaning of the provision. For example, the High Court has been asked on several occasions to determine the exact role and scope for decision-making of the federal conciliation and arbitration tribunal. As well, the Court has had to clarify what is meant by 'conciliation and arbitration', 'dispute', 'industrial' and 'interstate' in Section 51(xxxv) (see Figure 4.12).

There are a number of practical problems associated with the influential role the High Court has had in Australian industrial relations, including:
- the ability of the Tribunal to undertake activities seemingly appropriate for the 'prevention and settlement of industrial disputes'. Its actions have been curtailed in the past by decisions of the High Court regarding the limits of the Tribunal's powers; and
- the remoteness of the High Court from the workplace, where industrial disputes emanate. The decision-making of the judiciary, which is based on previous cases and historical concepts, often has little value in resolving contemporary industrial problems.

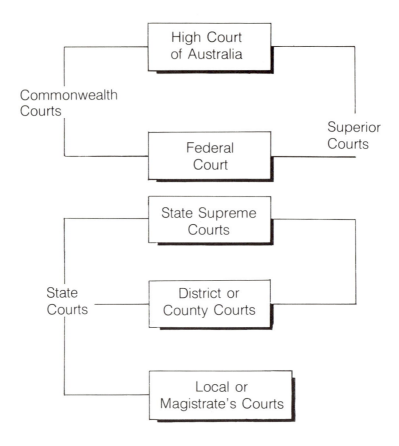

Figure 4.11: The court system.

One of the best examples of the juridical problems faced by the federal tribunal system in attempting to resolve industrial disputes is the issue of reinstatement of dismissed federal award employees. Until 1987 it was accepted that, as a result of a series of High Court cases, the federal industrial commission did not have the formal power to reinstate a dismissed employee. The constitutional problems for the commission in exercising this power included the issue of separateness of judicial and legislative powers, and whether an interstate dispute could be said to exist because of the dismissal of an employee in one state.

In December 1987 the High Court found, in the *Ranger Uranium Mines Case*, that a dispute over reinstatement which does not involve the enforcement of existing legal rights may be settled by the commission, using its conciliation and arbitration powers. This could include reinstatement of dismissed employees. However, in a subsequent decision in February 1989 involving Wooldumpers (Victoria) Ltd, the High Court determined that the Commission's powers for reinstatement depended on the specifics of the case and on how the claim was lodged with the commission.

IRC says it has jurisdiction to hear Shell super dispute

By BARRIE DUNSTAN

A Full Bench of the Industrial Relations Commission has ruled that it has jurisdiction to hear a dispute between the Shell Australia group and its employees over the surplus in the former Shell superannuation fund.

The decision, which may be subject to an appeal by Shell to the High Court, could pave the way for the IRC to become a judicial body which hears disputes on a variety of superannuation matters.

This could extend the IRC's powers into areas involving disputes over superannuation benefits flowing from disabilities or retrenchments.

The Shell case has been seen as the likely test case for employers who have old trust deeds which limit their ability to claw back surpluses. Companies in this position had been hoping to use the Shell approach of transferring the surplus into a new scheme with the appropriate powers.

But, if such matters could be decided by the IRC—more speedily and less expensively than in court hearings—employees would have the means of readily challenging such moves.

A Full Bench yesterday handed down its decision on the Shell superannuation dispute, which goes back to July last year when several Sydney employees challenged the proposed transfer of benefits from an old, $1 million-plus Shell fund to a new fund.

The Bench found there was a dispute relating to payment of $14.70 a week under award superannuation and that there was a dispute over the transfer of the surplus in the Shell fund. Justice Ludeke and Justice Peterson found there was a dispute in both cases. Commissioner Johnson agreed with the majority on the $14.70 dispute but found that the facts on the superannuation surplus did not give rise to a dispute under the Act.

The surplus dispute centred on a deed in May last year under which the Shell Australia Contributory Fund transferred members' entitlements to the new Shell Australia Superannuation Fund.

Justice LUDEKE

The deed of the new SASF empowered trustees to pay to Shell Australia any surplus, unlike the old SACF deed which did not give trustees any power to change the deed to allow any payment from the fund to Shell member companies.

The majority decision said that 'it is clear that the object of the exercise was to take a surplus which (whether or not it was confined in its application under the SACF deed for the benefit of members) was not available to Shell and to place it in a position where it was accessible to Shell'.

The decision said the matter of the compulsory superannuation scheme 'directly related to the employer and employee relationship' and so was within the IRC's jurisdiction.

A spokesman for Shell said the Company was studying the Full Bench decision.

Source: Australian Financial Review, 3 April, 1991.

Figure 4.12: Determining the jurisdiction of the industrial commission.

In a practical sense, it is ultimately the responsibility of the trade union official to explain to a meeting of workers whether a case for a dismissed employee can or cannot be argued before the Industrial Relations Commission because of a High Court decision. Workers' frustration, disbelief and confusion are understandable in this context, in that an institution as remote from the workplace as the High Court determines the fate of a co-worker.

The emphasis placed on minute questions of protocol and on technicalities dictated by the external legal system has historically distanced the industrial relations process from those in the workplace. Nevertheless, there is evidence that the High Court is beginning to allow the federal commission greater flexibility in decision-making. In addition, evidence suggests that the parties at the workplace are taking greater interest in developing their own machinery—such as grievance procedures—to resolve conflict amongst themselves, rather than relying on the more formal external system.

Federal Court (Industrial Division)

When the federal industrial relations framework was established in the early 1900s, the 'judicial' or enforcement aspects were embodied in the overall conciliation and arbitration machinery. However, in 1956 the High Court determined, as a result of the *Boilermakers' Case*, that the tribunal system was not able to exercise both 'judicial' (enforcement) and 'non-judicial' (administrative or arbitral) functions. The High Court held (in the same way the Constitution has determined that the legislative powers of government had to be separate from judicial powers) that the arbitral and judicial responsibilities of the tribunal system had to be clearly separate.

As a result of this High Court decision, the administrative and enforcement aspects of award-making were separated. Ultimately, in 1977 the Industrial Division of the Federal Court was designated to handle the judicial functions associated with the Federal Commission. The activities associated with the making of awards—that is, conciliating and arbitrating disputes—rested with the Commission. The Federal Court (Industrial Division) responsibilities fall into three principal areas:
- the interpretation of awards and other questions of law referred to it;
- the enforcement of awards or orders of the Commission; and
- the resolution of internal problems of registered organisations. The court adjudicates in disputes regarding observation of union rules, union elections, or irregularities in amalgamations of registered organisations.

To illustrate the kinds of issues which come before the Industrial Division of the Federal Court, the following case is summarised:

> In 1988/89, the Theatrical and Amusement Employees Association and the producers of the musical 'Les Miserables' were in dispute over meal breaks for stage crew members. The Federal Court was asked by both union and employers to interpret the clause on meal breaks of the Theatrical Employees Live Theatre and Concert Award.

The Court determined that the clause provided the employees with a half-hour paid meal break every four hours worked by the employees.

Applications are also made to the Federal Court in the case of breaches of Sections 45D and 45E of the *Trade Practices Act*. (This is discussed further in Chapter 6.)

Supreme Court

The conciliation and arbitration machinery which exists at the federal and state levels was designed to resolve conflict between the principal industrial parties. The opportunity still exists, however, for legal action to be taken in the Supreme Court under common or 'judge-made' law in the case of some forms of industrial action. (This is discussed further in Chapter 7.)

The State Supreme Court also resolves questions of legal interpretation of the respective state industrial acts.

Local or Magistrate's Court

The Magistrate's Court figures prominently in the enforcement of awards and state industrial legislation. If there is a breach of an entitlement under an award or industrial legislation, like the *Long Service Leave Act*, action can be taken in the local courts for recovery of any monies which have not been paid.

Summary

As has been shown, the role of government in industrial relations is far-reaching. Government acting on behalf of 'public interest' has the major part in shaping the framework for industrial relations through legislative measures. As well, government has considerable influence through its economic management and other executive responsibilities in establishing the environment within which the industrial relations system exists. Finally, the judicial system has a significant impact on the Australian industrial relations process.

Questions and Activities
1. After reading Figure 4.5 answer the following questions:
    a. Why is there less concern about a 'wages breakout' during a recession?
    b. Could the Federal Government set minimum wage regulations or is the argument 'fatally flawed'? If so, why?
    c. How would a tax cut 'appease' workers? What would employers' reaction be?
2. After reading Figure 4.8 answer the following questions:
    a. What does 'award-based superannuation' mean?
    b. What action is the government proposing to ensure workers receive their superannuation entitlements?
    c. Why would the government want employers to comply with the award-based superannuation schemes?

Questions and Activities (continued)
3. After reading Figure 4.12 answer the following questions:
   a. What was the composition of the full Bench?
   b. What is a 'majority' decision?
   c. On what basis would the employer appeal the decision to the High Court?
4. How does the government as an employer affect industrial relations? Give examples.
5. What is the 'social wage'? Give some examples. In your view, should employers and unions be involved in issues beyond strictly 'industrial' matters?
6. Governments have a range of industrial relations policies. Obtain information on them from either the state or federal Department of Industrial Relations/Labour. Discuss and evaluate one of them.

Chapter 5

Industrial Conflict

Objectives

At the end of this chapter, the reader should be able to:
- discuss the ways in which industrial conflict is demonstrated;
- review media coverage of industrial relations; and
- describe Australia's recent strike record.

Introduction

As outlined in Chapter 1, the essence of any industrial relations system is the manner in which conflict is regulated. In Australia, the recognised method of processing conflict occurs largely through institutions such as the Australian Industrial Relations Commission, especially conflict relating to national distribution of incomes and in the determination of awards.

Conflict is part of everyday life and it is not difficult to provide an array of industrial relations based examples:

- an employer may introduce a new form of technology into the manufacturing process which makes a number of employees redundant. A trade union would seek to protect the interests of its affected members;
- disputes often arise over the correct interpretation of an award;
- two trade unions may be in conflict over who can enlist certain workers as their members; and
- national employer bodies may not be able to agree on a common policy and submission to a National Wage Case hearing.

As these examples illustrate, conflict in industrial relations cannot be seen merely as a narrow spectrum involving trade unions 'against' employers. As the last item above demonstrates, a hallmark of peak inter-employer body relationships has been the deep conflict in determining a unified national wages position.

Approaches to industrial conflict

For some, industrial conflict is inevitable in a society such as Australia where, they argue, workers are 'alienated' from the full rewards of their effort and

Source: The Sun-Herald, 28 April, 1991.

labour. 'Rewards' are taken to mean not only economic benefits but also the achievement which comes with ownership and control over the means of wealth creation. Most workplaces are viewed as institutions in which employees do not have any real power and limited opportunity to fully develop their potential and their ability to serve socially useful purposes. In this view, the question is not why industrial conflict exists—rather, how it has been controlled. It isn't that strikes exist but that there are so few.

A pluralist approach similarly regards conflict as unavoidable, but with the task being to manage the conflict to optimise organisational performance. This was described in Chapter 1 as the 'face-to-face' approach. Conflict arises because of differences in goals and perceptions between individuals and groups. A successful manager is one who uses this conflict to remedy inadequacies in the organisation, and who harnesses it as a creative force: conflict is to be lived with and used.

The more traditionalist or unitary view, however, sees conflict as avoidable. Conflict usually occurs because of a failure by management to communicate (persuade/convince) to the workforce the significance of their objectives. Conflict can also occur through agitators and trouble-makers. It should be minimised or eliminated, if possible, as it disrupts work activity and prevents the organisation from achieving its optimum performance.

In a practical sense, these approaches help determine how an organisation designs its jobs, leadership style and skills which it expects of its managers, and its system of rewards. Whichever approach is dominant will have a significant impact on the industrial relations within any organisation. For example:

A. The issue of compulsory unionism: if a business were in a position of deciding by itself (i.e. without trade union or other pressure) whether to introduce as a work requirement that all employees must be in their relevant union, the management positions for and against union representation could be:

- *Against*: Trade unions will encourage complaints and claims and thereby increase conflict. The power of trouble-makers would be detrimentally increased.
- *For*: Trade unions will provide a vehicle for the employees' grievances to be aired. Inevitably there will be conflict, and the union may provide a useful collective line of communication.

B. Automatic wage and salary deductions for trade union membership fees; In response to a request to implement a system of 'check-off', an organisation's position for and against the policy could be:

- *Against*: the system will improve the trade union efficiency which will mean they can devote more resources into pursuing issues/claims against employers.
- *For*: agreeing to the request will contribute to building a positive working relationship with the trade union and thereby help manage conflict.

Of course, in both of these cases, an organisation would need to take into account factors and variables such as:

- the policies of their employer associations and industry practice;
- whether the compulsory unionism and 'check-off' system complied with all relevant law (statutes and awards);
- the likely impact on the current workforce if either change was implemented (adequacy of conscientious objection provisions, the possibility of discontinuing the check-off system during industrial disputes as a bargaining tactic); and
- if, in acceding to the requests, the trade union would be willing to accept some changes sought by the employer (a 'win/win' approach).

Each of these factors is important in determining how individual management responds to claims for compulsory unionism and automatic deductions of trade union membership fees. The attitudes of management (i.e. do they view industrial relations as a hand-in-hand or face-to-face process?) also markedly affect such decisions.

Manifestation of conflict

Employees have a number of ways to demonstrate concerns and dissatisfaction with their employers. These manifestations or symptoms of conflict can be either covert (concealed) or overt (open). Table 5.1 gives examples of the different ways in which conflict can be expressed. The overt manifestations tend to be by *group* action (strikes, work bans etc.), whereas the covert are usually limited to *individuals*. However, some of the manifestations listed here as 'covert' may be converted to 'overt' action—as, for example, when employees resign *en masse*. Also these overt demonstrations of conflict should be seen as part of the means employees may use to gain a change or concession from their management.

Table 5.1: Conflict in the workplace.

Overt manifestations		Covert manifestations
• Strikes • Stop-work meetings • Work bans (e.g. 'work to rule') • Lockouts • Boycotts • Transfer/termination of employees by employers	LEAKAGES ← Conflict present in the workplace → LEAKAGES	• Absenteeism • Resignations by employees • Sabotage/theft • Accidents • Low productivity • Lack of co-operation/ compliance

The most obvious manifestation of conflict, and the one which receives the most attention in the media, is the strike. While the cost of strikes to an employer and the economy is considerably less than that of accidents, for example, strikes are paradoxically the principal focus of attention.

The results of a major survey conducted by the federal Department of Industrial Relations (see Table 5.2) demonstrate that strikes, pickets, go-slows and other overt manifestations of conflict were not widespread. Indeed, 72 per cent of Australian workplaces had *never* had any such industrial action. Another 10 per cent had experienced no direct industrial action since 1989 (see Figure 5.1).

Expressions of conflict usually represent a 'leakage' from the efficient use of resources by an employer. Clearly, for example, an employer may need to sustain higher staffing levels than necessary to offset absenteeism. The effect of the 1989 Pilots Disputes on tourist resorts dependent on air travel was obvious. However, the extent of loss caused by conflict is not easily measured and in some instances, the strike or other action may not lead to any loss at all. An employer at a time when there is little demand for their products may in fact benefit from a loss of production due to a strike.

Table 5.2: Types of industrial action taken in the year 1989 by sector.

Type of industrial action	% of workplaces with industrial action			% of employees at workplaces with industrial action		
	Private	Public	All	Private	Public	All
Strikes	4	20	6	15	38	22
Stop work meetings	4	29	8	21	53	32
Overtime bans	1	12	3	10	26	16
Go slow	0	2	1	3	8	5
Picketing	0	2	0	2	9	4
Work to rule	0	13	2	3	14	6
Other bans	1	10	2	4	21	10
No industrial action	93	57	88	75	34	62

Population: Australian workplaces with at least five employees.
   Figures are weighted and are based on responses from 2 353 workplaces.
Note: Some workplaces had several types of action.

Source: Callus, R. et al., *Industrial Relations at Work*, The Australian Workplace Industrial Relations Survey, AGPS, 1991.

Strikes involve the removal of labour by employees from a part of an organisation, such as when aircraft refuelers may strike, or from the whole of an organisation. The latter is more likely to occur in single union plants and where shop committees (a body co-ordinating all the departments and trade unions involved) exists.

Employees generally will only strike as a last resort although in some instances a strike early in a dispute will be used to express the employees' depth of dissatisfaction or the seriousness of the issue involved. This, in turn, may affect the perceptions of those involved in resolving the dispute. Theories and practice of negotiation suggest that a party will achieve a better result if their opponents *perceive* them as having significant power. An early strike can be used to manipulate those perceptions.

'Wildcat' strikes are those which occur without the sanction of the trade union representing the employees. Also, courts have held that mass resignations and the mass taking of sick leave constitute a strike. Finally, absenteeism can be used to support an industrial campaign as the newspaper report on p. 99 illustrates.

Losses caused by covert expressions of conflict far outweigh the overt. Absenteeism, for example, has been estimated to account for up to 4 per cent of the workforce being absent on any one day, whereas, on average only one day per employee is lost each year to strike action.

Much of Australia's response to conflict involves the use of an array of industrial tribunals, which attempt to 'solve' conflict in the form of strikes and similar action. Ironically, comparatively few government agencies are equipped to assist businesses in their efforts to reduce conflict-based absenteeism

Survey shows 72pc of workplaces have never had strikes

By MARK DAVIS

Australia's first comprehensive survey on industrial relations at the workplace has called into question many assumptions and perceptions which have dominated policy debate in recent years.

The findings of the Australian Workplace Industrial Relations Study, issued by the Department of Industrial Relations yesterday, reveal that:

- The problems of multiple union and award coverage, which have been the central themes in much of the debate about reforming industrial relations, affect only a small minority of workplaces.
- In 72 per cent of workplaces, employees had never taken industrial action. In a further 10 per cent there had been no industrial action for at least two years.
- Just under half of the managers who felt they were being prevented from making necessary efficiency changes identified lack of resources and internal management policy as barriers to change. Only 7 per cent said industrial awards were barriers to change while 14 per cent blamed unions.

The survey, modelled on similar studies in Britain in the 1980s, provides the first comprehensive empirical database in Australia on workplace industrial relations.

According to the team of researchers commissioned by the Federal Government to conduct the survey, the project was designed to overcome the 'empirical vacuum' which has characterised the recent debate on workplace and enterprise industrial relations.

Most earlier Australian research on industrial relations at the workplace has been based either on individual case studies or surveys with sampling and methodological constraints, making it impossible to generalise on results across the economy.

The AWIRS sample of 2,353 workplaces with five or more employees, which were surveyed in late 1989 and early 1990, is said to be representative of workplaces employing some 4.3 million workers, allowing general conclusions to be drawn with a high degree of statistical confidence.

Among the more surprising results is the revelation that the problems of multiple unionism and multiple award coverage are largely confined to big business.

These are the problems which have been identified by the Business Council of Australia in surveys of its members and which underlie the ACTU and the Federal Government's policies on reforming union structures.

The AWIRS results show that 54 per cent of unionised workplaces with at least five employees had only one union. Only 2 per cent of workplaces had more than five unions.

But the extent of multiple unionism increased with the size of the workplace: 44 per cent of workplaces with more than 500 employees had more than five unions while only 6 per cent of workplaces with between 100 and 199 employees had this number of unions.

Similarly, the problems of multiple-award coverage are more pronounced in large workplaces than in small or medium-sized plants.

While only 3 per cent of workplaces surveyed said they were covered by more than five awards, multiple-award coverage still had a significant impact because of the proportion of workers employed in these larger workplaces (25 per cent of employees).

Further significant findings include:

- Over-award payments were made at 68 per cent of workplaces with 47 per cent of managers saying that the award rate was too low to attract suitable employees.
- Closed-shop provisions applied at 22 per cent of unionised workplaces, which employed 13 per cent of the workforce surveyed.
- The average voluntary annual labour turnover rate was 19 per cent.
- The average absenteeism rate was 4.5 per cent.
- Performance-related pay systems, such as piece rates and bonus payments for non-managerial employees operated at 39 per cent of workplaces.
- Half of all workplaces with 20 or more employees did not measure labour productivity in a quantifiable manner.

Source: Australian Financial Review, 1 March, 1991.

Figure 5.1: Report on the AWIS survey.

> # Air controllers 'use sickies as protest'
> **By BRAD NORINGTON** Industrial Editor
>
> The Civil Aviation Authority (CAA) yesterday accused air traffic controllers of using an "orchestrated campaign" of sick leave to protest against alleged staff shortages.
>
> The authority previously had alluded to high levels of sick leave, particularly at Sydney Airport, to suggest that controllers were engaging in a form of backdoor industrial action.
>
> But yesterday was the first time it bluntly accused conrollers of misusing "sickies".
>
> The CAA told an Industrial Relations Commission hearing a marked increase in sick leave taken by air traffic controllers had forced the closure of Sydney Airport more than 12 times since February.
>
> The CAA's advocate, Mr Michael Dowling, QC, said the CAA would argue that the controllers' union, the Civil Air Operations Officers' Association, had used sick leave as part of an orchestrated industrial campaign.
>
> Figures released by the CAA show that only 10 per cent of controllers are working their rostered shifts, with up to 25 of the 106 Sydney controllers calling in sick on any given day. They also show it is virtually impossible to find replacements on Fridays.
>
> A planned five-hour shutdown of Sydney Airport yesterday was called off to allow award restructuring wage claims to be heard in the commission in Melbourne.

Source: Sydney Morning Herald, 24 May, 1989.

and labour turnover. Organisations are expected to develop their own strategies and mechanisms to 'resolve' the non-dramatic expressions of conflict.

Not all manifestations of conflict are the sole domain of employees and their trade unions. Employers can use a variety of tactics in an effort to get their employees closer to management's objectives or to accept the changes employers wish to implement. These may include:

- a 'discipline' code, where workers are given a series of recorded warnings;
- temporary close-downs or lockouts;
- subcontracting out, where possible, work from conflict-prone parts of the business; and
- dismissals or retrenchments to reduce the power of the employees.

The media and industrial conflict

There are a number of reasons why the media's coverage of industrial relations concentrates on strikes. First, a strike by a group of workers is commonly regarded as a 'revolt' by employees against the power and authority of the employer. This action against what is seen as the status quo is newsworthy. Second, the media wants to win the attention of the consumer, and in doing so focuses on the effects of the strike rather than the issues behind the dispute. The result is that employees are often portrayed as being the sole perpetrators of disputes. Finally, the industrial relations system is complex, and journalists and editorial staff may have neither the time to familiarise themselves with its intricacies nor the opportunity to explain them to the consumer. This results, perhaps not surprisingly, in the highlighting of sensational aspects of industrial disputes.

In reality, much of industrial relations centres upon management and unions reaching amicable agreement on the issues in dispute. However, the picture of people sitting around a table discussing and arguing points—even if somewhat heatedly—is not considered very newsworthy by the popular media.

The outcomes of the industrial relations system—awards, agreements and industrial laws—are also not prone to ideal treatment in the media. The way in which national wage decisions are largely reported is a useful illustration: the emphasis is on calculations of 'what you will get', without a clear explanation of the reasoning behind the decision of the Australian Industrial Relations Commission. This inadequacy of reporting can lead to pressure at the workplace, especially if a decision is unfavourable to the ACTU's case.

Most reports of industrial relations events are written or subedited to a formula which increases the sense of drama ('threats', 'bans', etc.), and which tends to reinforce a bias against the legitimacy of industrial action. The headline in Figure 5.2 from *The Newcastle Herald* illustrates this point. The report emphasises the threat posed by the industrial dispute ('hit HSC papers') and does not directly explain the reason for the trade union action. An alternative headline could have been 'State printing closure—700 jobs lost'.

State printing ban to hit HSC papers

Staff occupied the NSW Government Printing Office in Sydney yesterday and banned all work on government publications after the announcement of the office's impending closure with the loss of 700 jobs.

The bans will affect the Higher School Certificate exams (which are being printed now), the Government Gazette and all ministerial correspondence.

The Minister for Administrative Services, Mr Webster, announced on Tuesday that the office, in the inner-Sydney suburb of Ultimo, would close in a month on economic grounds.

Source: The Newcastle Herald, 29 June, 1989.

Figure 5.2: Use of drama in headlines reinforces bias against industrial action.

Any review of the reporting of industrial relations—outside of the 'popular press' and its aligned electronic media—highlights the biases which operate. The article shown in Figure 5.3, 'Greiner fails in attempt to reduce workers wage claim rights', is reproduced from *Unity*, the newsletter/journal of the 'left-wing' Building Workers Industrial Union and the Federated Engine Drivers and Firemens Association. The words used in the article reflect the unions' own value system: 'in an unprecedented underhanded move', 'sneak', 'reduce workers [. . .] rights' and 'feeble excuses'. It is useful to reflect how this story would have been presented by the mainstream media.

> # Greiner fails in attempt to reduce workers wage claim rights
>
> The Greiner government has failed in its attempt to reduce the period for which under paid wages could be claimed for 6 years down to 12 months, and to similarly limit claim rights to long service leave and annual leave.
>
> In an unprecedented underhanded move, the state government tried to sneak the change through by including it in a minor amendment bill which accompanied a new apprenticeship training bill. The change was not included in the original draft bill supplied to the opposition and unions, and the final bill with the change only became available a day or two before it was put to the vote in parliament.
>
> Thanks to the diligence of ALP house member Jack Hallam (ex-AMWU official) the extra amendment in the bill was spotted, and the unions were alerted. When the bill then came up for debate in parliament on May 9, the ALP attacked the government on this late inclusion, and questioned it as to why it had included in the training bills general industrial matters which seriously affected all workers. The ALP also attacked the merits of the change being sought by the government.
>
> The government, having been caught out in their underhanded tactic, could only give feeble excuses. On the merits of the change, the industrial relations minister, John Fahey, gave the weak reason for the reduction to 12 months that this would save work for the DIRE inspectors and free them up to do other work.

Source: Unity, BWIU/FEDFA.

Figure 5.3: Wording in union journal highlights the union's own biases and value system.

Australia's recent dispute record

Since the early part of this century, the Australian Bureau of Statistics has collated and published data relating to industrial disputes where a stoppage of work (due to strike or lockout) has occurred. The statistics report on industrial disputes which involve stoppages of 10 working days or more at the place where the dispute occurred. A one-day strike by 10 workers would therefore be counted. Broadly, information is given on:

- the number of disputes;
- the number of working days lost;
- the reported causes of the dispute;
- how the dispute was resolved;
- the number and industry of workers involved; and
- the estimated loss of wages.

Figure 5.4 graphs the number of industrial disputes and working days lost in Australia since 1970.

Much industrial relations research involves attempting to explain the shifts in the level of disputes shown in Figure 5.4. Some of the explanations which have been developed include:

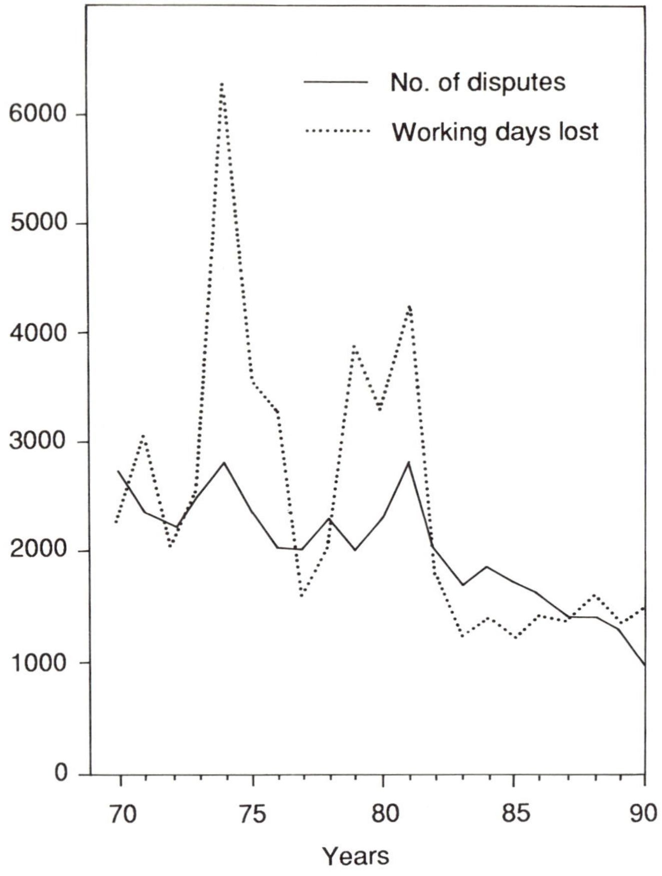

Figure 5.4: Australia's recent industrial dispute record.

Source: based on information from ABS, Industrial Disputes Australia, 1988.

- The level of economic activity approximately correlates with the number of working days lost especially in the recessions of the late seventies and mid-1980s and the resources 'boomlet' of 1982.

  This explanation relies on the relationship between trade union bargaining power and the strength/weakness of the labour market. High levels of economic activity with a strong demand for labour generally increases trade unions' power whilst unemployment diminishes their power. Indeed much of conventional macro economic policy regards certain levels of unemployment as a necessary instrument to reduce average wage settlements and thereby, it is argued, inflation.

- Penalties against industrial action largely fell into disuse after the Clarrie O'Shea case. O'Shea, an official of the Melbourne based Tramways union, was jailed for contempt of court for refusing an order of the court. The subsequent uproar and threats of widespread industrial action meant that a more 'pragmatic approach' to the use of sanctions evolved. The demise of these sanctions meant, it has been argued, that trade unions were more willing to take industrial action.

- Changes in government and their policies can also be seen as an explanation of changes in industrial disputation. For example, it could be said the election of the Whitlam Government in 1972 led to a greater willingness by trade unions to pursue claims. Four weeks annual leave loadings and a wages 'explosion' in 1974 occurred during the Whitlam Government's three year term of office. The Hawke ALP government's election in 1983, on a policy of 'national reconciliation' with the ACTU–ALP Accord is seen as driving the level of strikes down. The growth of 'corporatism' (i.e. business, government and unions co-operating in economic decision-making) has led to the ACTU and the Federal Government actively disciplining trade unions which have sought to pursue claims outside those sanctioned under the Accord.

Other explanations for the changes in the level of industrial disputes have been argued. For example, declining trade union membership, increases in the casualisation of the labour force, the shift from the unionised manufacturing sector to the less unionised service sector of the economy and the development and strict application of the no-extra claims conditions in National Wage Cases.

No one explanation provides a 'best-fit' for the changing level of disputes, moreover the marked variation from year-to-year should be seen as reflecting an intensively diverse number of variables and factors.

From the statistics, apart from the dispute record a number of other aspects of the way industrial relations is conducted in Australia, can be highlighted. Firstly, two industries, coal mining and stevedoring, are particularly 'strike-prone', historically accounting for up to 50 per cent of all strikes. In 1988, for instance, mining was responsible for 35 per cent of all working days lost. Specific theories have sought to explain this and have concentrated on mining's strong historical support for trade unionism, the camaraderie developed between miners because of their arduous working conditions and the social and geographic isolation often experienced by the mining communities.

Secondly, the great majority of strikes are 'settled' within five days by the employees returning to work. In 1990 less than one per cent of strikes lasted longer than five days. 67 per cent were over in one day.

Thirdly, most strikes are about managerial policy (50 per cent in 1990) eg. over reinstatement/unfair dismissals, computing employee entitlements and disciplinary matters.

Lastly, although the statistics do not provide a full picture, the system of industrial tribunals tend to play a changing role in resolving 'day-to-day' industrial disputes, ranging from just 6.5 per cent of all working days lost in 1984 to 38 per cent in 1990. A significant number of disputes are 'settled' by a resumption to work without negotiation (46.6 per cent in 1988) but the parties may then undertake steps to resolve the dispute.

Summary

Although the mass media tends to portray conflict as taking the exclusive form of strikes, conflict can be expressed in a variety of ways, both overt and covert. The bias of the popular media reflects the notion that conflict is to be avoided rather than managed.

Australia's dispute record reveals how the frequency of strikes can change in response to factors such as government policy, and that most strikes in Australia are short-lived and involve direct negotiation to reach resolution.

Questions and Activities

1. Conduct a survey using the form below to determine people's *'attitudes to industrial disputes'*. In the last column, write down what you think the community's view would be and compare it to your respondent's answers.

Attitudes to industrial disputes—A survey.

Factors causing Industrial disputes	Very Important	Fairly Important	Not Important	Expectation of community's attitude
Wages falling behind cost of living.				
Influence of trade union officials				
Frustration with industrial tribunals				
Unreasonableness of employers				
Government policies and attitudes				
Selfish attitudes of workers in key industries				

2. Read the article, ILO Scathing of anti-strike laws, *Australian Financial Review*, in Figure 5.5. Do you feel that the view expressed by the ILO is consistent with that projected by the mainstream media in Australia?

ILO scathing of anti-strike laws
By ROWLEY SPIERS

Virtually all strikes in Australia could be illegal, according to the International Labour Organisation.

The tripartite organisation has criticised the growing use of Australia's civil laws against striking workers and will investigate whether any right to strike exists in this country.

The decision of the ILO flows out of the pilots' dispute in 1989 during which the pilots' union, the Australian Federation of Air Pilots, and six of its officials were fined $6.5 million in damages after being found guilty of common law breaches.

The ILO, meeting in Geneva on Wednesday, found that Australia's law of industrial torts 'appears to treat all industrial action' as illegal and leaves any trade union initiating a strike open to heavy penalties.

'The cumulative effect of such provisions could be to deprive workers of the capacity lawfully to take strike action to promote and defend their economic and social interests,' according to a committee report unanimously adopted by the main body of the ILO.

The ILO report made a particular note of Justice Brookings' comment during the pilots' case in November 1989 that he was merely applying the current law and that 'any remedy must lie with Parliament'.

The international body has referred the examination of Australia's civil law to a specialist committee that will meet later this month. However, it is unlikely to report back until March next year.

Nevertheless, the ILO's condemnation will give added impetus to the push by both the Federal Government and the ACTU to curb the use of common law remedies during industrial disputes.

The Minister for Industrial Relations, Senator Cook, has raised the topic several times at the quarterly tripartite meetings of the National Labour Consultative Council and signalled his intention of reforming industrial law and perhaps creating a separate Labour Court to deal with industrial infractions.

His department is in the middle of producing an options paper. Apart from beefing up sanctions within the Industrial Relations Act and curbing access to the civil courts, it could also countenance separate legislation establishing a right to strike.

The Government attempted to make similar reforms when the IR Act was drafted in 1987. However, it withdrew the package when it was faced with vehement and well-funded employer opposition.

Source: Australian Financial Review, 1 March, 1991.

Figure 5.5: The ILO condemns the increasing use of civil laws against strike action.

3. Using the norms of the popular media, rewrite the article from *Unity*, 'Bosses use scabs and police against striking brickies' (Figure 5.6), so that it would be published.
4. Use the information contained in the Explanatory Notes to answer the following questions:
    a. If a company with 10 employees held a half-day (4-hour) stoppage, would this amount to an industrial dispute for the purposes of statistics?
    b. If an employer 'locked out' his employees, would that be reported in the statistics?
    c. How would a strike over a Federal Government policy on health insurance be classified in terms of cause?
    d. The Australian Bureau of Statistics reports conflict in terms of number of disputes, working days lost and estimated loss in wages. Which measure do you consider to be the most useful? Why?

Bosses use scabs and police against striking brickies

Verline bricklaying has been sacked from the Meriton Apartments job at Canley Vale and all striking workers reinstated with full pay for lost time in a successful outcome of the four week strike over the sacking of BWIU delegate Greg Hannon.

Verline used scabs, police and thugs to try and break a strike by bricklayers and labourers in support of Greg Hannon, who was sacked by Verline on May 4—two days after he attempted to organise a site meeting about safety problems on the job. Workers were set to return to work on May 19 when—after negotiations with the BWIU—Meriton Apartments and Verline agreed in writing to discuss final conditions for Greg's reinstatement at the BWIU office, but they failed to turn up to the meeting.

The following Tuesday, management brought scab labour on-site and used police to break a union picket line so that trucks could enter the site. Their action failed to break the resolve of the striking workers, who had full support from the union and workers on surrounding jobs.

When it realised that intimidation couldn't force the union to remove bans and pickets or end the strike, Meriton Apartments P/L agreed to sack Verline, and re-employ all striking bricklayers and labourers under the new contractor with full pay for lost time. The new bricklaying contractor will recognise site seniority.

Bricklayers who scabbed will not be allowed to work on the job. Assistant secretary Denis Matthews told 'Unity' that the outcome of the Meriton dispute was 'a major victory that will show other bosses that our members won't buckle in the face of intimidation'.

Source: Unity, BWIU/FEDFA.

Figure 5.6: Report of Strike and its outcome.

5. Using Tables 5.3, 5.4, 5.6 and 5.7, answer the following questions:
   a. Rank the industries according to the proportion of working days lost.
   b. Chart the working days lost (per cent) for each cause of dispute for the years 1984–1990 shown in Table 5.5.
   c. Using Table 5.6, has the pattern of duration of disputes changed significantly between 1984 and 1990?
   d. How are most disputes settled in Australia?

Table 5.3: Industrial disputes in Australia, 1970–1990.

Year	No. of disputes	Total no. of workers involved	Working days lost (in thousands)
1970	2738	1367.4	2393.7
1971	2404	1326.5	3068.6
1972	2298	1113.8	2010.3
1973	2538	803.0	2633.4
1974	2809	2004.8	6232.5
1975	2432	1398.0	3509.9
1976	2055	2189.9	3399.2
1977	2090	596.2	1654.8
1978	2277	1075.6	2130.8
1979	2042	1862.9	3964.4
1980	2429	1172.8	3320.2
1981	2915	1251.8	4168.3
1982	2060	706.1	1879.9
1983	1788	407.2	1284.6
1984	1965	560.3	1307.4
1985	1895	570.5	1256.2
1986	1754	691.7	1390.7
1987	1517	608.8	1311.9
1988	1508	894.4	1641.4
1989	1402	709.8	1202.4
1990	1177	726.2	1366.9

Source: ABS, Industrial Disputes Australia, December 1990. Catalogue No. 6321.0.

Table 5.4: Industrial disputes in progress during 1988, by industry, in Australia.

	Total industrial disputes in progress (no.)(a)	Employees involved (directly and indirectly) ('000)	Working days lost ('000)	Working days lost (per employee involved)
Agriculture, forestry, fishing and hunting	—	—	—	—
Mining	438	155.5	568.6	4.66
Ferrous metal ores	99	27.5	70.9	2.58
Coal	294	122.2	471.2	3.86
Other	45	5.8	26.5	4.58
Manufacturing	428	276.5	426.9	1.54
Food, beverages and tobacco	50	13.0	57.3	4.40
Meat products	33	9.1	35.2	3.87
Other food, beverages and tobacco	17	3.9	22.1	5.62
Textiles, clothing and footwear	5	0.7	1.1	1.62
Wood, wood products and furniture	13	1.4	3.5	2.52
Paper and paper products, printing and publishing	24	19.2	25.2	1.31
Chemical, petroleum and coal products	22	3.1	7.4	2.34
Non-metallic mineral products	15	1.7	15.5	9.26
Metal products, machinery and equipment	290	233.9	309.5	1.32
Basic metal products	139	207.1	239.8	1.16
Fabricated metal products	20	2.9	20.1	6.96
Motor vehicles and parts	15	3.9	19.1	4.88
Other transport equipment	81	16.3	14.8	0.91
Other machinery and equipment	35	3.7	15.7	4.22
Miscellaneous manufacturing	9	3.4	7.5	2.18
Electricity, gas and water	50	22.2	23.2	1.04
Electricity and gas	46	21.3	21.2	0.99
Water, sewerage and drainage	4	0.9	2.0	2.31
Construction	171	126.7	207.9	1.64
Wholesale and retail trade	56	13.4	39.9	2.99
Wholesale trade	47	8.3	29.7	3.59
Retail trade	9	5.1	10.2	2.00
Transport and storage	177	42.4	69.9	1.65
Road transport	17	5.0	7.0	1.40
Rail transport	15	11.0	31.2	2.84
Water transport	3	0.1	0.4	3.17
Air transport	19	4.4	6.4	1.45
Other transport and storage	5	0.3	0.8	2.46
Services to transport	118	21.5	24.0	1.12
Stevedoring	63	14.7	13.8	0.94
Other services to transport	55	6.8	10.2	1.51
Communication	29	5.4	5.2	0.96
Finance, property and business services	20	6.5	17.0	2.63
Public administration and defence	70	134.6	164.5	1.22
Community services	50	105.2	111.4	1.06
Health	10	7.0	12.8	1.82
Education, museum and library services	12	90.04	86.8	0.96
Other	28	7.8	11.7	1.51
Recreation, personal and other services	19	6.1	6.9	1.14
Total	1508	894.4	1641.3	1.84

Source: ABS, Industrial Disputes Australia, 1988.

Table 5.5: Industrial disputes alternate years 1984–1990, by cause of dispute, Australia.

Cause of dispute	1984	1986	1988	1990
WORKING DAYS LOST ('000)				
Wages	308.4	546.3	507.9	150.7
Hours of work	73.4	13.2	31.5	4.3
Leave, pensions, compensation	105.5	148.0	50.0	20.4
Managerial policy	407.0	486.0	897.7	1053.4
Physical working conditions	204.1	93.7	158.1	98.0
Trade unionism	109.5	45.7	34.0	52.3
Other(a)	45.5	33.3	34.6	24.4
Total	1253.5	1366.2	1713.8	1403.6
WORKING DAYS LOST (Per cent)				
Wages	24.6	40.0	29.6	10.7
Hours of work	5.9	1.0	1.8	0.3
Leave, pensions, compensation	8.4	10.8	2.9	1.6
Managerial policy	32.5	35.6	52.4	75.0
Physical working conditions	16.3	6.9	9.2	7.0
Trade unionism	8.7	3.3	2.0	3.7
Other(a)	3.6	2.4	2.0	2.0
Total	100.0	100.0	100.0	100.0

Source: Australian Bureau of Statistics, Catalogue no. 6322.

Table 5.6: Industrial disputes alternate years 1984–1990, by duration of dispute, Australia.

Duration of dispute	1984	1986	1988	1990
WORKING DAYS LOST ('000)				
Up to and including 1 day	187.1	441.0	732.9	417.4
Over 1 to 2 days	194.6	65.7	113.7	604.7
Over 2 and less than 5 days	213.8	98.9	144.2	97.4
5 and less than 20 days	202.8	219.4	547.5	92.9
10 and less than 20 days	183.5	398.4	132.7	67.8
20 days and over	271.6	142.8	42.7	123.3
Total	1253.5	1366.2	1713.8	1403.6
WORKING DAYS LOST (Per cent)				
Up to and including 1 day	14.9	32.3	42.8	29.7
Over 1 to 2 days	15.5	4.8	6.6	43.0
Over 2 and less than 5 days	17.1	7.2	8.4	6.9
5 and less than 10 days	16.2	16.1	31.9	6.7
10 and less than 20 days	14.6	29.2	7.7	4.8
20 days and over	21.7	10.5	2.5	8.9
Total	100.0	100.0	100.0	100.0

Source: Australian Bureau of Statistics, Catalogue no. 6322.

Table 5.7: Industrial disputes alternate years 1984–1990, by method of settlement, Australia.

Method of settlement	1984	1986	1988	1990
WORKING DAYS LOST ('000)				
Negotiation	314.6	165.1	176.1	213.7
State legislation	260.2	110.2	102.7	167.4
Federal and joint Federal-state legislation	80.9	576.8	788.2	364.0
Resumption without negotiation	585.9	467.8	598.4	654.5
Other methods(a)	12.0	46.3	48.3	3.9
Total	1253.5	1366.2	1713.8	1403.6
WORKING DAYS LOST (Per cent)				
Negotiation	25.1	12.1	10.3	15.2
State legislation	20.8	8.1	6.0	11.9
Federal and joint Federal-State legislation	6.5	42.2	46.0	25.9
Resumption without negotiation	46.7	34.2	34.9	46.7
Other methods(a)	1.0	3.4	2.8	0.3
Total	100.0	100.0	100.0	100.0

Source: Australian Bureau of Statistics, Catalogue no. 6322.

EXPLANATORY NOTES

DEFINITIONS

Cause of dispute. The statistics of causes of industrial disputes relate to the main cause of the stoppage of work and not necessarily all causes that may have been responsible for the stoppage of work. For these reasons, the statistics do not reflect the relative importance of all causes of disputes between employers and employees. The classification of causes is as follows:

Wages. Claims involving general principles relating to wages e.g. increase (decrease) in wages; variation in method of payment or combined claims relating to wages, hours or conditions of work in which the claim about wages is deemed to be the most important.

Hours of work. Claims involving general principles relating to hours of work e.g. decrease (increase) in hours; distribution of hours.

Leave, pensions, compensation. Claims involving general principles relating to holiday and leave provisions; pension and retirement provisions; workers' compensation provisions; insertion of penal clause provisions in awards.

Managerial policy. Disputes concerning the managerial policy of employers e.g. computation of wages, hours, leave, etc. in individual cases; docking pay, docking leave credits, fines; disciplinary matters including dismissals, suspension; alleged victimisation of union members or officials; principles of promotion and filling positions, transfers, roster complaints, retrenchment policy; employment of particular persons and personal disagreements; production limitations or quotas.

Physical working conditions. Disputes concerning physical working conditions and safety issues e.g. protective clothing and equipment; first aid services; uncomfortable working conditions; lack of, or the conditions of, amenities; claims for assistance; shortage or poor distribution of equipment or material; condition of equipment; new production methods and equipment; arduous physical tasks.

Trade Unionism. Disputes concerning employment of non-unionists, inter-union and intra-union disputes; sympathy stoppages in support of employees in another industry; recognition of union activities.

Other. Disputes concerning protests directed against persons or situations other than those relating to the employer/employee relationship e.g. political matters; fining and gaoling of persons; lack of work; lack of adequate transport; non-award public holidays; accidents and attendance at funerals. Stoppages for which no reason is given are also included in this category.

Disputes. For these statistics, an *industrial dispute* is defined as a withdrawal from work by a group of employees, or a refusal by an employer or a number of employers to permit some or all of their employees to work, each withdrawal or refusal being made in order to enforce a demand, to resist a demand, or to express a grievance.

A dispute affecting several establishments has been counted as a single dispute if it is organised or directed by one person or organisation in each State or Territory in which it occurs; otherwise it is counted as a separate dispute at each establishment and in each industry in which it occurred.

Duration of dispute. The *duration* of a dispute is the average number of working days lost per employee involved in the dispute.

Employees. Refers to wage and salary earners only. Excluded are persons who are self employed (e.g. building sub-contractors, owner-drivers of trucks) and employers.

Employees directly involved are those who actually participated in the dispute in order to enforce or resist a demand or to express a grievance.

Employees indirectly involved are those who ceased work at the establishment where the stoppages occurred, but who are not themselves parties to the dispute. Employees who ceased work at establishments other than those where the stoppages occurred are excluded.

Method of settlement. Statistics of the *method of settlement* of industrial disputes relate to the *method directly responsible for ending the stoppage of work* and not necessarily to the method (or methods) responsible for settling all matters in dispute. The classification of method of settlement is as follows:

Negotiation. Private negotiation between the parties involved, or their representatives, without the intervention or assistance of authorities constituted under State or Federal industrial legislation.

State legislation. Intervention or assistance of an industrial authority or authorities created by or constituted under State conciliation and arbitration or wages board legislation, or reference to such authorities or compulsory or voluntary conference, intervention, assistance or advice of State government officials or inspectors.

Federal and joint Federal–State legislation. Compulsory or voluntary conference or by intervention or assistance, of, or reference to, the industrial tribunals created by or constituted under the Conciliation and Arbitration Act, Coal Industry Acts, Stevedoring Industry Act, and other acts such as the Navigation Act; Public Service Arbitration Act. Intervention, assistance or advice of Federal government officials or inspectors.

Resumption without negotiation. This category may include some disputes which are settled subject to negotiation of a formal nature, such as industrial court hearings. Stop-work meetings are included, and this category may also include disputes settled by 'resumption' as stated, but about which no further information is available.

Other methods. Mediation; filling places of employees on strike or locked out; closing establishments permanently; dismissal of employees.

Coverage

The statistics of working days lost relate to the losses due to industrial disputes only. Effects on other establishments, such as standdowns because of lack of materials, disruption of transport services, power cuts, etc. are not included. Also, some employees involved in industrial disputes may obtain work at other establishments while a dispute is in progress. It is also possible that some or all of the total working days lost in any particular dispute may be made up through working longer hours or increasing the labour force at other establishments, or at the establishments involved in the dispute after work has resumed.

Sources

Reports of stoppages of work are obtained primarily from the Department of Industrial Relations, from trade journals, publications and newspapers. The statistics of individual industrial disputes are compiled from data obtained directly from employers and trade unions concerned. Particulars of some stoppages may have been estimated and the statistics therefore should be regarded as giving only a broad measure of the extent of industrial disputes (as defined).

Chapter 6

Resolving Conflict

Objectives

At the end of this chapter, the reader should be able to:
- discuss the various ways of resolving industrial conflict;
- define and describe grievance procedures;
- explain the composition and workings of the Federal Tribunal system;
- identify key aspects of relevant state industrial systems;
                and
- discuss other avenues of dispute resolution.

Introduction

The question of how to resolve disagreements or conflict which may arise between employers and their employees very much depends on one's approach to industrial relations. If conflict is regarded as abnormal, then disagreements will be seen as the outcome of inadequate communication, poor management or problem staff. Maintenance of a conflict-free workplace is therefore achieved through effective communication with staff, sound management practices, identification of 'problem' employees. On the other hand, if conflict between employers and employees is seen as inevitable the issue becomes one of resolution and regulation of the conflict.

In Australia discussion of the resolution of conflict between the parties in industrial relations has been governed historically by the conciliation and arbitration process. While attention has focused on the conciliation and arbitration process and its role in resolving industrial conflict, there are in fact other methods of resolving conflict as outlined in Figure 1.3.

There have been a number of contemporary economic, legislative and industrial relations developments which are expected to have significant impact on the way industrial conflict is resolved. These developments are discussed below, followed by a discussion of various means of resolving industrial conflict including:
- the use of workplace mechanisms such as grievance procedures;
- the traditional methods provided for by the tribunal systems;
- the potential recourse to the legal system; and
- the role of newer concepts, such as industrial democracy and employee participation.

A shift to a workplace focus

By and large Australian industrial relations has been described in terms of the dominating influence of its unique system of conciliation and arbitration in the resolution of industrial conflict. In more recent times, however, there have been a number of developments which have shifted attention away from the centralised nature of the tribunal systems to the practice of industrial relations at the workplace or enterprise level. These developments include:

- international economic pressures demanding a more flexible and efficient labour market which has shifted attention to workplace or enterprise reform;
- as a result of these economic pressures, there was a shift in versions of the 'Accord' between the Labor Government and the ACTU from 1986 onward, from macro-economic issues to micro-economic reform;
- the recommendation of the Hancock Report and endorsed in the Industrial Relations Act of 1988 for the development of local level dispute-settling mechanisms, e.g. grievance procedures;
- decisions by the Australian Industrial Relations Commission which have advocated greater consultation and conflict resolution by employers/management and employees/unions at the workplace.

As was noted in Chapter 2, since 1983 the Australian Council of Trade Unions and the Federal Labor Government have negotiated a number of versions of the 'Accord' which have formed the basis of wage determination for almost a decade. These agreements were generally supported by National Wage Decisions of the Australian Industrial Relations Commission. In the first two versions of the Accord (Accord Mark 1 and 2) the emphasis was on national economic and social concerns of the Government and the ACTU. From 1987 onwards, however, there has been a steady move towards greater enterprise determination of not only wages but also other aspects of award conditions.

This shift from a centralised focus represented by across the board wage settlements, to a workplace focus for wage determination became apparent as part of the two-tier wages system introduced in 1987. The second tier wage increases (4 per cent) were to be offset by the elimination of restrictive practices at the workplace, such as eliminating payment of wages by cash and replacing it with electronic funds transfer (EFTs). These changes to work practices had to be negotiated at the workplace and often included, among other things, the introduction or amendment of grievance procedures for local dispute resolution. This shift to greater enterprise bargaining was given even greater impetus (Accord Mark IV, V and VI) through the award restructuring process.

Greater use of informal workplace resolution of disputes between management and employees at the workplace was recommended in the 1985 Report of the Committee of Review into Australian Industrial Relations Law and Systems (the Hancock Report) which advocated greater utilisation of dispute settling/grievance procedures. Grievance procedures, as will be discussed, are designed to resolve workplace disagreements without resorting to the industrial tribunals. The Industrial Relations Act, 1988 which was based largely on the Hancock Report encourages the parties (s.91) to include grievance procedures in awards.

Finally, the federal commission in various National Wage Decisions throughout the 1980s impressed upon the parties, as a means to boost workplace efficiency and labour productivity, the need to increase the level of consultation at the workplace. Its National Wage Decisions, by and large, endorsed the 'devolution of industrial relations', that is, from itself to organisations and within organisations from industrial relations specialists and senior union officials to operational management and union representatives.

Grievance procedures

While considerable public attention is drawn to examples of industrial conflict which result in action such as strikes, most disputes are resolved amicably by the parties themselves. One of the principal ways of resolving disputes or disagreements in the workplace is through grievance or dispute-settling procedures.

From time to time, disputes which seem trivial receive public attention. Employees may seem to take industrial action simply because the lifts are out of order or the showers are unhygienic; in reality, however, conflict may have been brewing from some time over a number of managerial policies, which eventually erupts in an industrial dispute over a seemingly minor issue. Whether the circumstances of complaints are justified or unjustified, the effect of prolonged, unrecognised grievances can lower morale amongst employees and lead to reduced productivity.

In recent years, a number of studies considering the resolution of local level disputes have concluded that grievance procedures have certain advantages in that they:

- provide a 'strike free' flow of dispute resolution from lower to higher levels within the organisation;
- avoid the costs and delays of going to the tribunal, and are therefore cost efficient;
- maintain morale if problems are handled quickly and fairly;
- allow decision-making at the appropriate level of the organisation rather than involving senior management, union officials or outside parties such as industrial tribunals.

Grievance or dispute-settling procedures establish guidelines to resolve workplace conflict before it erupts into industrial disputation. Figure 6.1 outlines the major steps of a grievance procedure. Figure 6.2 is an example of an award clause dealing with grievance procedures.

Principles for the resolution of conflict through dispute-settling procedures have been adopted by employers, unions and government at the national level

116 □ UNDERSTANDING AUSTRALIAN INDUSTRIAL RELATIONS

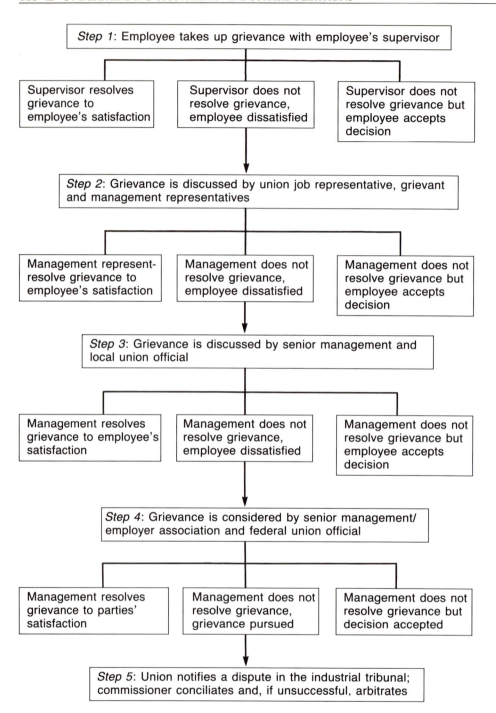

Figure 6.1: Steps in a grievance procedure.

Source: Adapted from Stone, T. H., and Meltz, N. M., *Human Resource Management in Canada*, Second edition, Holt Rinehart and Winston, Toronto, 1988.

Step 1

(a) Departmental Claims, Issues and Disputes
(i) Employee(s) and/or delegate(s) of the union(s) involved will place the claim, issue or dispute before the immediate supervisor. The immediate supervisor will take all reasonable steps to reply to the employee(s) and/or delegate(s) as soon as possible. If the reply cannot be given by the end of the next ordinary working shift, a progress report will be given.

Step 2

(ii) Failing agreement, employee(s) and/or delegate(s) of the union(s) involved will place the claim, issue or dispute before the superintendent or deputy. The superintendent or deputy will take all reasonable steps to reply to the employee(s) and/or delegate(s) as soon as possible. If a reply cannot be given by the end of the superintendent's or deputy's next ordinary working day a progress report will be given.

Step 3

(iii) Failing agreement, employee(s) and/or delegate(s) and/or official(s) of the union(s) involved will place the claim, issue or dispute before the company's Industrial Relations Department. The claim, issue or dispute and all relevant circumstances relating to it shall then be fully reviewed by the management of the company and by the union(s) involved and all reasonable steps shall be taken in an endeavour to resolve the matter.

Step 4

(iv) Failing agreement, the claim, issue or dispute shall be referred to the appropriate industrial relations tribunal, if the union(s) wants to pursue it further. (This final step is taken by a union official.)

Safety Matters

(v) The procedures in (i) to (iii) do not apply to claims, issues or disputes relating to genuine safety matters. In such matters the company will undertake immediate investigations including discussions with the employee(s) and/or delegate(s) and/or official(s) of the union(s) involved. As necessary the appropriate government authority will be involved.

(b) General Claims, Issues and Disputes
(i) The official(s) and delegate(s) of the union(s) involved will place the claim, issue or dispute before the company's Industrial Relations Department, which will take all reasonable steps to reply as soon as possible.
(ii) Failing agreement, the claim, issue or dispute shall be referred to the appropriate industrial relations tribunal, if the union(s) wants to pursue it further.

The provisions of the clause shall not affect in any way any other rights and duties of any party to this award pursuant to the Act or any other Act or at common law in relation to any matter.
The operation of this clause will be jointly reviewed by the parties at regular intervals.

Figure 6.2: Award clause for dispute-settling procedures, BHP Newcastle Steelworks.

for 20 years. However, it is only recently that procedures for the resolution of grievances or disputes at the local level have found their way into many awards, let alone practice.

The government-sponsored Australian Workplace Industrial Relations Survey (AWIRS) provided considerable insight into the existence of grievance procedures and the extent of their use at the workplace. Based on the survey, it would seem grievance procedures exist in almost 50 per cent of workplaces covering almost 70 per cent of employees. Figure 6.3 indicates that grievance procedures exist in substantially more public sector workplaces than private sector enterprises. This could be attributed to the larger size of public sector workplaces.

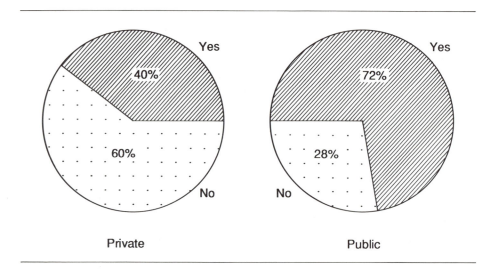

Source: Australian Workplace Industrial Relations Survey, Department of Industrial Relations, AGPS, 1991.

Figure 6.3: Formal grievance procedures, by sector.

While the existence of grievance procedures can be said to be fairly widespread, AWIRS suggests that they are not well utilised. In fact, the survey found that 60 per cent of managers never used the mechanism and of those who did, only 37 per cent had used it in the previous year. The primary reason for the poor use of grievance procedures could be ascribed to the fact they were introduced largely as a result of tribunal influence. In other words, the incorporation of a grievance procedure into an award was part of a tribunal decision rather than a workplace initiative.

In evaluating the usefulness of grievance procedures, AWIRS noted that managers saw their use in resolving individual grievances such as personality conflict, discipline promotion and discrimination. Given that almost 30 per cent of industrial disputes are attributed to 'managerial policy', which includes these kinds of grievances, this suggests there is considerable room for better utilisation of workplace measures to resolve grievances.

A number of reasons have been put forward for the relative poor success of grievance procedures to date in resolving workplace differences. These include:

- historical over-reliance on the tribunal structures to resolve employer/union differences. Further management has not insisted sufficiently that the procedures be observed;
- because the majority of procedures result from tribunal decisions, workplace personnel are not aware of their existence;
- workplace personnel do not have the requisite skills to handle grievances;
- unions are critical of grievance procedures if they are used as a delaying tactic in solving problems at the workplace; and
- the failure of grievance procedures to differentiate between an 'interest' dispute involving a claim for an award change and a 'rights' dispute involving the interpretation of an award condition.

Section 92 of the federal *Industrial Relations Act 1988* requires the Commission to assess the extent to which the parties have complied with existing dispute-settling procedures in determining 'whether or when' it will exercise its powers.

Despite the considerable efforts to encourage the parties to resolve differences themselves using grievance procedures, unless there is adequate local level communication of the procedures, acceptance of them by the parties, training of key personnel and involvement of the parties in review of the procedures, their effectiveness will be greatly diminished.

The presence of a grievance procedure does not prohibit the use of the tribunal system in resolving conflict. Most grievance procedures provide that, in the event of a matter not being resolved by the parties themselves, a dispute can be notified to the Commission.

The tribunal system

The tribunal system is the framework developed by governments to handle industrial relations disagreements which may arise between employers and unions. It is the institutional framework for resolving conflict. To illustrate the role and function of the tribunal system, the following hypothetical case demonstrates the way in which tribunals are involved in settling 'day-to-day' disputes.

Go For It Pty Ltd is a sporting goods manufacturer with 150 employees. The major union representing the employees is the OZ Workers Union.

Management filled several short-term job vacancies as they saw fit. Two employees felt that they had been unfairly overlooked, as these jobs provided an opportunity for them to gain new experiences and to develop further skills.

The matter was taken up by the employees according to the award's grievance procedure. Eventually the union became involved, arguing that the procedures laid down in the award clause 'Principles of promotion' had not been adhered to.

Despite a number of letters in which the employees' complaint was outlined and a series of subsequent meetings on the issue, the parties remained in disagreement.

The union notified the Commission that they were in dispute with the employer. (This does not mean there was any industrial action.) By notifying the tribunal of a dispute, the parties were seeking assistance in resolving the matter.

A Commissioner was appointed to help the parties resolve the dispute. He requested that the parties in dispute attend a compulsory conference for conciliation proceedings to take place.

During the conciliation process, the Commissioner conferred with the parties, clarifying the issues and offering suggestions in the hope the parties would come to some agreement.

Having no success with conciliation, the Commissioner had to arbitrate. During arbitration the Commissioner heard evidence from advocates for the employer and the union in support of their respective positions, and then made a decision.

The basic principles of resolving industrial relations problems and disputes through conciliation and arbitration apply to all industrial tribunals in Australia. However, there are variations in tribunal structures and practices, depending on the state in which the tribunal is located or whether it is a matter for the federal tribunal.

Tribunal structures

Industrial relations is both a federal and state government responsibility (as is discussed in Chapter 4). The concept of establishing conciliation and arbitration tribunals to process industrial relations problems was adopted by both federal and state governments. As Australia is a Federation, there are six state tribunal structures as well as a federal tribunal structure. Each industrial tribunal has been established and operates according to legislation passed by the state or federal government.

The federal system

The Australian Industrial Relations Commission is the most prominent industrial tribunal in Australia. Over the years the federal system has assumed a greater profile than the respective state systems in Australian industrial relations. The Commission determines national wage cases which state tribunals usually replicate with respect to the workers under their jurisdiction. Also

Source: Mitchell, Daily Telegraph.

a number of High Court decisions have increased the influence of the Federal Commission, in terms both of the issues it may consider and action it may take.

The decade prior to Federation in 1901 was notable for industrial unrest, including a number of crippling strikes. This influenced the persons drafting the Constitution to include reference to industrial relations. Section 51(xxxv) states that the federal parliament may make laws relating to 'conciliation and arbitration for the prevention and settlement of industrial disputes extending beyond the limits of any one state'. The effect of this section is that the federal government may only pass laws related to the prevention or settlement of industrial disputes.

Section 51(xxxv) of the Australian Constitution has been the single most important influence on developments in Australian industrial relations. The effect of the section is that:

- there must be a dispute (actual or pending) before the tribunal can intervene;
- the issue in dispute must be an 'industrial matter'. Some matters seen by employees as being related to work, therefore as 'industrial', have been

interpreted as *'managerial prerogatives'* by employers, the Commission and the courts; and
- the dispute must be beyond the limits of one state.

These prerequisites for a Federal Commission hearing have created a plethora of problems over the years between employers and unions, which have been left to the High Court to resolve.

Section 51(xxxv) and a number of other powers in the Constitution were used by parliament to pass the *Conciliation and Arbitration Act 1904*. This Act was amended at various times and finally replaced by the *Industrial Relations Act 1988*, as of 1 March, 1989, which now governs the federal industrial tribunal system.

The 1988 Act established the Australian Industrial Relations Commission as the industrial tribunal to handle—among other things—the resolution of conflict in the federal industrial relations sphere. Key aspects of the Commission are as follows.

- It is made up of a president, deputy-presidents (presidential members), and commissioners. While only the president must be legally qualified, appointees to the Commission must have 'appropriate skills and experience in the field of industrial relations'. They generally come from trade unions, employer bodies or government services. Commission members can have dual appointment to the Federal Commission and a particular State Commission. As at early 1991 there were 18 deputy presidents, five of whom were dual appointees, and 32 commissioners, two of whom were dual appointees.
- A sitting of the Commission can take place with one or more members of the Commission or a full bench.
- The composition of a full bench of the Commission is determined by the president and consists of at least three members of the Commission, two of whom must be presidential members.
- Full bench hearings are reserved for matters involving:
  a. primary decision making involving matters of significant national or industry interest;
  b. appeals against single member decisions; and
  c. claims for national or minimum wage increases or to alter hours of work etc.
- The president assigns each industry or area of employment to a panel of members of the Commission consisting of a presidential member and at least one commissioner. The presidential member organises and allocates and oversees the work of the panel members. (See Figure 6.4 for an example.) Section 37 of the Industrial Relations Act, 1988 gives the members of the panel the responsibility of exercising the powers of the Federal Commission in relation to that industry. There are normally about 12 panels.

Photo: Commissioner Griffin (right), Deputy President Marsh (left), and Justice Cohen were members of the first all female Full Bench in April, 1989 (*credit*: Peter Brennan, *The Weekend Australian*, 22–23 April, 1989).

INTERVIEW

COMMISSIONER PAULINE GRIFFIN

Position: A member of the Federal Commission since 1975. She has been on a number of industry panels, including building and construction, local government and most recently the Federal public service. Before joining the Commission, Commissioner Griffin worked for a number of years in the private sector in personnel management, which included industrial relations. However, her career began in the public sector as a social worker assisting in the settlement of migrants following World War II.

1. What do you see the role of the Commission as being?

While we work within the requirements of the Industrial Relations Act, particularly as it relates to dispute resolution, this includes a wider area of industrial relations. For instance a dispute doesn't have to be "alive" before the Commission gets involved. Sometimes matters come before the Commission too soon or before the parties have tried to resolve their differences themselves. Other times a matter arrives too late and the parties' positions are entrenched. Had the Commission been involved sooner conciliation proceedings may have helped the parties work through their differences. In conciliation proceedings, Commission members assist parties to reach agreement themselves. Hopefully this furthers the development of skills at the organisation level so that in future disputes, they can be better handled by the parties themselves.

2. What is a 'typical' day for a commissioner?

This is almost impossible to determine. Matters are set down for a Commission hearing but it is often difficult to speculate how long they are going to take. An award variation for meal money which affects thousands of employees may take a short time, whereas an individual grievance involving a demotion may be very lengthy.

There are site visits, particularly if the matter involves changes to the work environment. For example as a member of the building and construction panel a great deal of time was spent inspecting work sites as part of claims for site allowances and safety disputes.

Hearings are held as close to the dispute as possible, which can involve travel anywhere in Australia. All of which makes a 'typical' day difficult to define.

3. What are the qualities or characteristics of a good industrial relations practitioner?

Anyone in the field of industrial relations needs good communication skills, particularly a capacity to listen and a willingness to negotiate. Patience, tolerance, perception, integrity, objectivity and above all a liking for people are valuable attributes. Employer industrial relations practitioners should work with and be supported by the level of management seen as the decision-maker by employees. And there should be a good balance between personnel and industrial relations functions. They should be able to inform and influence management on industrial relations implications of policies and practices especially when change is involved. Similarly industrial relations practitioners in unions need to balance union policies with the aspirations and views of members, within the constraints of a variety of employment situations.

Deputy-President Marsh and Commissioners Cross, Lear and Harrison are the panel of Commission members responsible for the following industries and services.

Business equipment industry
More than 10 awards are classified as belonging to this industry, including:
- Business Equipment Industry (Clerical Officers) Consolidated Award 1985

Graphic arts
Five awards are classified as belonging to this industry, including:
- Commercial and Industrial Artists Award 1983

Journalism
Over 30 awards are classified as belonging to this industry, including:
- Journalists (Australian Associated Press) Agreement 1988
- Journalists' (Metropolitan Daily Newspapers) Award 1986

Northern Territory administration
The Federal Commission has responsibility for the determination of wages and conditions of work in the territories. This industry panel has responsibility for overseeing over 30 awards under Northern Territory administration, including:
- Northern Territory Public Sector Superannuation Award 1988
- Aboriginal Health Workers (Northern Territory Public Service) Award 1984

Private transport industry
Almost 40 awards are classified as belonging to this industry, including:
- Transport Workers Award, 1983
- Clerks' Avis Rent-a-Car System Agreement (1979)

cont.

> **Printing industry**
> Over 15 awards are classified as belonging to this industry, including:
> • Newspaper Printing Agreement 1987
>
> **Publishing industry, sanitary and garbage disposal services, scientific services, security services, technical services**
> Over 20 awards are classified as belonging to these industries, including:
> • Coin Operated Amusement Machines (Technical Service) Award 1974
> • Professional Scientists Award 1981, The
>
> In total over 150 awards are assigned to this industry panel.
>
> *Source*: Australian Industrial Relations Commission.

Figure 6.4: Example of an industry panel (as at 1 June, 1991).

Advantages of industry panels include:
- that they allow commission members to develop specialised knowledge of particular industries, which should theoretically ensure better uniformity of decision-making; and
- that they give the Commission greater flexibility. If one member is on other business there is sufficient back-up, and delays are avoided.

The 1988 Act also provides for an Industrial Registry, headed by an Industrial Registrar. Its functions include:
- to keep records of trade unions and employer organisations registered under the Act;
- to provide advice and assistance to organisations registered under the Act; and
- to provide administrative support to the Commission.

The basic principles underlining the *Industrial Relations Act 1988* are that disputes should be resolved through dispute-settling procedures or, if the matter reaches the Commission, through conciliation. The objects of the Act are relatively broad, and include (S.3[a]):

> to promote industrial harmony and co-operation among the parties involved in industrial relations in Australia.

In achieving this object, the Act (S.3[b]) provides the framework through the Australian Industrial Relations Commission:

> for the prevention and settlement of industrial disputes by conciliation and arbitration in a manner that minimises the disruptive effects of industrial disputes on the community.

In practice this means that, where a dispute between a union and an employer involving employees covered by a federal award cannot be settled by the parties themselves through negotiation, the IRC will settle the matter through conciliation and arbitration.

Table 6.1 compares the 1989–90 results with data on 1987–88 dispute notifications. Based on these statistics there has been a considerable increase in the number of dispute notifications resulting from dismissals. An example of a decision of the Australian Industrial Relations Commission to resolve a dispute involving the dismissal of an employee is in Figure 6.5. The steps taken by the Commission, as they relate to the appropriate sections of the Industrial Relations Act for resolving a dispute are illustrated in Figure 6.6.

Table 6.1: A comparison of 1987–1988 and 1989–1990 dispute notifications, by subject matter in the federal commission.

Subject matter	Notifications 1987–1988	Notifications 1989–1990
1. allowance	704	162
2. award respondency	2	2
3. bans clause	–	2
4. classifications	61	90
5. conditions of employment	107	119
6. employee discipline	–	48
7. employment	22	79
8. grievance procedures	8	9
9. health and safety	56	98
10. hours of work	87	170
11. leave	23	56
12. log of claims	441	508
13. other	1089	539
14. right of entry	10	11
15. staffing levels	62	64
16. stand-down	10	23
17. strike pay	33	27
18. superannuation	–	72
19. termination of employment	569	923
20. trade union membership	63	90
21. wage rates	831	444
22. work structure and process	–	124
Total	4178	3660

Source: Adapted from the 1987–1988 Conciliation and Arbitration Commission Report and the Second Annual Report of the President of the Australian Industrial Relations Commission 1 July, 1989 to 30 June, 1990.

AUSTRALIAN INDUSTRIAL RELATIONS COMMISSION

Industrial Relations Act 1988
s.99 notification of industrial dispute

The Clothing and Allied Trades Union of Australia
and
Venture Trial Pty Ltd trading as Impress Dry Cleaners
(C No. 30744 of 1991)

Dry cleaning employee   Dry cleaning industry
DEPUTY PRESIDENT RIORDAN   MELBOURNE, 18 APRIL 1991

Unfair dismissal

DECISION

The following decision was read into transcript on 18 April 1991:

"K was employed by T for a few months in a dry cleaning establishment and her employment was terminated on 2 April 1991. The Clothing and Allied Trades Union of Australia (CATU) seeks her reinstatement.

K's employmenbt was on a part-time basis and an overaward payment was made in order to attract a suitable person. Subsequently it was decided that full time weekly employment should be offered at the award rate of pay. This involved an additional ten hours of work and an additional $35.00 per week in wages.

It was suggested however that 5 percent of the profit of the business was also to be paid but K does not concede that this offer was made to her.

T takes the view that the employment contract is not capable of reinstatement.

There are several reasons for this view. At the outset there is an employee now working in the position who was engaged to replace K. There are also other factors flowing from events subsequent to the termination which could have an adverse effect on the commercial fortune of the business. It is not suggested that this effect is the consequence of an intention by K to cause damage to the business or any person involved. It is claimed that irrespective of K's intention the consequence is such as to make a future satisfactory relationship impossible.

It has been agreed by both parties that this matter should be resolved by the process of conciliation and that all concerned, including K, will accept a recommendation made as a result of these proceedings.

K was a short term employee, having been employed for some 3 months. I am mindful of the fact that she is likely to experience real difficulty in obtaining alternative employment in the current economic climate without some delay.

There are some aspects of fault on both sides of the relationship which would in all probability have been capable of resolution with proper counselling and consultation between both parties.

I am not able to recommend reinstatement, having regard to the likely problem of a future employment relationship in this very small enterprise.

In all the circumstances, however, it is my strong recommendation that K should be paid an additional 3 weeks' pay at the award rate as an ex gratia termination payment and that such payment be made within seven (7) days of today.

This payment is to be additional to monies otherwise paid to K at the time of termination."

Figure 6.5: An example of an arbitrated decision.

1. *Notifying a dispute (Section 99)*
   As soon as a registered union or employer becomes aware of the existence of an alleged industrial dispute it is required to notify the relevant presidential member (depending on panel) or the Registrar. A minister may also notify the Commission of an alleged industrial dispute or a member of the Commission may list a matter for consideration.

2. *Handling of a dispute (Section 100)*
   When an industrial dispute is notified under S.99 it will be forwarded to the relevant presidential member. The presidential member will either handle the matter him/herself or pass it on to a commissioner of that panel for conciliation.

3. *Finding of a dispute (S.101)*
   The Commission will determine:
   - the parties to the industrial dispute
   - the matters in dispute

   Its findings will be recorded.

4. *Conciliation Proceedings (S.102)*
   'the Commission shall do everything that appears to the member to be right and proper to assist the parties to agree on the terms for the prevention or settlement of the industrial dispute.'
   Including:
   - arranging conferences with the member of the Commission present
   - arranging conferences with the member of the Commission not present
   - calling compulsory conferences (S.119)

5. *Completing conciliation proceedings (S.103)*
   Conciliation proceedings are complete when the dispute is resolved. If the dispute involved the making of an award, conciliation is complete when a consent award (S.112) or certified agreement (S.115) is made. If the dispute is not resolved, conciliation is completed by the member of the commission being satisfied that no further conciliation is warranted.

6. *Arbitrating (S.104)*
   When a dispute is not resolved by conciliation, the Commission will arbitrate. The member of the Commission who conciliated will arbitrate unless one of the parties objects. The Commission will make an award or give a decision in the case of a dispute under an existing award or agreement.

7. *.Appeals (S.45)*
   An appeal can be made to the full bench under certain conditions (e.g. public interest).

Figure 6.6: Steps for resolving a dispute in the Australian Industrial Relations Commission.

The state systems

The states do not have the constitutional restrictions which constrain the federal system. As a result, they can legislate directly on conditions of employment, and have done so in relation to such areas as annual and long-service leave. Nevertheless, the federal system is paramount: that is, if a group of employees is covered by a federal award and the federal award contains provisions which are different to state legislation, the federal award provision will prevail. Federal long-service leave awards, for example, prevail over any state legislation, despite the fact that the state legislation might be more favourable.

New South Wales

Legislation: *Industrial Arbitration Act 1940*
Structure: The New South Wales industrial system is two-tiered, and consists of:

- conciliation commissioners, conciliation committees, industrial magistrates and the industrial Registrar; and
- the Industrial Commission.

Key elements of the Industrial Commission are listed below.

- The act specifies that 12 members may be appointed.
- The Industrial Commission consists of a president, judges and deputy-presidents. While the president and judges must be legally qualified, deputy-presidents must only have appropriate experience. As at June 1991 there were nine judicial members and two deputy-presidents.
- The Commission sits as a single member or as the Commission in court session (full bench).
- The Commission in court session consists of three members of the Commission. It is the supreme industrial tribunal, and is reserved for matters of importance, appeals, deciding questions related to cancellation of union registration, and any matters referred to it by the Minister for Industrial Relations.

Conciliation commissioners and conciliation committees can be described as follows.

- Conciliation committees are established by the Commission or upon application.
- Conciliation committees consist of equal representation of employers and employees, with a conciliation commissioner acting as chairperson (see Figure 6.7).
- There are over 400 conciliation committees in New South Wales. Their main function is to consider award applications.
- Conciliation commissioners are appointed on the basis of their experience and expertise in the field of industrial relations.

Processing of disputes

Either an employer or a union can notify a dispute under Section 25A of the Act. While Section 25A notifications can be lodged by telephone, a written notification should follow and include the following:

- the nature of the dispute;
- the parties to the dispute;
- a description of the conciliation process that has been undertaken; and
- a request for a compulsory conference.

The significance of the dispute and past practices will determine whether the dispute will be handled by the Commission or by the conciliation commissioner responsible for the relevant conciliation committee. In the financial

> **CONCILIATION COMMITTEES OF WHICH MR CONCILIATION COMMISSIONER PETER JOHN CONNOR IS TO BE CHAIRMAN, GENERALLY**
>
> **Building Trades**
>
> Asbestos Cement Fixers (State)
> Bituminous Roofing (State)
> Builders' Labourers (State)
> Carpenters, Bricklayers (State)
> Carpenters, Bridge and Wharf (State)
> Marble Workers, &c. (State)
> Painters, &c. (State)
> Plasterers, &c. (State)
> Plumbers and Gasfitters (State)
> Slaters, &c. (State)
> Stonemasons, &c. (State)
> Tilelayers (State)
>
> **Engine Drivers**
>
> Engine drivers, &c., General (State)
>
> **Government transport**
>
> Government Railways (Building Trades)
> Government Railways (Loco. and Stores)
> Government Railways (Permanent Way)
> Government Railways (Traffic)
> Government Railways (Building Trades)
>
> **Labouring, &c., industries**
>
> Gangers (State)
> Googong Dam Project
> Labourers, Railway and Road Construction, &c. (State)
> Rock and Ore Milling and Refining
> Shoalhaven Scheme
> Showground, &c., Employees (State)
> Surveyors Assistants (State)
>
> **Printing and allied industries**
>
> Air Brush Artists (State)
> Bookbinders, Letterpress Machinists and Lithographic Workers, Males (Cumberland and Newcastle)
> Commercial and Industrial Artists (State)
> Compositors, &c. (Country)
> Multigraph, &c., Operators (State)
> Printing Industry, Compositors, Cardboard Box Makers and Females (Cumberland and Newcastle)
> Printing Industry, Compositors, &c. (Sydney Daily Newspapers)
> Process Engravers, &c. (Cumberland and Newcastle)
> Process Engravers, &c. (Sydney Daily Newspapers)
> Type Foundry Products (State)
>
> *Source*: Labor Council of New South Wales Annual Directory.

Figure 6.7: Conciliation Commissioners chair a number of conciliation committees.

year 1989–1990 there were over 2000 disputes under S25A lodged of which over 75 per cent were handled by the conciliation commissioners.

In the first instance, a compulsory conference will be called at which conciliation can take place. If the parties cannot reach agreement during conciliation the matter can be referred to the Commission (if it is a conciliation commissioner or committee), or a decision can be made in the form of an award, order or recommendation.

Appeals can be made to the Commission of any decision made by a conciliation committee or commissioner. Appeal rights also exist to the

Commission in court session against a decision of a single member. Figure 6.8 is a diagram of a dispute settlement in the NSW industrial system.

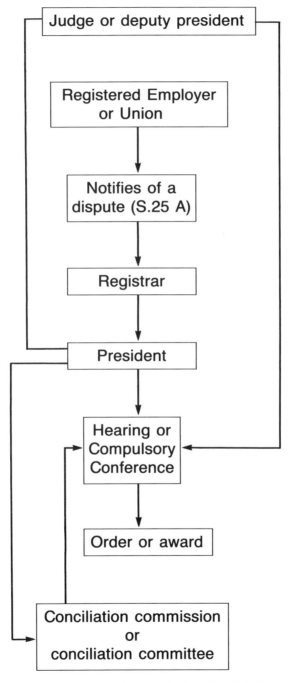

Source: Adapted from publication of Trade Union Training Authority.

Figure 6.8: Dispute settlement in the New South Wales industrial system.

Enforcement: Breaches of awards and related offences are dealt with by industrial magistrates, who have similar qualifications to stipendiary magistrates.

Arising from the 1989 Green Paper 'Transforming industrial relations in New South Wales' two significant pieces of industrial legislation have been passed. These are the Industrial Arbitration (Unfair Dismissal) Act, 1991 and the Industrial Arbitration (Enterprise Agreements) Amendment Act 1990. The first piece of legislation provides for individuals to have access to the industrial tribunal system in cases where unfair dismissal is alleged. Prior to this legislation only 'registered organisations' could lodge disputes. Conciliation Commissioners, under the legislation, can order reinstatement of the applicant, or require the employer to pay up to six months remuneration where it is found the dismissal was unreasonable or unjust.

The legislation on enterprise agreements which commenced from 25 January, 1991 allows employers and employees to formulate their own agreements outside existing awards. While Section 11 of the Industrial Arbitration Act, 1940 permits unions and employers to enter industrial agreements, it requires that one of the parties is a union. The new legislation allows the employer to make an agreement with its employees not necessarily represented by a union to regulate all or some of the conditions of employment at a particular enterprise. Three types of enterprise agreements are possible:

- between an employer and one or more unions;
- between an employer and at least 65 per cent of the employees in one or more trades or occupations; and
- between an employer and a works committee

Agreements must be registered with the Industrial Registrar and approved by the Industrial Commission.

Victoria

Legislation: *Industrial Relations Act 1979.*
Structure: Industrial Relations Commission, consisting of:
- a president (must have legal qualifications);
- deputy-presidents; and
- commissioners.

The commission has three levels:

a. *Commission in court session:* President (or deputy-president with legal qualifications) alone; responsibilities include 'judicial' functions (e.g. appeal against a conviction by a magistrate's court for an offence against the Act or 'clarification' of intent of an award).
b. *Commission in full session:* Three members, one of whom must be president or deputy-president; responsibilities include hearing appeals of decisions of a conciliation and arbitration board, jurisdiction of boards, interpretation of awards and agreements.

c. *Commissioner sitting alone:* Responsibilities include hearing any industrial dispute or any matters assigned by the president or by the conciliation and arbitration boards to the Commission. Awards of a commissioner sitting alone can be appealed to the commission in full session.

The Commission establishes conciliation and arbitration boards for any trade or occupation to handle the bulk of the work of the Commission. Each board (about 200 exist) consists of an equal number of employer and employee representatives appointed by the Commission, together with a chairperson who is a commissioner. Responsibilities of the boards are to make awards relating to 'any industrial matter', including days and hours of work, pay, wages and rights and duties of employers and employees. Decisions are arrived at by majority vote, with the chairperson having a casting vote in the case of a tied vote. Decisions of the boards can be appealed to the Commission.

While individuals can make applications of unjust dismissal to the Commission, there have been legal challenges to the jurisdiction of the Commission in hearing some cases. In particular the appropriateness of conciliation and arbitration boards in some instances has been disputed (see Figure 6.9).

Unfair dismissal of bosses 'outside scope of Vic IRC'

By JULIE POWER

The High Court has found that the Victorian Industrial Relations Commission does not have the jurisdiction to hear a case alleging unfair dismissal of an executive.

The decision has significant implications for the commission, whose jurisdiction on unfair dismissals has been held up in recent years partly as a result of an increasing number of award-free employees such as executives and managers lodging claims for reinstatement.

A backlog of unfair-dismissal claims has built up in the commission pending the outcome of an appeal in the High Court by Mr Patrick Cornelius Downey, a former group general manager employed by Trans Waste Pty Ltd, on technical grounds.

Dismissing the appeal, the High Court said that because there was no conciliation and arbitration board established to deal with Mr Downey's particular trade or occupation, there was no board with the power to refer his complaint of unfair dismissal to the commission.

However, the High Court does not rule out the possibility of a board being established to represent managers, other senior employees and non-unionised labour which could then refer claims of unfair dismissal to the commission.

Justice Dawson said that under the Victorian Industrial Relations Act, boards could be set up to represent trades including business and occupation.

Mr Downey was dismissed—with six months' salary—within three days of a takeover by an American company. Senior executives including Mr Downey had made an unsuccessful attempt to negotiate a management buy-out.

On the day of his dismissal, Mr Downey lodged an appeal with the Victorian commission, claiming his dismissal was harsh, unjust or unreasonable.

His complaint was referred to the Commercial Clerks Board. Trans Waste successfully argued that this board had no jurisdiction and was not relevant to Mr Downey. The commission deputy

> president said he had the jurisdiction to hear the matter because it was an industrial dispute.
>
> Trans Waste, now known as BFI Waste Systems Division, argued that there was no industrial dispute because the Act defined a dispute as occurring between an employer and more than one employee.
>
> However, Justice Dawson said the Act obviously extended to just one employee and to construe it otherwise would be 'unduly narrow and pedantic'.
>
> AAP reports that Trans Waste's instructing solicitor, Ms Aileen Ryan of Arther Robinson and Hedderwicks, said the decision meant similar applications now pending would not be heard.
>
> Ms Ryan said non-award employees could pursue unfair dismissal through common law, but in Victoria employees had tended to go through the VIRC, which was quicker and often awarded generous compensation payments.
>
> The executive director of the Victorian Employers' Federation, Mr David Edwards, said in a statement that the decision was a landmark.
>
> The VIRC had been prepared until now to deal with claims from non-award employees in particular circumstances.
>
> Mr Edwards said the commission dealt with at least 1,800 claims between 1983 and 1989, including one in which a manager sacked by a Melbourne company, Henderson Springs, was awarded $100,000 in compensation following a VIRC decision.

Source: *Australian Financial Review*, 26 April, 1991.

Figure 6.9: Jurisdiction of the Commission is determined by the courts.

Enforcement: Offences under the Industrial Relations Act are instituted in magistrates' courts.

Noteworthy features: Industrial agreements can be made between employers and unions which might vary conditions made under awards, so long as such conditions are not reduced. The agreements must be approved by and registered with the Industrial Relations Commission.

Western Australia

Legislation: *Industrial Relations Act 1979.*
The emphasis of the Act is on conciliation, which allows the industrial relations parties to reach agreement amongst themselves and allows the Commission flexibility in handling disputes.

Structure: The Industrial Relations Commission consists of:

- a president (must have legal qualifications of not less than five years' standing);
- a chief commissioner (who oversees administration of the Industrial Relations Commission); and
- commissioners.

The Commission has four levels:

a. *President alone:* Responsibilities include the overseeing of registration and regulations of unions.
b. *Full bench of the Commission:* President and two other members; hears appeals of any decision of commissioners sitting alone, matters of public interest, and applications to deregister unions.

c. *Commission in court session:* At least three commissioners sitting together; hears cases on general orders for wages and working conditions standards.
d. *Commissioner sitting alone:* Responsibilities include award interpretation and resolution of individual disputes.

The Industrial Appeals Court, which comprises four judges with supreme court status, deals with questions of law and jurisdiction relevant to the operation of the state's industrial relations system.

Enforcement: Industrial magistrates are responsible for award enforcement and wages recovery.

Noteworthy features: The state has a tripartite Labour Consultative Council, made up of representatives of major employer associations and the Trades and Labour Council of Western Australia. It is chaired by the minister responsible for industrial relations. The Labour Consultative Council functions as an advisory body to the minister on industrial relations policies in the state. The establishment of this council is seen as a strong commitment to the consultative approach. Under the Act, individual employees may apply to the Commission regarding claims of unfair dismissal and denial of benefits.

Queensland

Legislation: *Industrial Relations Act 1990.*
Following the tabling of the Report of the Committee of Inquiry into the Industrial Conciliation and Arbitration Act (the Hanger Report), new industrial relations legislation was introduced and commenced 23 June 1990. While the Act repealed a number of pieces of legislation, particularly relating to essential services and secondary boycotts, it does not represent a major departure from the pre-existing system based on conciliation and arbitration of industrial matters. Specific objects of the Act include the provision of a framework 'for the orderly conduct of industrial relations in Queensland and for adaptation to changes in technology and social and economic circumstances from time to time in the interests of employers, employees and the community.'

Structure: The Industrial Relations Commission constituted as:
a. Single member: Hears matters relating to dispute settlement and award making.
b. Full bench (three members): Determines such major issues as hours, basic wage.
c. Full Industrial Court (president and two members): Responsibilities include membership rules disputes, cancellation or registration.
d. Industrial Court (supreme court judge): Hears appeals from the full bench.

Enforcement: An industrial magistrate—that is, any stipendiary magistrate—has the power to undertake proceedings for offences against the Act.

Noteworthy Features: Grievance or dispute-settling procedures are mandatory in all awards and agreements. Individual agreements between an employer and employees (with or without union representation) can be registered. The Commission is obliged to take into account the 'public interest', e.g. state of the economy, when formulating a decision.

South Australia

Legislation: *Industrial Conciliation and Arbitration Act 1972.*
Structure: Industrial Commission, which consists of:

- a president, also president of industrial court (must be eligible for appointment as a supreme court judge);
- deputy-presidents (must be legal practitioners of seven years' standing); and
- commissioners, also presiding over conciliation committees. Half must have experience representing employers, while the other half must have experience representing employees.

The Commission can be constituted as:

a. *Member of Commission sitting alone:* Hears matters relating to disputes, makes awards.
b. *Full Industrial Commission* (two presidential members and a commissioner): Hears appeals from decisions by single members of Commission; establishes wages and standards of working conditions; establishes conciliation committees.

There are also conciliation committees, comprising equal numbers of employer and employee representatives and chaired by a commissioner. The parties have equal voting rights, with the chairperson determining the matter in the event of the parties not reaching agreement. The committees regulate the industrial affairs of a particular industry, including industrial matters, award-making and inspections.

Enforcement: The Industrial Court, including industrial magistrates, is responsible for such matters as recovery of wages, reinstatement, and award interpretation.
Noteworthy features: The South Australia Industrial Advisory Council, established in 1983, as a medium for consultation by the government with key representatives in industrial relations. This is seen as an indication of a strong commitment to consultation and co-operation in the state.

Under the Act, industrial agreements not exceeding two years can be made between parties, provided they are approved by the Industrial Commission.

Tasmania

Legislation: *Industrial Relations Act 1984.*
Structure: The Act established the Industrial Commission, which consists of:

- a president;
- a deputy-president; and
- commissioners.

The Commission can sit as:

a. *Single commissioner:* Responsibilities include dispute settlement, and the making of awards for the private and public sector.
b. *Full bench* (three members, including president or deputy-president): Responsibilities include appeals against decisions of single commissioners, and determination of major award matters, like wages and standard hours. Decisions of the full bench can be challenged in the supreme court only on questions of law.

Enforcement: Awards are enforceable in the magistrates court.
Noteworthy features: Under the Act, grievance procedures are the subject of a written agreement between the parties or subject to an award. The Act also allows for industrial agreements between a union and employer, with the approval of the Commission.

Non-compliance

The question is frequently asked: What can be done if an employer or trade union refuses to observe a ruling of the Commission?

Bans clauses

One avenue in the case of continuing industrial disputation is to apply to the Commission for the insertion of a bans clause in the award.

A typical bans clause prohibits any ban, limitation or restriction upon the performance of work in accordance with the award. Although a bans clause is directed at all parties, its intent is usually to preclude the union which is respondent to the award from being involved either directly or indirectly with the ban or limitation on or restriction of work.

The procedures for inserting a bans clause are not used extensively, as they are complicated and considered by many to work against the process of conciliation and arbitration. Figure 6.10 gives an example of the first case where a bans clause was used against an employer.

- S.4(1) of the Industrial Relations Act, 1988 defines a bans clause as:

    A terms of an award (however expressed) to the effect that engaging in conduct that would hinder, prevent or discourage:
    a) the observance of the award;
    b) the performance of work in accordance with the award; or
    c) the acceptance of, or offering for, work in according with the award;
    is to any extent prohibited.

> # Employers facing fines over super
> ### By MARK DAVIS
>
> Employers face fines of up to $500 for every day they breach award superannuation provisions, under a new legal sanction being invoked by unions.
>
> As part of the ACTU's superannuation compliance strategy, one of the legal weapons typically used by employers against unions in the Australian industrial relations system—the 'bans clause'—is being turned back against employers.
>
> In a decision handed down earlier this week, a deputy president of the Industrial Relations Commission, Justice Paul Munro, inserted a bans clause against a Newcastle car dealer, Young and Green Pty Ltd, into the Vehicle Industry (Repair, Services and Retail) Award.
>
> The bans clause, which was sought by the Vehicle Builders Employees Federation, is designed to force Young and Green to comply with the superannuation provisions of the award.
>
> It opens the way for fines of up to $500 to be imposed on the company and its officers for every day they hinder, prevent or discourage observance of their employees' award superannuation entitlements.
>
> The decision is the first time a bans clause has been used against an employer for failing to comply with superannuation obligations.
>
> Bans clauses are a legal sanction under the Industrial Relations Act almost always used by employers against unions taking industrial action. They are clauses which the commission may insert into awards to prohibit any action designed to hinder, prevent or discourage observance of the award or performance of work in accordance with the award.
>
> Justice Munro granted the VBEF application for a bans clause against Young and Green after finding that the company had set its own interests above the duties imposed upon it by the award. 'The award required that employees be given the choice of joining either [of two industry-based superannuation funds] fund,' Justice Munro said. 'The company has offered no evidence that it has in any real sense observed that obligation.
>
> 'The evidence that is available is consistent with the company having procrastinated in responding to its award obligations. It eventually adopted a course which, at the highest, offered a choice not sanctioned by the award.
>
> 'When money was paid over, it was paid in a form which was likely to bewilder fund managements in attempting to allocate entitlements.'

Source: Australian Financial Review, 3 May, 1991.

Figure 6.10: An illustration of the use of a bans clause.

The remedies under the Industrial Relations Act are primarily designed to ensure, through the use of penalties against those who do not comply, that parties adhere to the conciliation and arbitration procedures. In most instances this involves employers through the tribunal structure getting the union to adhere to a particular decision. However, some employers may also wish to seek compensation for damages caused by the industrial action.

Common law actions

An employer can initiate a common law action against a union for compensation of union-inflicted losses associated with industrial action. An employer can seek an injunction at common law for various actions, including:

- intimidation
- conspiracy
- nuisance
- trespass

An application is made to a state supreme court for an injunction under a particular aspect of common law. For the injunction to be granted the plaintiff (usually an employer) must demonstrate that the defendant (usually a union) is, for example, interfering with the ability of those persons wishing to enter the plaintiff's premises, thereby constituting a common law nuisance.

Considerable controversy surrounds the use of the common law to resolve industrial disputes. Many feel that there is no place for legal proceedings in relation to industrial action. In support of this view is the fact employers and employees will have to continue working together at the end of the dispute; the use of legal action, often involving heavy fines, is not conducive to on-going congenial industrial relations. Further action of this kind could be interpreted as antagonistic and cause the dispute to escalate. Others feel that the use of common law actions may be the only way to protect employer interests and force intransigent unions to co-operate.

On a practical level, common law actions are technical, time-consuming and costly; as a consequence, employers have tended to rely on Sections 45D and 45E of the *Trade Practices Act 1974*.

Sections 45D and 45E

Section 45D of the Trade Practices Act 1974 is generally known as the 'secondary boycott' section. A boycott is any combined refusal to deal with another in an attempt to bring about a certain result (as with people refusing to buy a particular product because of allegedly racist advertising). In industrial relations, employees who stop work in order to bring pressure to bear on their employer or some other 'target' are engaged in a boycott.

A boycott may be 'primary' or 'secondary' in nature, depending on the 'target' of the conduct.

- *Primary boycott*: Involves employees who strike in order to bring pressure to bear on their employer (target).
- *Secondary boycott*: Two or more persons prevent a third party (e.g. a potential customer or supplier) from doing business with the target business (see Figure 6.11).

Section 45D(1) of the *Trade Practices Act 1974* provides that a person shall not, in concert with a second person, engage in conduct which hinders or prevents the supply of goods or services by a third person to a fourth person. The conduct must—or be likely to—cause:

- substantial loss or damage to the 'target'; or
- substantial lessening of competition in certain relevant markets.

INTERVIEW

RICHARD CUSICK
Position: Industrial Officer with a large Australian manufacturing company.

1. Richard, briefly what does your organisation do and what is your role?

I work in one of my company's major production centres at which approximately 600 people are employed. My job description, in summary, specifies that overall my role is to provide advice on industrial matters and to assist in minimising the impact of industrial conflict on plant operations. I also assist in developing a healthy and productive employee relations climate. Some of my specific key tasks include: contributing to the development of industrial relations policies and procedures; communication and provision of information and advice on interpretation and application of policy, awards, legislation, regulations, agreements and decisions of industrial tribunals, maintenance of industrial relations information systems; working to resolve disputes; monitoring significant external industrial relations developments, for example changes in community standards which may affect our organisation; providing a research facility to assist in dispute resolution, policy development etc.; co-ordination, preparation and presentation of matters coming before industrial tribunals; providing the point of contact for the unions with the Company and vice versa; involvement in conferences with unions (of an industrial nature, e.g. chairmanship, record, adviser); a training and education responsibility in industrial relations areas for management, staff and wages personnel.

2. One of the views held about industrial conflict is that its 'hidden' manifestations (absenteeism, accidents etc.) cost far more to organisations than strikes and other collective expressions. Paradoxically though we have a tribunal system to deal with strikes but little support to companies to 'solve' the hidden manifestations. Do you agree?

Undeniably, industrial dislocation is a high profile and in many cases a newsworthy subject which attracts considerable public attention. This in itself contributes to the perception that the major form of industrial conflict is strike action. One aspect of this paradox is of course that these 'covert manifestations' are left largely to individual management/organisations to control, there is no high profile public body such as an industrial commission available to assist in resolving problems in those areas. For a number of years, my organisation has concentrated considerable effort on a range of policies aimed at maintaining high standards of performance in all areas of people management.

3. OK, now in dealing with industrial disputes, what would you see as the most important considerations?

- anticipate and plan—don't just wait for disputes to happen. A long term plan helps with day to day decision making;
- act promptly and be decisive;
- be sure you understand and are addressing the *real* problem;
- encourage positive problem solving (i.e. aim for a 'win-win' result);
- time spent training line management in dispute handling, is time well spent;
- treat all disputes as serious issues, don't assume matters are minor or unimportant;
- insist on compliance with agreed dispute settling procedures;
- maintain sufficient flexibility to be able to adopt to changing circumstances.

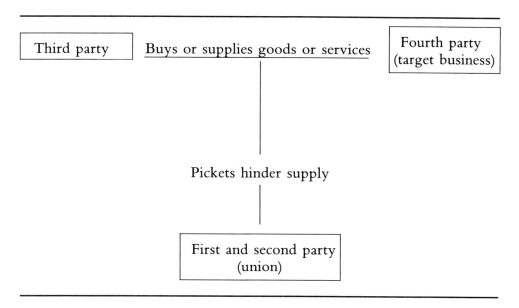

Figure 6.11: Diagram of a secondary boycott.

Section 45E was introduced in 1980, following the Leon Laidely case. Laidely was an independent petroleum supplier. Drivers employed by Amoco and members of the Transport Workers Union believed that Laidely drivers were supplying stations reserved for them. The union engaged in a secondary boycott against Laidely, and Laidely was granted an injunction against the union under Section 45D. To circumvent the injunction the union and Amoco reached an agreement not to supply Laidely, which meant that there was no secondary boycott. This action was seen as collusion between Amoco and the union, and consequently threatened the effectiveness of Section 45D.

The government then introduced Section 45E to the Act, which made it an offence for a person to enter a 'contract arrangement or understanding' with a trade union which has the purpose of preventing or hindering the supply or acquisition of goods or services by a person who has been accustomed to receive goods or services from that supplier.

As with common law actions, opinion is divided about the use of Sections 45D and 45E against those involved in industrial action. Many hold that, in the event of employees being forced to cease industrial action and go back to work, conflict will not necessarily terminate but will be manifested in other ways. Nevertheless, the option of 'penalties' is seen by employer groups as essential in solving difficult industrial disputes.

Industrial democracy and employee participation

Grievance procedures and the tribunal and legal systems are avenues for the resolution of industrial conflict. While legal machinery may always be necessary for resolving conflict, new approaches are being sought to lessen disputes—such as dispensing with the traditional 'them and us' view of industrial relations and introducing a 'joint problem-solving' approach.

Major issues like economic fluctuations, new technology, demands for social justice and equity have all contributed to the drive by major parties to seek new industrial relations practices. The concept of greater democratisation of the workplace through employee participation in decision-making is increasingly being seen as an answer to these issues.

Various employee participation schemes have operated for a number of years. Unlike those in other parts of the world, particularly Western Europe, the major industrial relations parties in Australia have been sceptical of these schemes. Unions have tended historically to see them as an employer 'con' to accept management plans. Australian employers have in turn guarded closely their 'right' to manage. Recent developments which have promoted greater acceptance of the concept of employee participation include:

- the 1986 Federal Government release of a Green Paper, 'Industrial democracy and employee participation';
- the government funding of a number of pilot projects in the area;
- the release of the CAI-ACTU 'Joint statement on participative practices';
- the insertion in awards of clauses requiring consultation on various issues;
- national wage decisions advocating a co-operative approach in restructuring awards;
- legislative requirements in some states for the establishment of employer/ employee occupational health and safety committees.

There is no precise formula for the introduction and operation of employee participation. However, it involves a commitment to the concept and the development of various participative practices designed to increase co-operation between the parties. These include:

- information sharing
- quality circles
- consultative committees
- shared decisions
- employee share-ownership

The adoption of participative practices cannot be expected to resolve all industrial conflict. It could, however, eventually assist in the development of an industrial culture which recognises and accepts the interests of the parties in industrial relations rather than continually confronting them.

Despite a commitment to a 'co-operative approach' to workplace decision-making at a national level as demonstrated by publications like the 'Joint Statement on Participative Practices' by the Confederation of Australian Industry and Australian Council of Trade Unions, recent evidence suggests that there is only limited ongoing union-management consultation at the workplace.

The Australian Workplace Industrial Relations Survey (AWIRS) found that union/management interaction was sporadic with less than 24 per cent of managers meeting workplace representatives on a regular basis. Further while it is often said unions are an impediment to organisational change the AWIRS evidence suggests that almost 75 per cent of management is not obliged to 'consult' with unions over proposed organisational changes. However, the level of management/union consultation varied dramatically between the public and private sector (see Figure 6.12).

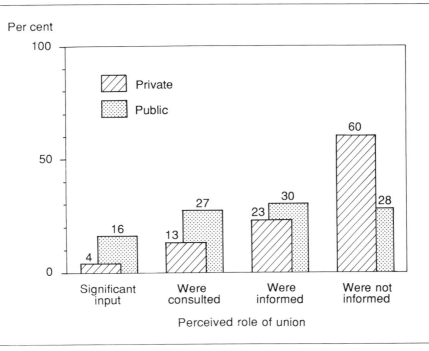

Source: Callus, R. et al., *Industrial Relations at Work*, Australian Workplace Industrial Relations Survey, AGPS, 1991.

Figure 6.12: Management's perceived role of unions in organisational changes that occurred in the two years prior to the survey.

Summary

Industrial conflict is often seen as being synonymous with industrial relations. It can therefore be said that the resolution of industrial conflict holds the key to improved industrial relations.

In Australia the tribunal systems, based on the concept of conciliation and arbitration, have been seen historically as the principal mechanism for resolving conflict. More recently, other avenues have been sought. The industrial relations parties are looking to mechanisms like grievance procedures to resolve workplace disputes, while concepts like industrial democracy and employee participation are being explored as a means of identifying potential conflict before it is manifested.

Questions and Activities
1. Compare and discuss grievance or dispute-settling procedures from different awards.
2. List the major principles involved in designing a grievance procedure. Draft one based on these principles.
3. After reading Figure 6.5 answer the following questions:
    a. Under what section of the Industrial Relations Act, 1988 was the dispute filed?
    b. How would the dispute have been handled by the IRC? Show the steps diagrammatically.
    c. Summarise the events which appear to have taken place leading up to the dispute.
    d. In the Deputy President's estimation how could this dispute have been avoided?
4. After reading Figure 6.10 answer the following questions:
    a. What is a bans clause?
    b. Why was the bans clause inserted in the award?
    c. Why is this particular case noteworthy?
    d. What are bans clauses usually used for?
5. In your view is the legal system an appropriate avenue for resolving industrial disputes? Why?
6. How could the concept of employee participation assist in reducing industrial conflict? Identify participative practices that would achieve this aim. Relate them to an organisation with which you are familiar.
7. Read the decision below of the Australian Industrial Relations Commission and answer the following questions:
    a. Who heard this case, and who were the parties involved?
    b. What did the Commission decide, and upon what grounds?
    c. Do you feel that the decision was justified?
    d. Draft a dispute notification letter to the IRC based on the facts in the case.

AUSTRALIAN INDUSTRIAL RELATIONS COMMISSION
Industrial Relations Act 1988
s.99 notification of an industrial dispute
Australian Institute of Marine and Power Engineers and others

and

Cape Lambert Services Pty Ltd
(C No. 65042 of 1989)

Tug crews
DEPUTY PRESIDENT POLITES
Crewing and classifications

Maritime industry
MELBOURNE, 11 May 1989

Decision
On 28 April, 1989, Commissioner Fogarty found an industrial dispute in the following terms:
"Consequently, I formally find that an industrial dispute within the meaning of the Industrial Relations Act 1988 exists between the Merchant Service Guild, the Australian Institute of Marine and Power Engineers and the Seamen's Union of Australia on the one part and Cape Lambert Services Pty Ltd on the other. The matters in dispute between these parties are the levels of manning and the classifications of manning on M.T. "Roebourne" and M.T. "Wickham" during voyages by those two tugs between Port Walcott in Western Australia and Darwin in the Northern Territory for the purposes of the tugs being dry docked in the latter port."

As objection was taken to Commissioner Fogarty hearing and determining the dispute, he having participated in conciliation proceedings, the matter came to me for determination.

On Saturday, 29 April 1989 when the proceedings were listed for hearing, I was informed that the tug "Roebourne" had sailed from Wickham to Darwin. A number of the crew who refused to sail, had their employment terminated. Since the dispute arising in relation to these terminations is before Commissioner Fogarty, I say no more about that matter in these proceedings.

I now turn to the merits of the matter. The unions seek a crew of ten comprising the following: master, mate, chief engineer, second engineer, three able seamen, greaser, cook and steward.

The company contends that a crew of seven consisting of master, mate, chief engineer, second engineer and three able seamen is both in excess of the minimum safety manning level required by the Minister for Transport and Communications in respect of the voyage and is fair in the circumstances.

The principles which have been applied by this Commission's predecessor and which should be applied by this Commission in relation to manning disputes are clearly set forth in the XPT case as follows:

"The principles which the Commission should apply in circumstances such as those before us have been the subject of a number of submissions to us and reference to a number of cases. The main case relied upon by the State Rail Authority is the decision of Coldham J in the Airline Hostesses' Case. In that decision Coldham J applied the test whether or not the work asked to be done was ". . . unjust . . . unreasonable, harsh or oppressive". In adopting this test his Honour referred to a decision of Wright J in an appeal under the Public Service Arbitration Act. In that case Wright J said ". . . this Commission, and the Arbitration Court before it, have throughout their existence acknowledged the right of an employer to manage and regulate his own business, subject to the protection of his employees from injustice or unreasonable demands". In that case not only did Wright J use that expression but Williams and Franki JJ in their separate decision referred to ". . . the right of an employer to manage and regulate his own employees" and said: "This approach has been accepted by the Commission and the Arbitration Court since the Conciliation and Arbitration Act became operative and has been reiterated from time to time since then." It is not clear why Coldham J added the words "harsh" and "oppressive". It seems to us that the proper test to be applied and which has been applied for many years by the Commission is for the Commission to examine all the facts and not to interfere with the right of an employer to manage his own business unless he is seeking from the employees something which is unjust or unreasonable. The test of injustice or unreasonableness would embrace matters of safety and health because a requirement by an employer for an employee to perform work which was unsafe or might damage the health of the employee would be both unjust and unreasonable. The ACTU submitted to us that we should apply the test as to whether the demand of the employer was just and equitable having regard to all the circumstances. It is our view that under any given set of facts the test suggested by the ACTU would not lead to a different decision from the test which the Commission has applied over time. Accordingly in reaching our decision we have approached the matter from the point of view of making a judgment whether the request of the SRA and the XPT be manned by one man is unjust or unreasonable."

The unions referred to the following passage in a case known as the 'Accolade' case:

"In the Commission's view manning claims must be looked at primarily as a matter of workload. The key question to be asked is "What are the man hour requirements for the work at hand?" Once this question is answered other matters such as safety, legal requirements and industrial relations issues can then be addressed."

In my view this is not inconsistent with what was raised in the XPT case but rather express a particular method of applying the test.

In this case I propose to review what was put to me and to determine in all the circumstances whether the manning level of seven proposed by the company is unjust or unreasonable. There is no issue before me as to the safety of that manning level.

Turning to the union case it was contended that by past custom and practice a crew of twelve should be the manning level for free-running voyages from Port Walcott. This manning level was consistent with the manning level of other tugs on the West Australian coast for free-running voyages. The unions were prepared to reduce the manning level to ten but anything less was to be regarded as unfair and unjust. In particular, it was said, the company's manning level was harsh, unfair and oppressive in view of the substantially increased work hours for deck and engine room officers. Such workload was excessive, especially if these persons were also required to perform catering functions.

The Commission conducted an inspection of the Port Walcott and the tugs "Wickham" and "Tai O" (a replacement tug on bare boat charter) and heard the evidence on the unions' behalf of five witnesses, being the Assistant Federal Secretary of The Seamen's Union of Australia, the Workboat Master for Cape Lambert Service Pty Ltd, a marine engineer employed on the tugs, two seamen employed on the tugs and the State Secretary and The Seamen's Union of Australia in Western Australia.

That evidence clearly established that in previous free-running voyages, crews of twelve had been used, that employees on these tugs during free-running voyages had not in the past been required to cater for themselves, that free-running voyages in the past had on occasions been rough, with repairs being required to be carried out during the voyages.

Evidence was also given that during cyclones in Western Australia, the tugs are moved to a special mooring on the other side of Nichol Bay, called Flying Fome Passage, where the tugs can remain for anything up to five days, with the engines kept running and with a constant sea watch. In these circumstances, the ordinary harbour manning level for the tug of six is maintained with the crew cooking their own meals.

For the company, three witnesses were called, being Captain Gouge, the Marine Manager, Captain Allen, the Marine Superintendent and Mr Maddison, a Security Officer with considerable naval experience who helped crew the tug "Roebourne" on the voyage from Port Walcott to Darwin. Evidence was given that in the voyage of the "Roebourne" to Darwin no difficulties occurred with both the deck and engine room officers keeping a six hour even time watch and that no problems arose during the voyage. Captain Gouge acknowledged the past custom and practice of using a crew of twelve but it was said that it was the policy of previous management of the company then owning the tugs to simply acquiesce to union demands and that the present management did not agree with this past practice.

In summary, the company's case was that it was the employer's prerogative to set manning levels, that the evidence showed the manning level was adequate and there was thus no basis, consistent with its own principles, for this Commission to intervene.

Stripped of all the rhetoric which has accompanied these proceedings, this is a dispute about three positions. The unions no longer press for a crew of twelve, and there is no difference between the crew proposed by the unions and the company in relation to the position of master, mate and two engineers. The position therefore comes down to the question of whether in relation to these voyages the tugs should carry a greaser, cook and steward.

Having considered all the evidence, I do not believe a greaser is required. The voyage is of some five days duration. On balance the evidence does not support the need for a greaser during this period. There was evidence of only one serious engine room problem in relation to previous free-running voyages of these tugs and even on that occasion all that could be concluded from the evidence is that the problem would have taken longer to fix in the absence of a greaser. Moreover, this assumes that able seamen should not be required to work in the engine room under the direction of an engineer. I do not believe this argument to be sustainable. Finally, the engines operate continuously for periods almost equal to the length of the voyage when the tugs are at cyclone mooring without a greaser, and in those circumstances the engineer is not assisted by a greaser. In all the circumstances, the claim for a greaser is rejected.

I now turn to the position of "steward". Having inspected the accommodation available on the tugs "Wickham" and "Roebourne" and the messing and kitchen areas, having heard evidence as to what occurred on the voyage to Darwin and as to what occurs when the tug is at cyclone mooring, it seems to me that the crew should be able to keep accommodation and passage ways clear without the need for a steward.

The position of "cook" is however more difficult. There is evidence that in the opinion of members of the crew who sailed the "Roebourne" to Darwin, a cook was unnecessary because the third able seaman was able to undertake most of the cooking. Moreover, a cook is not provided when the tug is at cyclone mooring at Flying Fome Passage. On the other hand, the evidence is overwhelming that with the exception of what can be described as unusual cases, a cook has invariably been provided on free-running voyages for tugs in Australia. In this case, the evidence is clear that it will be necessary for both deck and engine room officers to work twelve hours per day. It seems to me unreasonable on top of this work requirement to provide that they should also be required to cook their own meals. In attempting to counter this proposition which was put to Mr Buchanan during his address, he argued that the third able seaman should be required to undertake the cooking. This, however, seems to me would considerably reduce the availability of the able seaman to attend to other duties, including duties in the engine room and cleaning duties, which in my view, he should be able to undertake. Whilst it is true that a cook is not provided when the tug is at cyclone mooring at Flying Fome Passage, the evidence clearly shows that in these circumstances weather conditions are extreme and the tug is not provisioned as it is for free-running voyages. It seems reasonable to conclude, having regard to all that was said, that it would be unlikely that the cook could effectively perform any significant duties while the tugs were at cyclone mooring.

On balance, I believe that a cook should be provided for these voyages.

I emphasise that this decision relates only to these voyages and the award which ensues as a result of this decision to be known as "The Cape Lambert Services Pty Ltd Free-Voyage Tug Manning Award 1989" will be so confined.

Appearances:

Mr M. Byrne for the Australian Institute of Marine and Power Engineers.
Mr T. Rawlings and *Mr A. Papaconstuntinos* for The Seamen's Union of Australia.
Mr P. Rix and *Mr M. Fleming* for the Merchant Service Guild of Australia.
Mr M.W. Odes, Mr T. Caspersz, Mr J.P. Longo, M P. Kite and *Mr Buchanan Q.C.* for Cape Lambert Services Pty Ltd.
Mr H. Larratt for Peko Wallsend Ltd.

Dates and places of hearing:

1989. *Perth*: April 17; *Sydney*: April 24, 28 & 29. *Karatha*: May 3 & 4; *Melbourne*: May 9 & 10.

Chapter 7

Conditions of Employment

> **Objectives**
> At the end of this chapter, the reader should be able to:
> - list the three principal sources of law which affect an employee's terms and conditions of employment;
> - discuss their operation;
>   and
> - describe and explain the procedure used to make federal awards.

Terms and conditions of work

All employers must recruit and select staff; prior to a person's employment, the employer usually advises the prospective employee of their relevant salary, hours of work, annual leave entitlements and the like. Specifically, these can include, for example:

- the amount the person is paid (e.g. hourly wage or monthly salary);
- the designation the person is given (e.g. full-time, part-time or casual);
- the entitlements the person is to receive (e.g. eight days' sick leave); and
- the obligations the person has (e.g. to work efficiently and to be careful in the exercise of their duties).

The terms and conditions under which most persons are employed are governed by three complicated and interrelated factors;

- the contract of employment;
- awards and agreements; and
- legislation.

Conditions of employment are the critical outcome of an industrial relations system. They are significant, not only because there is conflict between unions, employers and government about the extent of the entitlements (and how they are taxed and otherwise affected by government policies) but also in the way the terms and conditions are interpreted and administered.

The contract of employment

The terms and conditions of employment established under the contract of employment have their basis in common or 'judge-made' law. These laws have been developed by judges over many centuries, originally in England but subsequently transferred and further developed by Australian courts. Common law utilises the concept of precedent (previously decided cases bind and influence courts in dealing with their current cases), and covers such areas as negligence, defamation, trespass and contracts.

Apart from the common law, statutes (laws made, and amended, by state and federal parliaments) and their regulations also determine rights and obligations of employers and employees.

The contract of employment is the first step in laying the legal foundation of the employer/employee relationship—or the 'master/servant' relationship, as it is sometimes known. It is the same as any other contract, in that it is an agreement made between two or more parties whereby legal rights and obligations are created that can be enforced by law. For the agreement to be a valid contract, it must contain a number of essential elements. Briefly, these are:

a. *The intention of the parties to create a legal relationship;*
b. *An offer by one party and the acceptance of that offer by the other party* (for example, an offer to pay $500 per week, to which the worker agrees);
c. *Form of consideration.* In essence, there must be some valuable 'trade-off' in the promises swapped by the parties (for example, 'I will make my skills as a stenographer available to you following your promise to provide me, and pay me, for one day's casual work');
d. *Capacity to contract.* Courts have decided that some people, such as children, cannot validly enter into contracts in certain circumstances;
e. *Genuineness of consent.* Where undue influence is used or if a mistake is made, a contract may be rendered invalid; and
f. *Legality of object.* It is possible for agreements which, for example, infringe upon the public safety to be held by courts to be non-enforceable.

All these six elements must be satisfied for there to be a valid contract of employment.

Only in rare cases, such as indentures of apprenticeship, is it mandatory for a contract to be in writing. Nevertheless, there are advantages to setting out a contract in writing, particularly as conflict may arise over what was intended in the original agreement. This difficulty cannot be understated: it is fairly common for a party to an employment contract to claim that the agreement provided for some condition (e.g. that the employee would work every second Sunday), but if the condition was never recorded it is much harder to prove.

Some written contracts are lengthy, setting out the fine details of the agreement. A more common method is a letter confirming the person's employment. In Figure 7.1, a letter to a prospective employee, all the six essential elements of a valid contract are present:

- an intention to contract;
- confirmation of the offer and acceptance;
- consideration (payment for providing services as an office manager);
- Didge's capacity to contract;
- her agreement to work for the Child Care Centre; and
- its object does not contravene any public interest (i.e. its objective is legally acceptable).

Contracts of service and contracts for service

Not all contracts of employment give rise to an employee/employer relationship. Using the Christina Stead Child Care Centre from Figure 7.1 as an example, could the people who clean the building during the evening be classed as employees? Similarly, the Centre needs to know its legal relationship with the gardener who mows the lawns and prunes the trees.

THE CHRISTINA STEAD CHILD CARE CENTRE

Dear Didge,

    This letter confirms your appointment as the Centre's office manager from 20th January, 199X on the following basis:-

(a) Your conditions of employment are set out in the relevant award;
(b) The centre agrees to pay you $50 p.w. above the prescribed award rate;
(c) You will be allowed one full day's paid absence per month to continue your studies in bookkeeping during 199X;
(d) You will join the appropriate trade union from the commencement date of your employment.

I take this opportunity to welcome you and sincerely trust that you find the position rewarding and stimulating.

Yours faithfully,

President

Figure 7.1: All the six elements of a valid contract are present.

In administering terms of employment, it is important to be able to distinguish between that of an employee (contract *of* service) and those that have a different legal relationship, usually that of principal and an independent contractor (contract *for* services). There are different legal entitlements depending upon the nature of the relationship. Many cases have reached courts in which a person has argued that they were an employee, in order to sustain a claim for award payment or some other entitlement. The employer has maintained that the person was not an employee. Even though the parties may have agreed to an independent contractor arrangement (in writing or otherwise), courts can 'look behind' the contract and define the true relationship. So, while the Christina Stead Child Care Centre may have signed contracts with their cleaners which state that they are independent contractors and not employees, it needs to ensure that this in fact is the case. The status agreed to by the parties, while often helpful to a court, does not stop the court from deciding otherwise.

In instances where it is unclear whether a person is an employee, courts have applied a legal principle known as the *control test*. This says that the employer/employee relationship exists when: *one party has the right of continuous, dominant and detailed control over the other*. Hence, a 'servant' is a person subject to the command of his/her 'master' regarding how the work shall be done. An independent contractor is one who undertakes to produce a given result but, in the actual execution of the work, is not under the order or control of the person for whom it is done.

A gardener at the Child Care Centre is an employee then if the management of the Centre has the right to direct which tasks shall be performed (e.g. 'please fertilise the roses this week') and how they shall be carried out (e.g. 'you must use this organic spray, as it does not cause an allergic reaction in the children').

In instances where there is no definite indication of control, courts often consider factors such as the right of one party to delegate or to subcontract. Other tests include:

1. Payment of regular wages or salary.
2. Deduction of tax, especially PAYE (Pay As You Earn).
3. Performance of work in the employer's place of business.
4. Continuity of work.
5. Regular and defined hours.
6. Use of employer's plant and equipment.
7. Right of the employer to dismiss for disobedience or misconduct.
8. Workers' compensation cover by employer.

Each element is carefully weighed by the courts. Other tests have been developed, but the control test is the one which dominates the court's decisions. An example of its application can be found in the case *AMP Society v. Chaplin*. This case reflects how complex and often difficult it is to define the true legal relationship between two parties. It also strongly reinforces the need to understand how the law operates when employing people.

The case came about when Mr Chaplin, an insurance representative, claimed long-service leave under a state long-service leave act. The act entitled an 'employee' to long-service leave after a specific period of service. To justify his claim, Chaplin had to convince the court that he was an employee. In making their judgment, and in applying the control test, the court considered the following factors:

1. There was a written agreement between the AMP Society and Chaplin. The document, 'Benefits and conditions of appointment as an AMP Representative', detailed the specific terms and conditions of Chaplin's appointment.
2. The actual duties performed by Mr Chaplin in his agency work: e.g. use of his own house as an office; employment of subagents and his own clerical staff; conversion of a spare room in his home into an office; and the fact that he was not required to report his whereabouts or activities in agency work or to ask for leave of absence when he took a holiday.
3. Although Mr Chaplin regularly attended 'sales' meetings at the Society's office this was not considered significant by the court, even though 'such attendance [. . .] should be regarded as obligatory' because 'the reason for attendance was that it was necessary for the agents to be kept informed and instructed about new forms of insurance contracts, changes in the relevant law and other current matters'.
4. The relatively large amount that Mr Chaplin claimed in business expenses (60%–80%) as a deduction from his gross income was 'much more consistent with the view that the tax payer was carrying on a business of his own than with the alternative view that he was an employee under a contract of service'.

In weighing these factors up, the Court decided that Chaplin was an independent contractor, and he therefore lost his claim for long-service leave.

In another case, *Inspector L. P. Crawford v. Katherine Ivkovitch*, (1989), the NSW Chief Industrial Magistrate was required to determine whether a worker was an employee for the purposes of the Annual Holidays Act. The person would gain an entitlement under the Act if they could prove they were an employee.

In his decision, the Magistrate referred to another judgment in the case *Stevens v. Broadribb Sawmilling Co. Pty Ltd*, (1985–86), in which Justice Mason said:

> A prominent factor in determining the nature of the relationship between a person who engages another to perform work and the person so engaged is the degree of control which the former can exercise over the latter. It has been held, however, that the importance of control lies not so much in its actual exercise, although clearly that is relevant, as in the right of the employer to exercise it (*Zuijs v. Wirth Brothers Pty. Ltd.* (1955); *Humberstone v. Northern Timber Mills* (1949) . . .
>
> But the existence of control, whilst significant, is not the sole criterion by which to gauge whether a relationship is one of employment. The approach of this court has been to regard it merely as one of a number of indicia which

must be considered in the determination of that question... Other relevant matters include, but are not limited to, the mode of remuneration, the provision and maintenance of equipment, the obligation to work, the hours of work and provision for holidays, the deduction of income tax...

Source: CCH, *Australian Industrial Law Report* (31) 25, 22 December, 1989.

Stevens v. Brodribb Sawmilling, a decision of the High Court, is regarded as a leading authority on the issue of determining whether a contractual relationship is that of employer/employee.

INTERVIEW

HOWARD HARRISON
Position: Partner, Carroll and O'Dea, Solicitors.

1. Briefly Howard, what sort of work and cases would your firm undertake in the industrial relations area?

Carroll and O'Dea advise and act in a range of matters relevant to the industrial relations area such as industrial disputes (which includes disputes between unions and employers and unions and unions); union mergers; wages and related entitlements recovery; superannuation advice and claims; and personal injury, workers' compensation and/or damages claims.

2. Presumably you act for both unions (and their members) and employers?

We do act for unions and employers, but primarily for unions and their members.

3. Using the example of a disputed claim for workers compensation, what specific tasks such as organising referrals to doctors and so on would your firm do?

Well, the specific tasks we would undertake include: obtaining all relevant medical and other information and instructions; undertaking any necessary legal research; preparing, filing and serving initiating process and other documents relevant to interlocutory processes such as subpoenae; organising referrals to medico-legal specialists if necessary and obtaining reports from necessary medical, actuarial, accounting or liability experts; supplying particulars and serving documentary evidence on solicitors for defendant and obtaining from the solicitors all material they must produce in connection with a particular type of claim including particulars of any matters raised in a defence; retaining, briefing, conferring with and instructing Counsel if applicable; and attending and advising the client at various times from inception to conclusion of claim and of course throughout any hearing.

4. If a government was to introduce legislation which your firm felt was inappropriate or ill advised, how would you convey this to the government?

Through the Law Society, individual members of parliament, discussions with trade union officers and/or members of Labor Council and through discussions with clients.

5. Finally, although you are a partner in a firm of solicitors, do you feel aspects of the industrial relations system are too legalistic?

Whilst particular procedures seem at times cumbersome and somewhat ineffective, generally the existence of legal structures and mechanisms are, in our experience, necessary for the protection of individuals' award rights, and a highly desirable structure for the orderly resolution of industrial disputes, either by the process of negotiation or third party determination. Overall, Australia's system of compulsory conciliation and arbitration of industrial disputes has served this country, and both employees and employers, very well. That system must necessarily have a degree of legalism to ensure its proper operation and its credibility with the parties before it.

What does a contract of employment mean?

A contract of employment gives rise to certain legally enforceable rights and obligations for the employer and the employee. Much care must be exercised in specifying these rights and obligations, and individual cases vary with the detail of each circumstance. Nevertheless, these implied common law conditions in contracts of employment are worthy of review. Employers, for example, must provide their employees with a safe place of work. Courts have decided that an employer who does not ensure that machinery is guarded in such a way as to stop a reasonable person from being injured has been negligent in satisfying their duty of care. Courts have also held that at common law an employee must:

- *obey the lawful and reasonable commands of the employer*. This has its basis in the idea of the employer 'controlling' the activities of the 'servant'. If an employee fails to obey such an order, it may lead to summary (instant) dismissal. It is often difficult, however, to determine what is a 'reasonable' command.
- *display care and be competent in the performance of her/his duties*. As an example, in the English case *Lister v. Romford Ice and Cold Storage*, the court decided that Mr Lister, a truck-driver for the Romford Ice Company, did not exercise reasonable care in the performance of his duties when he reversed his truck into a workmate, who, sadly, was his father, causing him serious injury.
- *be faithful to her/his employer's interest*. This can arise, for example, when employees are not allowed to reveal confidential information to business competitors. Many employers put clauses in their contracts forbidding employees from revealing information and unfairly taking advantage of what they have learnt in their employment even after the employment relationship has terminated. Yet courts are reluctant to enforce this type of term if it will have the effect of limiting the former employee's future employment activities (restraint of trade). However, where such a restraint is necessary because it is in the interests of both the employer and the employee as well as in the public interest, the restraint will be enforced by the courts.

Obligations of employers include:

- *indemnifying employees for expenses legitimately incurred in the course of their employment*. Cases can sometimes arise to determine whether the expense was reasonable and employment-related; and
- *providing work*. At common law, an employer generally does not have the right to 'stand-down' an employee; that is, even when there is no work, the employee must be paid. So, for example, if a salesperson could not sell the employer's product because the business had depleted its stock, the salesperson would still have an entitlement to be paid at common law.

All these obligations are implied in contracts of employment and exist even though the parties may not have discussed them nor specifically agreed to them. If any of these obligations are not met, then a variety of 'remedies' may be available to the concerned party. Damages (a money payment) have often been awarded by courts—for example, in cases where employees have been injured as a result of the employer's negligence.

The obligations on the employee under the contract of employment seem quite stringent in comparison to those on the employer. The reasons for this include:

- the common law dealing with the contract of employment significantly reflects the power of the 'master' and the obedience expected of his/her 'servants'.
- many of the obligations on employers have been codified into relevant legislation and awards.

How are contracts of employment terminated? This can occur through a number of ways:

- *By giving notice*. Where the contract has no fixed term then it may be terminated by the method set out in the contract and/or award, or in the absence of any such condition by either the employer or employee giving reasonable notice. What is reasonable is dependent on factors such as custom and practice in the relevant industry, and how wages are paid.
- *By frustration*. Sometimes events can arise which are no fault of either party but which mean that the contract is terminated because it cannot be fulfilled. This may arise when an employee becomes ill for an extended period.
- *By breach*. When a party commits a fundamental breach of their contract

it can bring the contract to an end. If a bank teller was convicted of theft, even if committed outside of the employment relationship, it would probably be seen as justifying dismissal. Gross neglect of duties and wilful disobedience of a reasonable command are other examples. In these circumstances an employer can 'summarily dismiss' the employee, i.e. without the notice required under the contract.

Employment legislation

State governments have passed laws which contribute to an employee's conditions of employment, especially in the fields of annual and long-service leave and workers' compensation. Other statutes, such as the *Sex Discrimination Act 1984* and the *Affirmative Action Act 1986*, have been enacted by the Federal Government. These laws protect employees against unfair treatment on the basis of gender, marital status and other grounds, and provide for employers to adopt measures to improve the employment status of women and other groups. Similar laws exist in most of the states. The absence outside of the territories of federal laws setting out annual leave conditions and the like reflect limitations imposed by the Australian Constitution on the industrial relation powers of the Commonwealth Parliament (as discussed in Chapter 4).

To illustrate the operation of employment legislation, an employer in New South Wales would need to administer the following laws in respect to all or part of their workforce, depending upon their workers' award coverage:

Long-Service Leave Act
- Allows an employee to take 13 weeks' paid leave after 15 years' continuous service.

Annual Holidays Act
- Entitles an employee, after 12 months' service, to four weeks' paid leave. Casuals and part-time workers also have benefits under the Act.

Anti-Discrimination Act
- Prohibits an employer from making decisions on the basis of a person's race, gender, sexual preference, etc., in a wide array of employment-related fields (e.g. recruitment, selection, and access to training).

Workers' Compensation Act
- Provides employees with payments when they have been injured as a result of or in the course of their employment.

Industrial Arbitration Act
- Provides maternity leave benefits, which include the right of an employee with the requisite service to return to her job after the period of leave.

Figures 7.2 and 7.3 reproduce a number of sections from these Acts.

NEW SOUTH WALES

TABLE OF PROVISIONS

1. Short title
2. Construction
3. Interpretation
4. Long service leave
5. Exemptions
5A. Review of exemptions
6. Savings as to powers, etc.
7. Contracting out prohibited
8. Records to be kept by employers
9. Powers of inspectors
9A. Disclosure of information
10. Penalties and offences
11. Recovery of penalties
12. Recovery of long service leave pay
13. Amendment of Act No. 2, 1940 and savings
14. Provisions as to enforcement of orders, etc.
15. Regulations

Recovery of long service leave pay

12. (1) Any worker may apply to a court of petty sessions holden before a stipendiary magistrate sitting alone, or to any industrial magistrate appointed under the Industrial Arbitration Act 1940, for an order directing the employer to pay to the worker the full amount of any payment which has become due to the worker under this Act at any time during the period of 6 years immediately preceding the date of the application but not earlier than 2 years before the date of assent to the Long Service Leave (Amendment) Act 1980.

The magistrate may make any order the magistrate thinks just in the matter and may award costs to either party, and assess the amount of such costs.

Such costs shall be according to a scale to be fixed by the Industrial Commission of New South Wales.

Source: Long Service Leave Act 1955 No. 38 (reprinted as at 4 February, 1987), NSW Government Printer.

Figure 7.2: Extract from Long Service Leave Act.

New South Wales

ANNO OCTAVO
GEORGII VI REGIS

* *

Act No. 31, 1944 (1), as amended by Act No. 28, 1958 (2); Act No. 31, 1964 (3); Act No. 33, 1965 (4); Act No. 50, 1967 (5); Act No. 37, 1969 (6); Act No. 44, 1970 (7); Act No. 48, 1972 (8); Act No. 97, 1974 (9); Act No. 54, 1976 (10); Act No. 184, 1980 (11); Act No. 91, 1983 (12); and Act No. 31, 1984 (13).

An Act to provide for holidays for workers; to amend the Industrial Arbitration Act, 1940, and certain other Acts; and for purposes connected therewith.

Annual holidays with pay.

3. (1) Except as otherwise provided in this Act, every worker shall at the end of each year of his employment by an employer become entitled to an annual holiday on ordinary pay.

Such annual holiday shall—

(a) where any such year of employment ends upon or before 30th November, 1974, be of three weeks;
(b) where any such year of employment ends after 30th November, 1974, be of four weeks.

(2) An annual holiday shall be given and taken either in one consecutive period or two periods which shall be of three weeks and one week respectively, or if the worker and the employer so agree, in either two, three or four separate periods and not otherwise.

(3) If the worker and the employer so agree, the annual holiday or any of such separate periods may be taken wholly or partly in advance before the worker has become entitled to the annual holiday.

Source: Annual Holidays Act, 1944, No. 31 (reprinted 1972), NSW Government Printer.

Figure 7.3: Extract from Annual Holidays Act.

Awards

Awards are the third major source of law affecting the employment relationship. They can be defined as: *a formal document, made by an industrial tribunal, setting out terms and conditions of employment which are legally enforceable*. Most awards contain *minimum* rates and conditions. Paid rates awards however prescribe the *actual* rates and conditions.

There are currently in operation over 1000 federal awards (those made by the Australian Industrial Relations Commission; and many more state awards (those made by tribunals such as the NSW Industrial Commission). As a result, many employers need to administer a variety of differing awards. This reflects, to some extent, the fact that some unions are industry-based, while others can enrol as their members only those working in occupations and trades. Figure 7.4 gives examples of the awards that would typically be dealt with by a moderately sized printing company in Sydney.

JOB	AWARD
Printing employees, e.g. compositors, printing machinists, tablehands	Federal Graphic Arts Award
Clerks, typists and stenographers	Clerks (State) Award
Truck-driver	Transport Industry (State) Award
Cleaner	Miscellaneous Workers General Service (State) Award
Sales Representative	Commercial Travellers (State) Award

Figure 7.4: An illustration of award coverage in the printing industry.

The Australian Workplace Industrial Relations Survey published in 1991 found that all but 1 per cent of workplaces were covered by at least one award with an average of two awards at the 2351 workplaces surveyed. Figure 7.5 shows the distribution of awards and the percentage of employees covered. The report summarised that:

> While recent policy debates have highlighted the problems of multiple award coverage at workplaces, this type of coverage usually occurs in relatively few large workplaces. Almost half of all workplaces had no more than one award. On the other hand, 3 per cent of workplaces reported having six or more awards; one large workplace even reported it was respondent to forty-six or more awards. While relatively few workplaces had multiple award coverage, its impact was pronounced because of the proportion of employees that were employed in these predominantly large workplaces (a quarter of the workforce surveyed).

Fifteen per cent of the workforce is not covered by awards, and this is usually restricted to managerial employees. Care should be exercised in determining whether a person is actually 'award-free' because, while their job may not be specifically included in an award's list of job classifications, the employee could still be covered as a result of performing award-related tasks.

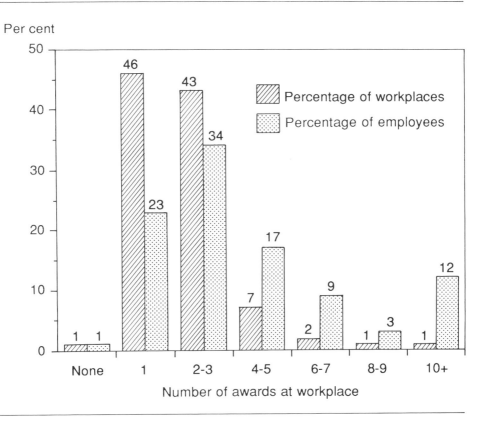

Source: Callus, R. et al., *Industrial Relations at Work*, The Australian Workplace Industrial Relations Survey, AGPS, 1991.

Figure 7.5: Workplaces and employees in Australia, by number of awards at the workplace.

Table 7.1 sets out the incidence of awards, by industry, in Australia in May 1985. The main features of the system of awards detailed are that:
- eighty-five per cent of all employees are covered by awards or their equivalent, such as industrial agreements. These have the same effect as an award;
- approximately half (49.8%) of those covered are under the awards of the state tribunals and 32.6% under federal awards; and
- almost all employees in the public sector (government departments) and in communication agencies such as Australia Post and Telecom are covered by awards, with the incidence of awards lowest in the wholesale trade industry.

To provide an understanding of the array of awards in Australia, Table 7.2 lists a number of major federal and state awards, and the number of employees each covers.

Content of awards

As can be seen from the first page of the (Federal) Theatre Managers Award 1986 in Figure 7.6, awards regulate a diverse range of employment conditions. Some, as might be expected, relate to particular aspects of the industry (Clause 18, Midnight Performances/Clause 19, Additional Performances), while the others (such as Clause 17, Overtime/Clause 21, Meal Hours) are found in most awards. Four clauses from the Theatre Managers Award are set out in Figure 7.7. These clauses illustrate the detailed rights and obligations of awards.

Table 7.1: Incidence of awards, all employees by industry, Australia, May 1985

Industry	Number of employees (in thousands)	Covered by awards, determinations and collective agreements (%)			Not covered by awards etc.
		Federal	State	Total[a]	
Mining	88.1	50.8	26.3	79.9	20.1
Manufacturing	991.8	46.6	36.0	85.0	15.0
Food, beverages and tobacco	174.3	24.1	59.9	87.3	12.7
Textiles, clothing and footwear	85.3	60.8	27.8	89.2	10.8
Paper, paper products, etc.	103.1	42.1	33.0	83.7	16.3
Chemical, petroleum and coal products	55.8	31.9	40.3	73.8	26.2
Metal products, machinery and equipment	410.3	60.2	24.6	86.0	14.0
Basic metal products	72.8	38.1	46.4	85.1	14.9
Fabricated metal products etc.	218.2	57.1	22.8	81.8	18.2
Transport equipment	119.3	79.3	14.5	94.3	5.7
Other manufacturing	163.0	36.8	43.8	82.2	17.8
Electricity, gas and water	137.6	39.2	59.4	98.5	*
Construction	224.3	31.6	39.4	73.8	26.2
Wholesale Trade	326.4	23.1	42.3	69.6	30.4
Retail trade	616.9	17.9	63.8	82.9	17.1
Transport and storage	277.1	54.0	31.2	88.8	11.2
Communication	133.6	99.8	*	99.9	*
Finance, property and business services	543.2	30.5	38.0	77.0	23.0
Public administration and defence	302.7	57.3	40.2	98.5	*
Community services	1053.4	9.6	79.0	90.0	10.0
Recreation, persona and other services	307.7	29.1	52.4	83.5	16.5
All Industries	5002.9	32.6	49.8	85.0	15.0

a Includes a small number of employees covered by unregistered collective agreements.
Source: Australian Bureau of Statistics, Catalogue no. 6315.0.

Table 7.2: Major awards—Australia, May 1985.

Jurisdiction	Name of award, determination, or collective agreement	No. of employees covered
Australia	Metal Industry Award	221 800
NSW	Clerks (State) Award	116 600
VIC	Commercial Clerks Award	80 700
Australia	Bank Officials (Federal) Award	75 500
Australia	Vehicle Industry: Repair, Service and Retail Award	70 500
QLD	Clerks and Switchboard Attendants (State) Award	50 300
NSW	Crown Employees (Teachers: Education Teaching Service) Award	44 200
VIC	Hospital and Benevolent Homes Award	37 900
Australia	Insurance Officers (Clerical and Indoor Staff) Consolidated Award	29 900
Australia	Hotels and Retail Liquor Industry Award	
VIC	General Shops Award	27 900
SA	Clerks (South Australia) Award	26 400
WA	Shop and Warehouse (Wholesale and Retail Award	25 600
SA	Teachers' Salaries Board Award	20 000
Australia	National Building Trades Consolidated Award	14 300
Australia	Engineering (oil Companies) Award	13 800
Tasmania	Retail Trades Award	12 600
Australia	Liquor and Allied Industries Accommodation, Catering Food Services, Drink Cafeteria and Canteens Award	12 600
SA	Hotels, Clubs (etc.) Award	10 400
QLD	Hospital Nurses Award (State)	10 100

Source: Australian Bureau of Statistics, Catalogue no. 6315.0.

TO11 A B Print G9991

In the matter of a notification of an industrial dispute between the
Theatre Managers' Association

and

The Cinematograph Exhibitors Association and others
in relation to wages and working conditions for theatre managers
(C No. 3934 of 1983)

MR COMMISSIONER MANSINI   BRISBANE, 12 NOVEMBER 1987

AWARD
1 — TITLE
This Award shall be referred to as the Theatre Managers Award 1986.
2 — ARRANGEMENT

Subject matter	*Clause number*
Accident make-up pay	29
Additional performances	19
Annual leave	26
Arrangement	2
Boards of Reference	35
Casual managers	11
Clothing and footwear allowances	22
Compassionate leave	28
Confectionery shops, stalls and/or milk bars and/or snack bars and licensed liquor bars	9
Daylight saving time	13
Definitions	3
Determination of previous award	36
Hours	12
Intermittent managers	10
Leave reserved	37
Locality	6
Locomotion allowance	24
Meal hours	21
Midnight performances	18
Mixed functions	30
No extra claims	8A
Operation and duration	5
Overtime	17
Parties bound	4
Payment of wages	32
Preference of employment	31
Prosecutions	33

Figure 7.6: Illustrates the diversity of employment conditions regulated by one award.

7 — TERMS OF ENGAGEMENT

(a) All employees on the permanent staff shall be engaged by the week unless a longer period of engagement be agreed to between the parties.

(b) During the first twelve months of employment such employment shall be terminated on either side only by giving two weeks' notice. After the first twelve months of employment such employment shall be terminated on either side only by giving four weeks' notice. Notice may be given at any time during the week and the employee shall only be entitled to payment up to the time of the expiration of the notice.

(c) Nothing in this Award shall affect any legal right of an employer to dismiss without notice any employee for whatever period engaged, for malingering, inefficiency, neglect of duty or misconduct; in the case of such dismissal, wages shall be payable for the employment up to but not after the time of dismissal.

(d) Notwithstanding anything elsewhere contained in this Award, an employer may deduct payment of wages for any day on which an employee cannot be usefully employed because of:
   (i) any strike;
   (ii) any breakdown of machinery; or
   (iii) any stoppage of work unavoidable by the employer.

17 — OVERTIME

(a) All time worked outside the time of beginning and ending work as prescribed in Clause 12—Hours of this Award, shall be paid for at the rate of double time.

(b) All time worked within the times of beginning and ending work in excess of the hours fixed for a week's work shall be paid for at the rate of time and a half for the first two hours and double time thereafter.

(c) Time off shall not be given in lieu of payment for overtime.

(d) The calculation of rates in this clause shall, except where it is agreed that the actual rate paid includes an amount to compensate for overtime worked or to be worked, shall be on the actual rate paid to the employee. The rates payable under this clause shall not be cumulative.

(e) An employee recalled to work overtime after leaving his place of employment, except for the partaking of a meal, shall be paid for a minium of three hours' work at the appropriate rate.

27 — SICK LEAVE

(a) Any employee engaged by the week absent from duty shall lose pay proportionate to such absence unless he provides or forwards to his employer within twenty-four hours of the commencement of such absence, evidence satisfactory to the employer that the absence was reasonable because of either:
   (i) any illness of himself due neither to his own default nor to accident arising otherwise than out of and in the course of his employment; or
   (ii) any bodily injury to himself caused by accident arising out of and in the course of his employment.

(b) If any dispute shall arise as to the deduction of pay on the ground that satisfactory evidence has not been produced or forwarded, the question whether the evidence should have been accepted by the employer as satisfactory may be determined by the local secretary or other authorised representative of the Theatre Managers' Association and the employer or his representative and if they do not agree shall be determined by the Board of Reference appointed hereunder and the employer and the employee shall treat the evidence as satisfactory or not satisfactory for the purpose of subclause (a) hereof according to the tenor of the determination.

> (c) This clause shall not affect any right of the employer to determine the employment in accordance with clause 7 of this Award.
>
> ### 33 — PROSECUTIONS
>
> Where the screening of a film classified as "restricted" under the relevant legislation governing the censorship classification of films results in a prosecution against a manager or assistant manager, the employer shall pay all fines and costs resulting from such prosecution unless the prosecution results from the wilful default of such manager or assistant manager.
>
> ### 34 — RIGHT OF ENTRY OF ASSOCIATION OFFICIALS
>
> (a) For the purpose of interviewing employees on legitimate Association business, a duly accredited representative of the Theatre Managers' Association shall have the right to enter employers' premises wherein members of such Association, or persons in the same calling as such members are engaged, on the following conditions:
>
>   (i) that he produces his authority to the manager or such other person as may be appointed by the employer for that purpose.
>
>   (ii) That not more than one representative of the said Association be on the premises at any one tiome.
>
>   (iii) That not more than one representative be permitted to visit the premises more than once a week, provided that such representative shall not make his visit earlier than 30 minutes after the commencement of the performance.
>
>   (iv) That if any employer alleges that a representative is unduly interfering with his work or is creating dissatisfaction amongst his employees or is offensive in his methods or is committing a breach of any of the previous conditions herein, such employer may refuse the right of entry, but the representative shall have the right to bring such refusal before a Commissioner or a Board of Reference.
>
> (b) A person shall be a duly accredited representative of the Theatre Managers' Association if he be the holder for the time being of a certificate which has not been cancelled or revoked, signed by the Secretary and bearing the seal of the Association and bearing the signature of the holder.

Figure 7.7: Sample clauses from the Theatre Managers Award.

The procedure for making awards

Federal awards

Section 51(xxxv) of the Australian Constitution requires that the Australian Industrial Relations Commission strictly limit itself to dealing with industrial disputes which extend beyond two or more states (interstate). To satisfy this constitutional requirement, trade unions have developed a 'legal' device known as a 'log of claims'. Essentially, this process involves the union serving a set of claims for improved wages and conditions upon employers and their associations, together with a letter of demand stating that unless the employer agrees with the log they will be in dispute with the union and the matter can be referred to the Commission. Difficult though it is for non-practitioners in the industrial relations field to appreciate, the union is creating merely a 'paper' dispute—that is, the dispute in the customary sense of threatened or actual industrial action does not strictly exist.

Although the log of claims exists as a technical device, the conditions must still satisfy the requirements determined by Section 51(xxxv): that is, it must be an interstate industrial dispute. Relevant decisions, especially those of the Industrial Relations Commission and the High Court must be kept in mind: for example, that the log of claims must be sufficiently specific for the employers genuinely to evaluate it. A log which is phrased too broadly will not satisfy this requirement. In all of these award-making processes, it is available to the parties to seek the intervention of the High Court where they feel that a constitutional aspect has not been satisfied. Indeed, much of the work of the High Court since Federation has involved interpreting Section 51(xxxv) of the Constitution. Figure 7.8 provides an example of a 1990 case where the Commission determined it had the jurisdiction to deal with a claim seeking portability of job entitlements.

The nature of Section 51(xxxv) requiring that a dispute exists has also created the concept of *ambit*. In order to avoid the costly exercise of creating a dispute by serving each employer with a log of claims, the initial claims are made sufficiently broad that a subsequent dispute can be within the ambit of the first claim. For example, a union might make a claim for a weekly wage of $1000. If the parties settle on $500 per week the ambit is the difference between $500 and $1000. Consequently, the 'dispute' will (or can) continue to exist until the wage level reaches $1000 per week.

Serving logs of claims by registered mail (to prove delivery) to many employers (up to 5000 or 6000 in the metal industry) is a costly and onerous task, which unions do not undertake lightly. They therefore try to maximise the ambit created within the limitations imposed by the relevant decisions of the High Court. Once the dispute has been created, the union notifies the Australian Industrial Relations Commission. The member of the relevant panel to whom it has been allocated then decides:

- that a dispute exists;
- the parties to the dispute (the applicants and the respondents); and
- the matters in dispute (the ambit).

This is discussed further in chapter 6. The detailed method of settling this dispute by the Commission making an award is shown in Figure 7.9. Examples of the documents used in the award-making process are shown in Figures 7.10 and 7.11. If an agreement is reached during negotiation, the parties can apply to have it made a certified agreement. Provided the agreement is not outside stipulations laid down in the Act, including 'public interest' criteria, it will be certified. If the parties reach agreement during conciliation, a consent award can be made. Finally, if the parties go to arbitration, an award will be made.

Decision opens way for portable job entitlements

By MARK DAVIS

The Australian Industrial Relations Commission has opened the way for unions to seek 'portability' of accrued employment entitlements when workers change jobs.

In a decision earlier this week, Commissioner Justine Oldmeadow held that the commission had jurisdiction to consider claims by unions for the transfer of entitlements such as annual leave, long service leave and sick leave when workers change jobs from one employer to another.

The matter before Commissioner Oldmeadow involved a log of claims by the Independent Teachers Federation effectively seeking preservation of teachers' accrued employment entitlements and benefits every time they change jobs.

Employers from the various non-government school systems had opposed the finding of a dispute, arguing that the commission had no jurisdiction to consider the claim because its subject matter—portability of entitlements—did not constitute an industrial matter as defined in the Industrial Relations Act.

The employers argued that the ITF was seeking to impose a liability on existing employers for work performed by teachers for previous employers and that such a claim could not give rise to an industrial dispute within the meaning of the Act.

But Commissioner Oldmeadow held that a dispute existed.

Although the merits of the ITF's claim, for a new employer to recognise past employment in calculating employees' entitlements, will still have to be argued out, Commissioner Oldmeadow's decision removes an initial legal hurdle standing in the way of moves by teacher unions to secure portable entitlements.

A similar claim was lodged some time ago by the union covering teachers in government schools, the Australian Teachers' Union, although the government employers did not raise jurisdictional issues at the dispute-finding stage of the proceedings.

The push by the teacher unions for portable entitlements is part of their strategy to seek greater national consistency in salaries for teachers in different States and between the State school system and the non-government school systems.

The teaching unions, supported by the Federal Government, are seeking a more unified national teaching service with portability of both teacher qualifications and entitlements across different State teaching services.

This is designed to make it easier for teachers to transfer from State to State to alleviate skills bottlenecks which emerge in teaching.

Last week, the South Australian Government agreed to allow teachers from its schools to take up three-year contracts in NSW schools and to pay their travel costs, superannuation and leave entitlements. SA has a significant oversupply of teachers while NSW is facing shortages.

Source: *Australian Financial Review*, 12 December, 1990.

Figure 7.8: The Australian Industrial Relations Commission determines it has jurisdiction.

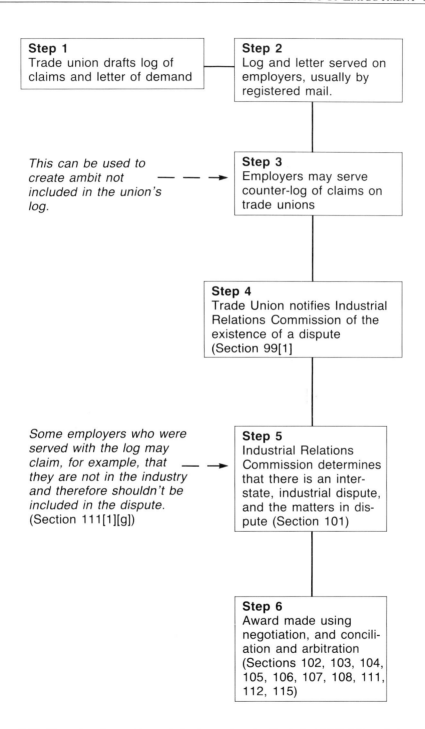

Figure 7.9: Procedure for making a federal award under the Industrial Relations Act.

MJ:LL

3rd June, 1988

Dear Sir/Madam,

By the direction of the Australian Bank Employees Union, an organisation registered under the Conciliation and Arbitration Act, I hereby claim of you the conditions of remuneration and employment contained in the attached Log of Claims, for all your employees in Australia, in or in connection with the industry of banking. Such conditions to apply from 10th June, 1988.

In the event that you fail to agree to grant the claim within seven days of the date of this letter, the Union will regard the subject matter of the Log as being in dispute and will take the appropriate steps under the Conciliation and Arbitration Act to notify the Conciliation and Arbitration Commission of the existence of a dispute and seek the assistance of the Commission in its settlement.

Please note we have advised the Victorian Credit Co-operative Association (V.C.C.A.) at 69 Wellington Street, Windsor, Victoria of this service.

Yours faithfully,

L. N. HINGLEY
Federal Secretary

Attach:

Australian Bank Employees Union
Log of Claims

1. Title

2. Scope

3. Term of operation

4. Salaries
Employees shall be paid at the rate of $20,000.00 per annum upon commencement with automatic annual increments of $2,500,00 for every year of service.

5. Industry allowance
An industry allowance of not less than $5,000.00 per annum shall be paid to each employee.

6. Special rates
A minimumn of $5,000.00 per annum shall be paid to each employee in addition to all other payments.

7. Part-time employees
Part-time employees shall receive pro rata salary rates according to the hours worked appropriate to their age, adult year of service or classified position occupied.

8. Payment of salary
All salaries and allowances shall be paid weekly.

9. Travelling allowance
Each employee shall be paid a travelling allowance of $50.00 per day.

10. Removal expenses
An employee who because of transfer is required to change his/her place of residence shall receive reimbursement of all removal costs and in addition will receive an allowance of $500.00 for each such transfer.

11. Transfers
The Credit Union shall give not less than three months' notice of intention to transfer any employee.

12. Hours of work
The ordinary hours of work of each employee shall not exceed 30 hours per week to be worked between 9.00 a.m. and 4.00 p.m., Monday to Friday inclusive.

13. Meal money
An employee qualifying for meal money shall receive the sum of $10.00 for a meal.

14. Overtime
Overtime in excess of the ordinary hours of work shall be paid at four times the ordinary rate.

15. Shift work
Employees engaged on shift work shall not work in excess of 30 hours per week and shall receive a loading of 40%.

Source: Australian Bank Employees Union.

Figure 7.10: Sample letter of demand of extract from accompanying log of claims.

IN THE MATTER of a notification of
an industrial dispute between the

AUSTRALIAN BANK EMPLOYEES UNION

and

AAFCANS EMPLOYEES CREDIT UNION
CO-OPERATIVE LIMITED AND OTHERS

NOTIFICATION OF INDUSTRIAL DISPUTE

In pursuance of Section 25 of the Australian Conciliation and Arbitration Act, 1904 the *AUSTRALIAN BANK EMPLOYEES UNION HEREBY NOTIFIES YOU* of the existence of an industrial dispute *BETWEEN* the Australian Bank Employees Union of 18 Drummond Street, Carlton South, Melbourne, Victoria *and* the employers mentioned in the attached Schedule 'A' with respect to the following matters:-

1. On 3rd June, 1988 a claim was made on the employers in the attached Schedule 'A' in relation to employment conditions in terms of the accompanying letter of demand marked 'B', Log of Claims marked 'C' and Certified Mail Posting Receipt marked 'D'.
2. The employers referred to in paragraph 1 herein did not accede to the claim within the time specified in the said letter of demand.
3. The Australian Bank Employees Union therefore seeks the assistance of the Australian Conciliation and Arbitration Commission in the settlement of the dispute.

Dated this   day of   1988

A. S. MASON
Assistant Federal Secretary

To: The Industrial Registrar
     Australian Conciliation and Arbitration Commission
     Nauru House
     80 Collins Street
     MELBOURNE Vic. 3000

Figure 7.11: Sample notification of an industrial dispute.

All awards, once they are made, cannot, generally speaking, be varied during their 'life'. For example, Clause 4 of the Federal Shipping Officers (Consolidated) Award, 1989 specifies:

4–TERMS OF OPERATION

This award shall come into operation on and from 1 September 1989 and shall continue in force until 30 June 1991.

This means that neither the employers nor the trade union could agree to nor seek the Industrial Relations Commission's approval to change any of the awards clauses. A Leave Reserved Clause may be included in an award to allow the parties to raise issues through or during its 'life'. In the shipping award it includes Clause 44:

4–LEAVE RESERVED

(a) Salaries
(b) 35 hour week.
(c) 9 day fortnight.
(d) Sick leave.
(e) Annual leave loading.
(f) First class air travel.
(g) Holidays.
(h) On-call and contact officers.

Finally, as a result of National Wage Case decisions, trade unions have had to formally undertake to promise the Commission that they will make no additional claims other than those allowed under the wage case principles. Without such an undertaking the increases would not be passed into the relevant award. Clause 4A of the Shipping Award states:

4A–NO EXTRA CLAIMS

It is a term of this award (arising from the decision of the Australian Conciliation and Arbitration Commission in the National Wage Case of 12 August 1988, the terms of which are set out in Pring H4000) that the association undertakes, until 1 July 1989, not to pursue any extra claims, award or overaward, except where consistent with the National Wage principles.

The association agrees "that it will co-operate in a review (to be monitored by the Commission) of the award to give effect to the structural efficiency principle". In this regard, it is noted that "It is not intended that this principle will be applied in a negative cost-cutting manner or to formalise illusory, short-term benefits. Its purpose is to facilitate the type of fundamental review essential to ensure that existing award structures are relevant to modern competitive requirements of industry and are in the best interests of both management and workers".

State awards

All the state industrial tribunals make and vary awards in accordance with procedures and rules determined by the relevant state legislation. Importantly, because they are not limited by the constitutional constraints which bind the federal tribunal's operation, the process is much simpler. Unions generally are required only to make an application to the tribunal and to notify the employers affected and their associations. There is no need to create the dispute or ambit in the way required in the federal jurisdiction. Trade unions in the state systems often do claim more than they expect to achieve, but this relates more to the bargaining process rather than to the formal requirement to establish ambit.

How awards are applied

As detailed above, federal awards cover those employers who were served with the log of claims and who were subsequently found by the Australian Industrial Relations Commission to be a party to the dispute, and those employer associations that were also found to be party to the dispute. These are known as the respondents, as stated in Clause 4 (Parties Bound) of the Theatre Managers Award 1986 (see Figure 7.12). All the theatre managers working for Hoyts Theatres Ltd, for example, are covered by this award, as the company is listed as a 'named' respondent in Schedule B.

A situation can be imagined, however, in which a new cinema company was formed and, because it was not in existence when the log of claims was served, it could not be a named respondent to the award. It could still be covered by the award if it joined the Cinematograph Exhibitors Association, as Clause 4 specifies that the award shall be binding on the 'Association and its members'. Equally, the new company would lose coverage if it resigned its membership of the association.

This shortcoming allows employers who are not named respondents potentially to try and avoid a federal award's coverage. To reduce their vulnerability, unions will:

- try to serve the log of claims on all the employers they believe to be in the industry.
- create a *'roping-in-award'* if a substantial number of employers 'escaped' the original dispute or came into being after that time. This technical device involves the serving of logs of claims on these employers and thereby binding them to an equivalent award. (The Theatre Managers Association could, for example, ask the Industrial Relations Commission to make a Theatre Managers (Roping-In) Award to cover any new employers in the industry.)
- establish 'counterpart' state awards. Thus, if an employer did resign their membership of a respondent employer association they would then be covered by an equivalent state award. A 'counterpart' state award is

4 — PARTIES BOUND

This Award shall be binding on the Theatre Managers' Association and its members and on The Cinematograph Exhibitors Association and its members and the Motion Picture Exhibitors' Association of New South Wales and its members and the employers whose names are set out in Schedule B—Respondents, in respect of the employment by them of any persons, whether members of the Theatre Managers' Association or not, engaged in any of the classifications specified in clauses 8, 10 and 11 of this Award.

SCHEDULE B
RESPONDENTS

Canberra Theatres Pty Ltd, Capitol Theatre, Canberra, ACT 2600
Australian Cinema, 59 Goulburn Street, Sydney, NSW 2000
Bel-Air Drive-in Theatres Ltd, Bel-Air Drive-in, Broken Hill, NSW 2880
The Greater Union Organization Pty Ltd, Box 1609, GPO, Sydney, NSW 2001
Hoyts Theatres Limited, 600 George Street, Sydney, NSW 2000
Motion Picture Exhibitors Association of NSW, 119 York Street, Sydney, NSW 2000
Regent Theatre, 149 Windsor Road, Richmond, NSW 2753
Theo Goumas Theatres, Lyrique Theatre, Wolfe Street, Newcastle, NSW 2300
Young Municipal Council, Box 436, PO, Young, NSW 2594
Birch, Carrol and Coyle Ltd, Edward Street, Brisbane, Qld 4000
Far Northern Theatres Ltd, Box 1102, PO, Cairns, Qld, 4870
Leisure Time Entertainments Pty Ltd, Second Floor, Film Centre, 164 Melbourne Street, South Brisbane, Qld 4101
Sourris Bros, Redcliffe Drive-in, Redcliffe, Qld 4020
Bel-Air Drive-in Theatre, Waikerie, SA 5330
City Projects Pty Ltd, 76 Kensington Street, Rose Park, SA 5067
Clifford Theatre Circuit, 163 Halifax Street, Adelaide, SA, 5000
Wallis Theatres, 139 West Beach Road, Richmond SA 5053
Mrs V.J. Watson, 8 Edgesmbie Street, Woodville North, SA 5102
Cinematograph Exhibitors Association, 414 Lonsdale Street, Melbourne, Vic. 3000
Tasmanian Amusements Pty Ltd, C/- Village Theatres Pty Ltd, 500 Collins Street, Melbourne, Vic. 3000
Village Theatres Limited, 500 Collins Street, Melbourne, Vic. 3000
Albany Investments Ltd, 258 York Street, Albany, WA 6330
Allan Jones Circuit Pictures, Busselton Drive-in Theatre, Busselton, WA 6280
Carnarvon Cinema Pty Ltd, 1 Howard Street, Perth, WA 6000
Central 70 Drive-in Theatre, Stead Road, Albany, WA 6330
Collie Drive-in Pty Ltd, Laurie Street, Collie, WA 6225
Consolidated Theatres Pty Ltd, 96 St George's Terrace, Perth, WA 6000
Esperance Drive-In Pty Ltd, Drive-in Theatre, Esperance, WA 6450
Goldfields Pictures Ltd, 13 Alvan Street, Mt Lawley, WA 6050
Harvey Drive-in Theatre Pty Ltd, Box 197, PO, Bridgetown, WA 6225
Independent Film Distributors (W.A.) Pty Ltd, 96 Stirling Highway, Nedlands, WA 6009
Jones Cinewest Drive-Ins, Box 77, PO, Busselton, WA 6280
Mandurah Drive-in Pty Ltd, Box 64, PO, South Perth, WA, 6151
Merredin Drive-in Theatre Pty Ltd, Merredin, WA 6415
New Oxford Theatre Ltd, Box G404, GPO, Perth, WA 6001
T.V.W. Enterprises Ltd, Trading as City Theatres Group, 166 Murray Street, Perth, WA 6000
Twin City Drive-in Theatre Pty Ltd, Box F346, GPO, Perth, WA 6001

Figure 7.12: Clause 4 of the Theatre Managers Award 1986

therefore an award which mirrors a federal award; and can dissuade employers from 'swapping' jurisdictions in an effort to alter or manipulate their award coverage. The NSW Engineers (State) Award is a counterpart of the (federal) Metal Industry Award.

State awards not bound by the strictures of the federal jurisdiction apply by a system known as *common rule*. This means that there are no specific respondents, and that the awards apply generally to employers operating within the industry of the award or employing people in the classifications covered by the award. Clause 34 of the NSW Club Employees Award demonstrates the absence of specific respondency; 'Industries and Callings' of the relevant conciliation committee is also significant (see Figure 7.13).

---

34. Area, Incidence and Duration

This award rescinds and replaces the Club Employees (State) Award, published 2 June 1982 and all variations thereof.

It shall apply to all employees in clubs in the State, excluding the County of Yancowinna, within the jurisdiction of the Club Employees (State) Conciliation Committee.

The award published 2 June 1982 took effect from the beginning of the first pay period to commence on or after 30 September 1981 and the variations thereof incorporated herein on the dates set out in the attached schedule.

Pursuant to section 87 of the Industrial Arbitration Act, 1940, the award, as varied, and now reprinted, remains in force until varied or rescinded, the period for which the said award was made having already expired.

Club Employees (State) Conciliation Committee
Industries and Callings

Employees in clubs, including markers and lift attendants, in the State, excluding the County of Yancowinna;

Excepting—

Engine-drivers and firemen, greasers, trimmers, cleaners, and pumpers, engaged in or about the driving of engines, electrical crane, winch, and motor drivers;

Carters, grooms, stablemen, yardmen, and drivers of motors and other power-propelled vehicles;

Persons within the jurisdiction of the Club Managers and Secretaries (State) Conciliation Committee.

Figure 7.13: Extract from the NSW Club Employees Award.

Conflict between the sources of law

From time to time an employer and employee may agree to a condition which is in conflict with an award provision. For example, the worker may work beyond a certain period of time when a break is deemed mandatory by the award. Similarly, although a law requires that an employee take annual leave and not be paid in lieu, sometimes the employer and employee agree to such a payment. In both situations, even though there was agreement, these arrangements were invalid as the award's or law's *minimum* requirements were not met.

Conflict can also arise between federal and state law. Consider, for example, a situation in which a state law requires an employer to grant long-service leave to an employee after 10 years' service but a federal award covering that employer prescribes that the entitlement should only occur after 15 years' service. Clearly, there is a conflict between these two. Which must the employer obey? Does she/he grant leave to the employees after 10 or 15 years?

First, the High Court has decided that an award has an effect very similar to that of statutes. The federal award, then, has the same legal 'status' as the state Act of Parliament. Second, Section 109 of the Australian Constitution states that where a law of the Commonwealth is inconsistent with the law of a state then the federal law is paramount to (overrides) the state law to the extent of the inconsistency. In this case, therefore, the federal award would be paramount, and the entitlement to long-service leave would occur after 15 years' service.

Section 152 of the Industrial Relations Act, set out below, reinforces the effect of Section 109 of the Constitution:

> **Awards to prevail over State laws, awards etc.**
> 152. Where a state law, or an order, award, decision or determination of a State industrial authority, is inconsistent with, or deals with a matter dealt with in, an award, the latter prevails and the former, to the extent of the inconsistency or in relation to the matter dealt with, is invalid.

Many High Court cases have revolved around the application of Section 109. Indeed, the notion of 'inconsistency' itself has been defined and redefined. As a 'rule of thumb', most industrial relations practitioners will ask whether it is possible to obey both laws. Obviously, the case on which one law grants long-service leave after 15 years and the other after 10 years do not satisfy this test. The High Court, however, has developed more intricate tests of inconsistency (especially the 'covering the field' test), which means that expert legal advice is often needed to determine accurately which law takes precedence.

Award interpretation and enforcement

Once an award is made or varied, it becomes the legal entitlement of those employees covered under that award. As with any document, argument can occur as to the specific meaning of the various clauses. The drafters of awards can not envisage all employment situations that may arise, and this often leads to disputes over the award's interpretation.

An employee may claim, for example, that they have been underpaid because the employer's interpretation of the award has incorrectly classified their position and hence their rate of pay. Unions often represent their members in these cases and, if the conflict is not resolved, it is open to the union on behalf of their member to argue the case before courts which have the power to interpret and enforce awards. Inspectors from government departments with the responsibility for enforcing awards and employment legislation can also take action for employees which may require courts to interpret the appropriate award or law. Any condition which is part of the contract and not specified in an award or employment legislation can be enforced in an appropriate common law court. Typically, this involves making a claim before a magistrate.

Federal and state laws allow employees to seek 'back-pay' for up to six years. This makes it particularly important that employers correctly interpret and apply awards, and that they keep the required time and wages records. Courts also have the power to fine the parties for breaches of an award. Employees can be found to have breached an award by, for example, not having given the required amount of notice to terminate their employment. Awards usually specify that the relevant amount of pay (say, one week's pay in the case of one week's notice) can be deducted from any monies due on termination.

The way in which the wording of an award can lead to conflicting interpretations is illustrated in the case *Nyamirandu v. The War Veterans Home*, decided in the South Australian Industrial Court. The employee, a registered nurse, claimed that she was entitled for $4254.88 back-pay because she had not been granted the meal breaks prescribed by Clause 10 of the Nurses (South Australia) Award, which states:

> (4) By arrangement with the employees an unpaid meal break shall be allowed on each shift of a duration of not less than 30 minutes but not more than 60 minutes which shall be free of all duty, provided that the meal break on the night shift shall not exceed 30 minutes. Such meal breaks shall not be regarded as working time.
> (5) When an employee is interrupted during a meal break by a call to duty the extent of the interruption shall be counted as time worked and the employee shall be allowed to continue such meal break as soon as practicable; should it be impracticable for the employee to complete such meal break during the remainder of the ordinary working hours, the employee shall receive the appropriate overtime pay for the time so worked.

Nyamirandu was the only nurse employed on night shift and, because a nurse had to be on duty at all times, she was told that, although she must take her meal breaks in accordance with the award, she was not allowed to leave the nursing home.

The court then had to interpret the meaning of the words 'free of all duty' in subclause 4 of Clause 10. Two possible constructions of the words were considered:

a. the meal breaks taken by the nurse were free of all duty, as she had not been required to work and therefore had no entitlement to the penalty pay prescribed by 10(5); or
b. she had not been free of all duty, and so was entitled to the penalty payment.

The court found in favour of interpretation (b)—that is, the employee's construction—by reasoning:
a. the break must logically be free of all work to be regarded as non-working time; and
b. her inability to leave the nursing home during the meal breaks implied she was not 'free of all duty'.

In reading an award, it is important:
- that the problem be exactly understood with supporting detail; and
- that the relevant award be used and that all the clauses which refer to the problem by carefully consulted.

Summary

The terms of a person's employment are the essence of any industrial relations system. The employer's and employee's obligations and rights are set out in the common law contracts, awards and employment legislation. Industrial relations practitioners and those with responsibilities for staff must be able carefully to apply and to interpret these three sources of employment law.

Questions and Activities
1. Why do most practitioners in human resources management consider the terms and conditions of a person's employment as a 'complex web of rules'?
2. In the article 'Your 'Subbie' can be an employee' (Figure 7.14), Peter Townsend outlines a ruling of the Taxation Department. How does this ruling affect the question as to whether a person is an employee?

Your 'Subbie' can be an employee

Labor cost blow-out can mean disaster for businesses of any size. The most serious source of a potential labour cost blow-out for your business is *not* from the excessive wage demands of your employees' trade unions, but rather from an area you may have never considered—your sub-contractors.

Turning one's employees into subcontractors is the great dream of every business person who utilises a substantial amount of labor. Contractors are marvellous—no sick pay, no holiday pay (or loading), no long service leave, no workers compensation, no payroll tax, no wards controlling the terms of hire and much less administration of the labor force.

Is it any wonder that this area causes constant conflict between the users of labor, who try to pull the worker towards the delights of allegedly being his own boss, and the trade union movement, which wants all workers to assert their employed status and thereby win all the benefits listed above as well as have union membership?

Australia has various laws that turn a subcontractor into an employee regardless of what you and your "subbie" agree to. When that happens you may have all the obligations toward your subcontractor that you thought you only had toward your employees, and these obligations can be expensive.

Here is an illustration. X operated a business removing both rubbish and cullet (discarded glass). The business was small but healthy and in 1984 it began to expand, forcing X to seek extra labor. He weighed the pros and cons of employing more staff against using a subcontractor and chose the latter mainly because of the fluctuations in the available work.

X was a cautious opertor and so made it abundantly clear to all his contractors that they were contractors first and last and were not employees. He even suggested that they take out their own insurance cover. All the people he contracted were aware that X wanted to have them work only as contractors.

Due to the nature of his business, X had to instruct the contractors where to pick up the rubbish and cullet. He also gave the contractors the use of his collection trucks. Everything went smoothly until a worker was hurt in an accident while collecting cullet. Consequently, the worker lodged a claim for compensation against X for loss suffered while employed.

If X was surprised that the contractor had made such a claim (he was sure the fellow involved had no right to workers' compensation as he was not an employee), he was horrified when he was ordered by the workers' compensation board to compensate the contractor for loss of wages, loss of use of a finger and medical expenses.

The simple fact is that the workers' compensation legislation in most states deems "contractors" to be "workers" in certain situations so that the head contractor has the obligation to take out workers' compensation insurance to cover these "non-employees". In many areas the law further reduces the distinction between employees and contractors by making the employer more responsible for contractors and other people who provide him with services.

X's case highlights a fundamental error made by many employers—that of incorrectly assessing their relationship with their workers. X presumed that his relationship with his workers was a contract relationship because it did not fit into what he commonly understood to be an employer/employee relationship. But, like Shakespeare's rose, what you call the relationship is irrelevant. The real issue is the rights and obligations of the parties concerned.

The performance of work by one person for the benefit of, or at the direction of another, may come within a wide variety of social and legal relationships. The law today recognises that work may be done pursuant to myriad relationships including partnership, subcontracts, employment agreements, bailment and tenancy—to name but a few. The law recognises these different relationships and applies different rules to them. As a result different consequences flow.

What distinguishes the employment relationship from an independent contract? There is no single test and no standard list of characteristics. Each circumstance is different. However, at common law, different tests have evolved which help in making a determination. Two of the more commonly used tests are the control test and the integration test.

The control test: The presence of a right to control how, where, when and whom, points strongly to an employment relationship. The greater the obligation on a worker to obey the orders of the person he has contracted with as to the manner of performance of the work the greater the relative weight that can be attached to the control criteria and the more certain it is that the individual is an employee.

In 1985 the Taxation Department issued ruling IT2129 in which it gave an efficient and thorough summary of the common law distinctions between contractor and employee and went on to show how it would rely on these distinctions in deciding whether a group employer should be deducting PAYE income tax from the salary of a worker.

Ruling IT2129 summarises the many aspects of the relationship between the parties that need to be carefully considered before deciding whether the worker is an employee. The PAYE provisions of the Income Tax Assessment Act are limited to income derived from personal exertion of individuals and are made from "salary and wages"—the definition of which, under the Act, encompasses payments to any individual who is virtually in a position of an employee. It therefore includes those independent contractors who are, in reality, employees.

If you have independent contractors working for you it is advisable to check this list carefully to ensure that at least in the majority of the tests the contractor complies with the taxman's requirements. Failure to do so could mean that the Taxation Department will make *you* liable for all the PAYE tax that you should have paid *plus penalties*. That could be an amount so great it could put you out of business.

Figure 7.14.

Source: Peter Townsend, *Rydges*, September 1987.

3. Try to obtain a copy of an indenture of apprenticeship. Look at such aspects as whether an employer can terminate that indenture by providing notice in the normal way.
4. *Case studies*
   a. Under the Theatre Managers Award, if there were an argument about whether an employee provided satisfactory evidence to support their claim for sick leave, how would this be resolved? (*Answer*: See Clause 27.)
   b. A theatre manager is fined for allowing a person under 18 years into their cinema contrary to the 'R'-rated classification of the film. Would the manager have to pay the fine? (*Answer*: See Clause 33.)
   c. If a Cinema owner told their manager to start work late the following day because he had worked late, would the cinema still have to pay overtime? (*Answer*: See Clause 17[c].)
5. Obtain five federal and five state awards. Compare and contrast the following award provisions:
   - overtime
   - sick leave
   - bereavement/compassionate leave
   - annual leave loading
   - notice of termination of employment.
6. You are the Federal Secretary of the Computer Operations Union. How would you go about gaining a new federal award for your members?
7. An official from the NSW Branch of the Storemen and Packers Union recently visited the ABC Printing Company in Newcastle and, after checking the company's time and wages records, argued that the company's storemen were being underpaid. To support her case, the official showed the manager a copy of the current wage rates which applied under the Storemen and Packers (Newcastle) Award. The award applies to 'all storemen and packers employed within 20 kilometres of the Newcastle G.P.O.'

   The company is situated within the geographical area specified by the award. Also, the company is a member of the Printing and Allied Trades Employers' Federation of Australia, which is named respondent to the Graphic Arts Award. This is an award of the Industrial Relations Commission, and applies in all states of Australia. The company's storemen were being paid the appropriate rate prescribed by the federal award. Under which award should the storemen have been paid? (*Answer*: The Graphic Arts Award, because ABC Printing is a named respondent and with award classifications for storemen the federal award overrides the inconsistent state award—Section 109 of the Constitution.)
8. The article from *The Australian* dated 14 January, 1991 (Figure 7.15) illustrates the general misunderstanding in the community of how the constraints imposed by the Australian Constitution affect federal award-making procedures. Prepare a letter to the editor for the trade union explaining why the log was served, the notion of ambit, and the rights of the recipients of the log to argue that they should not be included in the dispute.
9. After reading the letter confirming Didge's employment with the Christina Stead Child Care Centre (Figure 7.1), would she be entitled to a national wage increase, or could the employer absorb the increase into her over-award payment?
   (*Answer*: As her contract specifies that she shall receive $50 per week above the award, if the award rate is increased she must receive the increase. It cannot be absorbed into the over-award payment, as the contract guarantees her $50 above the award rate.)

Claim for $38,600 a week 'stupid'

By TREVOR CHAPPELL

A SENIOR union official has admitted a wages claim made by his union for workers to be paid up to $38,600 a week for less than two hours' work was 'stupid'.

The NSW secretary of the National Union of Workers, Mr Frank Blean, said yesterday the ambit claim, served on 2000 companies in the rubber, plastic and cable-making industries, would tarnish the image of the trade union movement.

'We don't usually serve ambit claims that look or sound stupid,' he said.

'We like to be seen as a serious and responsible organisation.'

The claim seeks a 30-hour week, eight weeks' annual leave, 23 public holidays a year, superannuation worth 50 per cent of wages, childcare and 10 weeks' pay for voluntary resignations, as well as extra payments and allowances.

In each eight-hour day, workers would get rest breaks for two hours and 20 minutes, a 'wash-up' period for two hours and 20 minutes, an hour's lunchtime and two hours for job training.

They would work for only 20 minutes a day or less than two hours a week.

All up, a shift worker in a supervisory role with five years' experience could take home $38,593 a week.

Mr Belan said ambit claims were usually extremely generous but this was 'outrageous'.

'It describes us as idiots ... when people around the country are talking about changing conditions,' he said.

Mr Belan said he had no idea how the union came to make such a claim.

'It was not done in consultation with the NSW branch of the NUW,'' he said.

The NSW industrial relations director of the Chamber of Manufactures, Mr Mark Paterson, said he was not concerned about the ambit of the claim.

He said the claims were always ridiculously high so they would create a dispute between the unions and the employers in a number of States.

He said a 'paper dispute' had to be created over a log of claims in order to fulfil constitutional requirements which dictated the IRC could only deal with interstate disputes.

Mr Paterson said if unions submitted realistic claims they would run out of ambit and have to file another claim.

Source: *The Australian*, 14 January, 1991.

Figure 7.15: Log of claims and ambit.

10. In a case in the NSW Supreme Court, *Logue v. Thomas* (13 March 1990), a dentist (the plaintiff) sought an injunction restraining a former employee from working as a dentist at a surgery which was within an 8 km radius of the plaintiff's practice.

   The plaintiff relied upon a written agreement that had been entered into when the dentist had been employed by him.

   Clause 12 of the agreement read:

   'The employee hereby ... agrees ... that upon termination of the employee's engagement ... she ... shall not without the written consent of the employer first had and obtained:

   (a) For a period of two years from the date of such termination within the boundaries of 8km aforesaid:

(i) Practise ... the business of the profession of a dentist.

(ii) Enter into or be directly or indirectly engaged in such business or profession or solicit or endeavour to obtain professional business for any dentist firm of dentists practising within such radius other than the employer.

(b) Directly or indirectly solicit or interfere with or accept or transact any professional business in the practice of dentistry for any person firm or corporation who or which is at the date hereof or was at any time heretofore or may at the date of such termination have become a client of the employer.

Source: CCH, *Australian Industrial Law Report* (32) 20, 15 October 1990.

The court granted the injunction because it held the restrictive covenant was not unreasonable given that, in a competitive market, the dentist would have come into contact with her previous patients.

(a) Draft an employment contract clause which would prohibit a sales representative from working for a firm's competitors.

(b) Do you feel restraint of trade is appropriate?

Appendix 1

Glossary

Below are a number of terms used in industrial relations which are not defined in detail in the text.

Advocate
A person who represents either party by presenting their case before an industrial tribunal.

Ambit
In the Federal industrial system, there must be a dispute for the Commission to intervene. The difference in the dispute between the employer and the union is the 'ambit' of the dispute. The initial claim is made sufficiently large so the 'ambit' will allow the parties to go back to the Commission without having to recreate another dispute.

Arbitration
The process whereby an independent third party makes a decision based on the merits of the evidence and submissions made to the tribunal. The parties are bound to abide by the decision.

Award restructuring
This is a process which arises from the Structural Efficiency Principle developed in the August 1988 National Wage Case decision. It covers the review of awards to reduce outmoded provisions and to make them more relevant and appropriate to the needs of industry and employees. This includes developing new career paths, major reforms to skill formation and revised job classifications.

Black ban
A ban placed by a trade union against an employer, their goods or processes. A ban could be placed against using new equipment, for example, until the union negotiated revised workforce levels.

Board of reference
A special board established in some Federal awards to resolve minor disputes over issues such as apprenticeships and employee classifications. The Board generally consists of an equal number of employer and employee representatives and an independent chairperson such as a nominee of the Industrial Registrar.

Bona fide
In good faith, genuine.

Certified agreement
A memorandum of agreement between the parties to apply for a specific time period, certified by the Australian Industrial Relations Commission. A certified agreement has the same status as an award.

Collective bargaining
The method of determining, interpreting and administering the terms and conditions of employment through direct negotiation between trade unions on the one hand and employers and managers on the other.

Common law
Or 'judge-made' law is that body of cases which have been decided by the courts.

Common rule
Where the terms and conditions of an award apply to all parties in a particular industry or trade even though they may not be respondents to the award. The concept only has application in the State jurisdiction and in the Commonwealth territories (NT and the ACT).

Compulsory conference
A summons by an industrial commission compelling the attendance of particular persons to appear before the commission.

Conciliation
The process whereby a member of an industrial tribunal brings the parties to a dispute together with a view to having the parties themselves come to an agreement. Conciliation can take place with the parties meeting alone, separately or together with the member.

Consent award
An award where the parties reach agreement themselves on a particular matter/s and apply to the Commission to give effect to their agreement.

Counterpart award
An award made in the state system which is the equivalent of its 'parent' federal award.

Damages
Indicate the loss a person has incurred as a result of a dispute, breach of contract or another person's negligence. It is usually a monetary amount awarded by a court to compensate for the loss.

Demarcation dispute
A dispute between two or more unions over the question of which union has the exclusive right to cover certain work. One union believes it is a job for their members while another feels it is their job.

Enterprise bargaining
A method of making, interpreting and administering terms and conditions

of employment between employers and employees (with or without union representation) at the workplace or enterprise level.

Flow on
The process by which a wage increase in one section is applied to others to maintain the wage structure.

Grievance/dispute settling procedures
Procedures for the settlement of grievances or disputes at the workplace. The procedures usually incorporate a number of steps starting with the first line of contact. If the matter cannot be resolved, increasingly senior personnel are involved.

Industrial democracy
The concept of making the workplace more democratic through maximum employee participation in decision-making.

Industrial matter
This is a term used to define the subject matter which falls within the jurisdiction of the various industrial tribunals.

Interest disputes
Disputes which arise out of the making of an award.

Jurisdiction
Involves the power of a tribunal or court to deal with a matter. With its interpretations of the Australian Constitution for example, the High Court has often determined the jurisdiction of the Industrial Relations Commission to deal with certain industrial disputes.

Log of claims
A list of demands (claims) made by one party (usually the union) on the other party (usually the employer). It covers any number of issues related to employment, e.g. hours of work, sick leave and other entitlements.

Managerial prerogatives
Managerial 'rights' perceived by employers as being non-negotiable. Union efforts have reduced the issues regarded as managerial prerogatives.

National wage case
The universal wage review conducted by a Full Bench of the Australian Industrial Relations Commission. Submissions are heard from a number of interested parties, including governments, employer associations and trade unions. A new award is determined to apply to the award wage rates.

Negotiation
Discussions carried out directly between the industrial parties themselves with a view to reaching an acceptable agreement.

Paid rate award
An award which prescribes the complete salaries and conditions which are granted to the employees subject to the award. There is no scope for over-award benefits.

Paper dispute
A dispute which is created 'on paper' as opposed to involving industrial action so that the Federal Commission has jurisdiction to deal with the particular matter.

Paramountcy
When a State law or award is inconsistent with a Federal one, the Federal one shall prevail. This is based on Section 109 of the Constitution which makes Federal laws 'paramount'.

Pattern bargaining
A method adopted by trade unions in industry-wide negotiations. It involves making a claim against one employer with possible industrial action. When the employer makes concessions, the union seeks to have them applied to other employers in the industry.

Private arbitration
When a tribunal does not strictly have jurisdiction to deal with a claim or where an informal hearing is desired, the parties may ask the tribunal member to deal with the case privately. Both sides are required to be committed to accept the outcome of the arbitration.

Preference of employment
A system where an employer must give preference to union members when filling job vacancies.

Registration
In order for an organisation to have access to the industrial tribunal system it must be registered. Various requirements and conditions must be met.

Respondents
Those parties which are bound by a particular award made in settlement of a dispute.

Roping-in award
The procedure used in the Federal system to bind additional respondents to an existing award.

Rights disputes
Disputes arising out of the interpretation or application of existing awards or agreements.

Stand down clause
This refers to a clause in an award which gives an employer the power to stand down an employee without pay if the employee cannot usefully be employed for reasons beyond the employer's control.

Statutory law
Law which has been enacted by Parliament. It overrides any common law which is inconsistent with it.

Sympathy strike
A strike by workers not directly involved in a dispute aimed at supporting the union in the dispute.

Test case
A case before the industrial tribunal which establishes a standard which will be applied in subsequent decisions.

Tort
A wrongful act, other than a breach of contract, which entitles the affected person to seek damages. Some torts are negligence, defamation and intimidation.

Further Reading

Aldred, J., (ed.) (1984), *Industrial Confrontation*, Allen and Unwin, Sydney.
ACTU/TDC (1987), *Australia Reconstructed*, AGPS, Canberra.
Berry, P., Kitchener, G. (1990), *Can Unions Survive?*, BWIU (ACCT Branch), Dickson, ACT.
Brooks, B. (1986), *Contract of Employment*, 3rd ed., CCH Australia, North Ryde.
Brooks, B. (1982), *Let's Negotiate*, CCH Australia, North Ryde.
Brooks, B. (1988), *Why Unions?*, 2nd ed., CCH Australia, North Ryde.
Business Council of Australia (1989), *Enterprise Based Bargaining Units, A Better Way of Working*, BCA, Melbourne.
Callus, R., Morehead, M., Cully, M., Buchanan, J. (1991), *Industrial Relations at Work, The Australian Workplace Industrial Relations Survey*, Commonwealth Department of Industrial Relations, AGPS, Canberra.
Caroll, J. (1988), *Australian Industrial Relations Handbook*, 3rd ed., CCH Australia.
Clark, R. (1988), *Australian Human Resources Management*, McGraw-Hill, Sydney.
Cole, K. (1982), *Power, Conflict and Control in Australian Trade Unions*, Penguin, Ringwood.
Dabscheck, B. (1989), *Australian Industrial Relations in the 1980s*, Oxford University Press, Melbourne.
Dabscheck, B., Niland, J. (1981), *Industrial Relations in Australia*, Allen and Unwin, Sydney.
Deery, S., Plowman, D. (1991), *Australian Industrial Relations*, 3rd ed. McGraw-Hill, Sydney.
Dufty, N. F., Fells, R. E. (1989), *Dynamics of Industrial Relations in Australia*, Prentice-Hall, Sydney.
Eaglebook (1989), *Jobs and the Law*, 2nd ed., CCH Australia, North Ryde.
Ford, G. W., Hearn, J. M., Lansbury, R. D. (1987), *Australian Labour Relations: Readings*, 4th ed., Macmillan, Melbourne.
Ford, G. W., Plowman, D., (eds) (1989), *Australian Unions*, Macmillan, Melbourne.
Hearn, J. M., Howard, W. A. (1984), *Australian Industrial Relations: Case Studies*, Macmillan, Melbourne.
Holdsworth, W. J. (1987), *Advocacy and Negotiation in Industrial Relations*, 3rd ed., Law Book.
Jones, G. P. (1988), *A Guide to Sources of Information on Australian Industrial Relations*, Pergamon Press, Sydney.
McCarthy, P. (1989). *Developing Negotiating Skills and Behaviour*, CCH Australia, North Ryde.
Mathews, J. (1989), *Tools of Change: New Technology and the Democratisation of Work*, Pluto Press, Sydney.
Moore, P. J. (1974), *Industrial Relations in Australia*, 3rd ed., John Wiley, Brisbane.
Punch, P. (1989), *Law of Employment*, CCH Australia, North Ryde.
Rawson, D.W. (1986), *Unions and Unionists in Australia*, 2nd ed., Allen and Unwin, Melbourne.
Sexton, M., Maher, L.W. (1982), *The Legal Mystique*, Angus and Robertson, Sydney.
Trade Union Training Authority, *Reading Your Award*, Sydney.
Windshuttle, K. (1984), *The Media*, Penguin, Melbourne.

Journals and periodicals

Asia Pacific HRM, Institute of Personnel Management Australia in association with the Institute of Personnel Management New Zealand and the Institute of Personnel Management Papua New Guinea.
Australian Industrial Law Reports, CCH Australia Ltd.
Australian Journal of Labour Law, Butterworths.
Journal of Industrial Relations, Industrial Relations Society of Australia.
Labour & Industry, A Journal of the Social and Economic Relations at Work.
Labour Law Reporter, CCH Australia Ltd.
Workforce, Published by Seabind Pty. Ltd., Manly, NSW.

Videos

Working It Out: An introduction to the world of industrial relations, 1988, produced by Commonwealth of Australia, CAI and ACTU, Curriculum Development Centre, PO Box 34, Woden, ACT 2606.
Talking Turkey, Living with the Law Series, Australian Broadcasting Corporation, Gore Hill, NSW.
Smart A.L.E.C.C., Living with the Law Series, Australian Broadcasting Corporation, Gore Hill, NSW.
Working Agreement, Film Australia, 1980.

Index

Accord, 23, 103
Act of Parliament, 69–70
ACTU, 22–25, 30, 31, 37, 42
Affirmative Action Act 1986, 72
Affirmative Action Agency, 78
Air traffic controllers, 99
ALP, 38
ALP–ACTU Accord, 23, 103
Ambit, 169
Amoco, 141
AMP Society, 153
Annual Holidays Act, 157, 159
Anti-Discrimination Act, 157
APHEDA, 38
Arbitrated decision, 127
Australian Chamber of Manufacturers, 46
Australian Council of Trade Unions, *see* ACTU
Australian Industrial Relations Commission, 120–126
Australian Labor Party, *see* ALP
Australian Meat Industry Employees Union (AMIEU), 53
Award restructuring, 25, 114

Bans clauses, 137–138
Boilermakers' Case, 90
Broadribb Sawmilling Case, 153–154
Building Workers Industrial Union, 100
Business Council of Australia (BCA), 49, 50, 51

CAI–ACTU Joint Statement on Participation Practices, 142
Cause of dispute, 109
Chamber of Manufacturers of NSW, 61
Collective bargaining, 40
Conciliation and Arbitration Act 1904, 122
Confectionery Workers' Union (CWU), 57
Confederation of Australian Industry (CAI), 43, 48, 49, 84
Conflict, resolution of, 113–144

Conflict, *see* Industrial conflict
Constitution, 70, 71, 72, 121, 157, 177
Contracts of employment, 150–151
Control test, 152–154
Corporatism, 103
Craft unions, 32

Demarcation disputes, 32
Department of Industrial Relations (DIR), 78–84
Direct negotiation, 40
Dispute record in Australia, 101–102, 107
Disputes, 101–104
Dollar Sweets Case, 56–57
Duration of dispute, 103, 109

Economic management, 75–78
Electrical Trades Union (ETU), 32
Employer organisations, 43–68
    administration, 63
    commercial services, 61
    types of, 45–48
    militancy, 55–59
    services, 59–63
    unity, 53–55
Employers' Federation of NSW, 47, 59
Employers' Review, 60
Employment, 149
Enterprise bargaining, 17–18, 25, 50, 52, 114
Equal employment opportunity, 82
Equal pay, 22

Face-to-face industrial relations, 4–8
Federal Commission, 120–126
Federal Court, 90–91
Federated Engine Drivers and Firemens Association, 100
FIET, 38

General unions, 32–34

Government
    employer, 85–87
    executive responsibilities, 75–78
    functions of, 71–72
levels of, 69–71
powers of, 69–71
Governor-General, 70
Grievance procedures, 116–119

H.R. Nicholls Society, 56
Hancock Report, 114–115
Hand-in-hand industrial relations, 4–8
Hawke Government, 23, 25, 103
High Court, 72, 87–90, 120–121, 133
House union, 134
Human resource context, 10–12

Income taxes, 76–77
Industrial Arbitration Act 1940 (NSW), 129, 157
Industrial Conciliation and Arbitration Act 1972 (SA), 136
Industrial conflict, 93–144
Industrial Registry, 125
Industrial relations, 1–18
    definition, 1–4
    human resource context, 10–12
    specialist, 12–14
Industrial Relations Act (Victoria) 1979, 132–134
Industrial Relations Act 1984 (Tas), 136–137
Industrial Relations Act 1988, 28, 74, 75
Industrial Relations Commission (WA), 134–135
Industrial relations legislation, 72–75
Industrial unions, 32
International Labour Organization (ILO), 73, 81, 82, 105
International Metalworkers Federation, 38

Job Protection Test Case, 23
Job representative, 34–35
Judicial system, 87–91

Local Court, *see* Magistrate's Court
Log of claims, 169
Long Service Leave Act, 157, 158

Magistrate's Court, 91
Master Builders' Federation, 53
Maternity leave case, 23
McNaughton, Ald., 56

Media, 99–101
Metal Trades Industry Association, 25, 52, 62, 63
Method of settlement, 103–104, 110
Mudginberri case, 55, 58

National Farmers Federation, 53, 58, 66, 67
National Labour Consultative Council (NLCC), 84
National Occupational Health and Safety Commission, 78
National Union of Workers, 32
New Right, 56, 57
New South Wales Act, 129, 157

O'Shea Case, 102–103

PATEFA, 45, 61
Personnel Management, 59
Pilots' dispute, 57
Prices and Income Accord, 23, 103
Prime Minister, 69
Printing and Allied Trades Employers' Federation of Australia, 45, 61
Public servants, 85–86

Queensland Act, 135–136

Ranger Uranium Mines Case, 88
Registered Clubs Association of NSW, 45
Registration of unions, 34
Respondents, 174
Retail Traders' Association, 44, 55

Safety and Occupational Health, 11
Secondary boycott, 139, 141
Sex Discrimination Act, 1984, 157
Social wage, 78
Social welfare policies, 78
Staff association, 34
State organiser, 36
State systems, 128–137
Strikes, *see* Industrial conflict
Structural Efficiency Principle, 26
Supreme Court, 91

TAFE, 63
Tasmanian Act, 136–137
Trade Practices Act, 91, 139, 141
Trade Union Training Authority (TUTA), 78

Trade unions, 19–42
   aims and objectives, 37–38
   development, 19–23
   organisation, 25–31
   size, 28–29
   structure, 34–37
   type, 32–34
Trades and Labour Council of Western Australia, 135
Training and development, 11
Tribunal system, 120
   structures, 120–137

Unemployment, 76, 102

Victorian Act, 132

Wage/tax trade-off, 76–77
Western Australian Act, 134
Williams, Pamela, 57
Wooldumpers (Victoria) Ltd, 88
Workers' Compensation Act, 157
Working days lost, 101
Worksafe Australia, 78

Zuijs v. Wirth Brothers Case, 153

(Tape shut)

No postage stamp required
if posted in Australia

BUSINESS REPLY POST
Permit No. 7323 - SYDNEY
Postage and fee will be paid on delivery to

Managing Editor, College Division
Harcourt Brace Jovanovich, Australia
Locked Bag 16
MARRICKVILLE NSW 2204

TO THE OWNER OF THIS BOOK

We are interested in your reaction to the *Understanding Australian Industrial Relations,* by Robyn Alexander et al.

1. What was your reason for using this book.

   _____ university course   _____ continuing education course
   _____ college course   _____ personal interest
                             _____ other (specify)

2. In which school are you teaching? _____

3. Approximately how much of the manual did you use?
   _____ 1/4 _____ 1/2 _____ 3/4 _____ all

4. What is the best aspect of the manual?

5. Have you any suggestions for improvement?

6. Would more diagrams help?

7. Is there any topic that should be added?

Fold here

- -